Américo Paredes

Number Thirty-Four
Jack and Doris Smothers Series in Texas History, Life, and Culture

« JOSÉ E. LIMÓN »

Américo Paredes

CULTURE AND CRITIQUE

University of Texas Press ↬ AUSTIN

Publication of this work was made possible in part by support from the J. E. Smothers, Sr., Memorial Foundation and the National Endowment for the Humanities.

The poem "The Four Freedoms" by Américo Paredes is reprinted with permission from the publisher of "Between Two Worlds" by Américo Paredes (© 1990 Arte Público Press—University of Houston).

First edition, 2012
First paperback edition, 2013
Requests for permission to reproduce material from this work should be sent to:
    Permissions
    University of Texas Press
    P.O. Box 7819
    Austin, TX 78713-7819
    utpress.utexas.edu/index.php/rp-form

LIBRARY OF CONGRESS CATALOGING-IN-PUBLICATION DATA

Limón, José Eduardo.
Américo Paredes : culture and critique / by José E. Limón. — 1st ed.
    p.   cm. (Jack and Doris Smothers series in Texas history, life, and culture ; no. 34)
Includes bibliographical references and index.
ISBN 978-0-292-75682-3
1. Paredes, Américo—Criticism and interpretation.   I. Title.
PS3531.A525Z73   2012
813′.54—dc23
    2012000875

For Teresa and Renata

Contents

Acknowledgments

The writing of this book would not have been possible without a 2009–2010 Faculty Fellowship from the College of Liberal Arts at the University of Texas at Austin. My thanks to Dean Randy Diehl and Senior Associate Dean Richard Flores. The Department of English at the University of Texas at Austin provided a supportive intellectual home for Américo Paredes during his academic career, as it has for me during the last thirty years and before that as a student. I thank them all, but especially the two fine chairs under whom I have served, Jim Garrison and Elizabeth Cullingford.

At the University of Texas I have also learned much that has been central to this work from the many fine graduate students and the thirty wonderful faculty affiliated with the Center for Mexican American Studies (CMAS). I am especially grateful for the personal and intellectual presence of Emilio Zamora and John Moran González. I especially thank Interim Director Domino Perez and Associate Director Deborah Paredez for their competent and creative administration of CMAS during my leave of absence with the always able and loyal support of the fine CMAS staff: Luis Guevara, Johannah Hochhalter, Natasha Saldaña, Ileana Cerda, and Alberto González.

Américo Paredes was the founding Director of CMAS in 1970 with only two faculty including him. He would be pleased beyond measure to see CMAS today.

Once again, I continue to be so grateful for the superb University of Texas at Austin libraries, but especially the rare books and manuscript holdings at the Benson Latin American Collection and the Mexican American Library Project, which house the Américo Paredes Papers.

This book was written mostly in Long Beach, California, directly after my marriage to Teresa McKenna, professor of English and American studies at the University of Southern California and a former postdoctoral fellow with Américo Paredes. She has provided sustaining love and unfailing support; informed, critical conversation; a close reading of the manuscript; a lovely study in which to work; and Kiki, *el perro chihuahuense*, who rose with me every morning to make sure I was under way in my writing before going back to sleep. For sustaining this writing in their own way, I also thank the entire McKenna family, especially my wonderful new sisters-in-law, Amelia and Irene, for taking this wayward Tejano into their warm embrace. Ollie provided ample, grounded, and solid support as well.

I completed the final prepublication phase of the book during my first semester at my new academic home in the Department of English and the Institute for Latino Studies at the University of Notre Dame. For their warm welcome and nurturing support, I thank my new chairpersons: first, John Sitter and now Valerie Sayers; the department, the Institute and its former director, Gilberto Cárdenas; and my close friend Dolores García. I am also very grateful to Dean John T. McGreevy of the College of Arts and Letters for his generous support.

Finally, of course, once again, I must acknowledge Américo Paredes for changing my life at a critical moment and sustaining me throughout my academic work even in his passing.

Portions of this study appeared in the *Journal of American Folklore* as well as in *American Literary History*. These and yet other sections were also presented as public lectures at the universities of California-Berkeley, California–Los Angeles, Illinois-Urbana/Champaign, Málaga, Michigan State, New Mexico, Texas-Austin, Texas–San Antonio, and at the annual meetings of the American Studies Association, the American Literature Association, and the American Ethnological Society. A portion of Chapter 3 was presented as the Distinguished Phillips Barry Lecture on Folksong at the 2004 meeting of the American Folklore Society. I thank them all for these opportunities.

The anonymous readers of the manuscript are much thanked for their very useful commentary. Virginia Raymond read the entire manuscript with great care and editorial attention. Its failings are all my own.

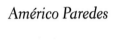

Américo Paredes

Introduction

Américo Paredes (1915–1999) became and continues to be the foremost U.S. literary and cultural studies intellectual of Mexican ancestry, a figure who focused his creative and scholarly efforts largely on the cultures and peoples of what he called "Greater Mexico." By that he meant "all of the area inhabited by people of Mexican culture—not only within the present limits of the Republic of Mexico but in the United States as well—in a cultural rather than a political sense" (Paredes 1976: xiv). He was also one of the primary founders of the institutional academic enterprise called "Mexican-American studies."[1] It is therefore not surprising that his work has been the subject of much scholarly commentary, most focused on his fiction and mostly of article length, but not entirely.

In what follows I offer an extended analytical treatment of most of Paredes's work—scholarly and creative—and thus join three other book-length assessments (López-Morín 2006; Saldívar 2006; Medrano 2010).[2] Serious intellectual and social issues surrounding Paredes's or any intellectual's work are not automatically settled forever when the scholarly growth reaches any particular plateau, especially when one is in honest and serious disagreement and debate with some or even all of that scholarship, or notices that certain issues have not been fully addressed. Moreover, a leading critic of Mexican-American cultural studies, the late Juan Bruce-Novoa, once suggested that, as of 1994, all commentary about Paredes was uncritically reverential toward this body of work and its author (Bruce-Novoa 1994: 234–237). If true, I offer the present work as a continuing corrective intervention in Paredes studies.[3] I began this book in the early 1970s as Américo Paredes's graduate student, specifically Chapter 3, and gradually added to it as more of Paredes's early and forgotten work was retrieved and published in the 1990s, until I began to see the coherence of a possible book. While some of what follows in these chapters will no doubt show my admiration of Paredes and much of his work, other parts of it will clearly demonstrate my critical discomfort with certain other aspects of his writing.

My general thesis is that previous treatments of his work have not closely examined many of the specific contributions, but also the contradictions, in the Paredes corpus. In each chapter that follows I hope to show just such previously unrecognized or underappreciated contributions, as well as contradictions.

The accessibility of academic writing to a more general though intellectually literate public has become much more important for me in the later stages of my career, and I have been trying to make amends with my last book (1998) and now perhaps this one. As part of that accessibility, I have tried to lend sharp and, I hope, clear focus and critical argument to some specific key issues, even as these foci broach larger questions in such areas as literary ethics, scholarly genealogies, folklore, transnationalism, and cultural studies that were also of concern to Américo Paredes, or that his work raised, and that have either been ignored or not specifically addressed in the extant scholarship on his work. Since I am interested in focusing on these specific issues, I have not addressed other parts of his work that seem to me not as central to my concerns, or I have done so only tangentially.

As I discuss the specifics of the chapters that follow, my preliminary introduction to these areas and genres will also take on a chronological structure that corresponds to different significant periods in Paredes's life; these also occur in the context of a Mexican-American social history, with some emphasis on Texas, where he spent most of his life. These periods and some of his biography have been well known to Paredes scholars and even to the lay public at least since 1980, when I offered the first public overall interpretation of his life and work, also the subject of later work (Limón 1992, 1994). Nevertheless, for new and, especially, younger readers, a brief rehearsal of these historical and biographical periods may be helpful, together with my delineation of the specific concern of each chapter. For a far more detailed biography than is warranted here, I refer the reader to Saldívar, López-Morín, and Medrano, and for more detail on the historical context, the reader may consult a host of excellent histories.[4] Indeed, though these recent histories fully inform and flesh out the account that follows, it is highly probable that those of us who write on such matters—including these historians—acquired our first sense of this history from

"The Country," the first chapter of Paredes's classic work *"With His Pistol in His Hand": A Border Ballad and Its Hero* (1958), as many younger students continue to do today.

Américo Paredes's ancestral family was part of the Spanish settlement of what is now southern Texas and parts of northern Mexico in the mid-eighteenth century as part of Spain's last extension into the Americas. Ranchers and agriculturalists, these Euro-American settlers coming from central New Spain subdued or integrated the indigenous populations and established a society of small to large ranching settlements with three major towns: Laredo to the west, San Antonio to the northwest, and Matamoros to the east and to the Gulf of Mexico—defining and governing the internal settlement, although the Nueces River offered a kind of natural boundary as well.

Despite being a trading society, it remained relatively isolated even after becoming part of the new Republic of Mexico in 1821, until encountering the expanding and imperial power of the United States in the years 1826 to 1848, marked by two decisive events: first, the war for independence and the formation of the Republic of Texas from 1836–1848, a successful war against a Mexican central authority that had permitted these rebels with Anglo-Saxon origins in the United States to first settle in what is now central and east Texas, but who now in their independence also claimed the largely Mexican southern area to the Rio Grande as well; and, second, the eventual military invasion and political-economic incorporation of the area into the United States as part the U.S.-Mexico War supporting the Texas claim, and the formal annexation of Texas into the Union in 1848.

More U.S. citizens then began a gradual expansion into the previously all Spanish-Mexican, now legally southern, Texas, although even with the military violence of the wars and continuing, sporadic ethnic violence, there developed largely what historian David Montejano (1987: 34) calls a "peace structure" between these two groups sharing a common ranching culture—but one marked by a gradual erosion of Mexican land ownership.

This erosion, as well as a corresponding erosion of Mexicans' civil and human rights, intensified toward the end of the nineteenth century and well into the twentieth with the introduction of large-scale crop agriculture—agribusiness—to the area led by a new kind of Anglo-American, largely midwestern farmers with no attachment to the peace structure. This new agribusiness was built on the exploited labor of Mexicans, who at the same time were being racially segregated and socially marginalized—particularly, but not exclusively, in public education. We must also add another major component to this mix—namely, the entrance of thousands of largely destitute Mexicans from national Mexico across the Rio Grande into south Texas and other parts of the United States. Many were fleeing the repressive dictatorship of Porfirio Díaz (1876–1911) and the terrible vicissitudes of the prolonged revolution against him from 1910 to 1920. For Mexicans, and Mexican Americans, in southern Texas, and for most of those living elsewhere in the United States, second-class status became the order of the day, although they did maintain some controlling presence in interesting sectors of southern Texas such as Brownsville, Starr County, the Laredo area, and parts of San Antonio.

It was perhaps this sense of continuing presence in these areas, together with the experience of marked social subordination, that sparked the armed Mexican-American insurrections of 1915–1916 by *los sedicio-sos*, a group operating under a revolutionary manifesto called the Plan of San Diego. If 1915 is a watershed year, then we may speak of its aftermath as extending through the Second World War. Some would argue that the violence of that unsuccessful and bloody insurrection led Mexican Americans, especially their leaders, to seek other routes to social equality. Principal among those was the formation of a series of civil rights organizations, including the still very active League of United Latin American Citizens, better known as LULAC, a group akin to the NAACP (Johnson 2008). Such efforts were based on the emergence of a small, entrepreneurial middle class, itself a harbinger of a coming structural change (García 1991). This is not to say that ethnic and ethno-nationalist, left-of-center efforts keyed on labor ceased to exist, as Emilio Zamora (1995, 2009) has shown us. Zamora also tells us of the continuing role of a resistive and critical Mexican-American culture in this conflicted arena, a culture that others have discussed and that included newspapers, education, and literature, but perhaps centrally folklore, including ballads of heroic Mexican Americans resisting the Anglos, known as *corridos* (Flores 1992; Limón 1992; Peña 1983, 1999; Gonzalez 2009).

Here we may take momentary leave of such a delineated, cursory history and take up our principal subject, Américo Paredes, because his story begins precisely in 1915 with his birth and subsequent upbringing in Brownsville, Texas, in a largely Mexican-American–dominated town, but one not at all physically and psychologically far from the continuing social inequities felt by most Mexican Americans elsewhere in Texas, particularly the neighboring counties in what was then coming to be called "the Lower Rio Grande Valley." Paredes would grow into young manhood with such sensibilities, including a sharp sense of anger at inequalities, even while experiencing a stable and culturally nurturing home and social life in Brownsville that included a public education, which was not always available to Mexican Americans in other parts of Texas.

This combination of sensibilities and welcome privilege, together with that ineffable and unpredictable quality sometimes called "the muse," led the young Paredes into the spheres of intellect and creative writing, even though he might well have become something else, such as a lawyer. That was the chosen profession of the Mexican-American central protagonist of his first major literary work from this period, who also gives the novel its title: *George Washington Gómez: A Mexico-Texan Novel* (1990), a work that speaks out of and to the south Texas history noted above. Together with *Caballero: A Historical Romance* (1997)—coauthored by Jovita González and Eve Raleigh—the novel has become a foundational text of Mexican-American literature, especially its Texas lineage, and as such has drawn the most scholarly critical work of any of Paredes's other intellectual and creative labors, including *"With His Pistol in His Hand."*

I join these efforts in Chapter 1, titled "Radical Hope," with an assessment of this body of criticism and my own critical sense of what I take to be a more interesting and compelling argument offered by this early novel, informed by the work of literary critic Anne Lenne Cheng and philosopher Jonathan Lear.

The next major phase of this history—which is to say, the period including and following the Second World War—brought significant changes to the Mexican-American community in Texas. In part these changes resulted from extensive and largely male participation in the U.S. armed forces in all services and all theatres of the war, but other factors entered into expanding civil, political, educational, and economic opportunity, including the growth of a middle class (Montejano 1987). Yet this expansion would never have been achieved without continuing struggle in the civil and political arena, including a resurgence of ethnic militancy in the 1960s known as the Chicano movement, in emulation of the black civil rights and militant efforts of that period (I. García 1997, 2000, 2002).

Paredes played a paradoxical role during this latter historical period. As with so many others, he joined the army, but toward the end of the war, and thus did not fight but did serve in the army of occupation in Japan. Although one might have expected an immediate return to the United States at the end of his tour of duty, he chose to remain in Japan and other parts of Asia for almost six more years. During this time in Asia, principally in Japan, he continued to write, principally journalism, but also a series of short stories that explore the relationship of Americans, including those of Mexican origin, to Asians, primarily the Japanese. This Asian period, and these stories, are the focus of Chapter 2, "Asian Américo," where I argue that this period and its relationship to what was going on in the U.S.-Mexico borderlands, especially Texas, may be at once more simple and more complicated than his previous critics, principally Ramón Saldívar, have made them out to be.[5]

Paredes returned to the United States in 1950 but kept his distance from the ongoing practical processes of social change among Mexican Americans. Rather, and now hearkening to the muse of scholarship which he had also practiced as early as 1942, he embarked upon an intensive academic career, studying at the University of Texas at Austin (BA 1951, MA 1953, and PhD 1956) and later joining its faculty. As his academic specialty he chose the professionalizing field of folklore studies, and as his principal subject, folklore—theory and method, but also the folklore of what he soon came to call "Greater Mexico," with a decided emphasis on southern Texas. Among his principal published work from this period, which would extend to 1990, is the ballad study *"With His Pistol in His Hand": A Border Ballad and Its Hero* (1958), based on his doctoral dissertation and a series of articles on the Mexican-American joke form.

In Chapter 3, "The Folklorist," I revisit these two bodies of work, on balladry and jokes, to argue that they merit a critical evaluation in explicit relationship to the field of folklore as that discipline was gaining momentum and status in the academy—an evaluation that they have never really received. *"With His Pistol in His Hand"* and, by implication, Paredes's broadened scholarly formation as a ballad scholar have been largely overlooked for what they most manifestly are: namely, a *ballad* study produced by a figure who critically, comprehensively, and with great subtlety commands yet goes beyond the international ballad scholarship and theory of his time, a command acquired in a few short years of intense study. By somewhat of a contrast, Paredes's work on joke narratives now seems limited given recent theoretical and historical approaches to joking behavior in culture and society that were not fully available to him at the time of his writing in the early sixties, or so I shall argue.

In our time, which for me extends from ca. 1968 to our present moment, Mexican America has gone through paradoxical changes. Mexican Americans of a third generation or later continue to experience some upward mobility, although in measured terms, with most still in a working-class status albeit in semiskilled and skilled occupations. Mexican Americans also experienced much greater political participation, including the election of Mexican-American mayors in two major cities: San Antonio,

Texas, and Los Angeles, California. Of more specific significance to the present argument, such an expansion of opportunity was predicated upon a gradual, if also measured, greater access to higher education.[6]

The increased access to higher education that began in the 1960s had another long-term effect that directly involved Américo Paredes and his work. As a direct outgrowth of the militant Chicano movement of the 1960s, we saw the creation and development of Mexican-American studies, including cultural studies.[7] In the early development of Chicano cultural studies, *"With His Pistol in His Hand"* was discovered and quickly became the beginning point and model, or standard, for the enterprise, but less as a work on academic folklore and more as a history of cultural resistance, even as the author himself began to take on the aura of scholar-hero and foundational figure. For example, in an early and influential collection of articles of Chicano literary criticism published in Maynard Mack's then-definitive "Twentieth Century Views" series, Paredes was invited to author the opening essay, "The Folk Base of Chicano Literature" (Sommers and Ybarra-Frausto 1979: 4–17).[8] However, since then and in our time, Paredes's presence in a thriving Chicano (and now Chicana) cultural studies seems to have been set aside, especially with regard to folklore work.

In Chapter 4, "Cultural Studies," I explore this contradictory relationship with Paredes to argue that Chicano/Chicana contemporary cultural studies has neglected Paredes's work at a cost, overlooking the experience of everyday life and vernacular culture. This evasion is not surprising, since, I will also argue, it also affected the development of cultural studies in general, from its inception in the early work of Raymond Williams and Richard Hoggart, and the formation of the Birmingham School in Great Britain in the early 1960s, at the same moment that Paredes's own brand of cultural studies was emerging.

Yet even though younger Chicano-Chicana cultural studies scholars seem distanced from it, such vernacular culture continues in the present day. Américo Paredes died in 1999, almost living to see the twenty-first century, and quite aware of the new fundamental technological and cultural changes that were taking place, which some have called "postmodernity." Necessarily, Mexican Americans have also entered into such a new cultural milieu, as I have argued elsewhere (Limón 1994: 97–117).

If, by definition, the postmodern works in idioms of pastiche, intertextuality, and emergent transformations, my final, substantive Chapter 5 takes up the field-based analysis—the ethnography—of two major instances of such an everyday and present-day Mexican-American vernacular culture—instances that were paradoxically generated by the influence of Paredes's scholarly work. Echoing the material of Chapter 3, these are what I shall call the new Mexican-American joke form and a popular, mass-media musical transformation of the ballad of Gregorio Cortez.

Finally, and before a closing farewell, I review Paredes's entire career under the rubric of the "public intellectual," evaluating his uneven participation in the salient public affairs of his time, principally as these concerned Greater Mexico, to which he devoted most of his intellectual career. This inquiry will also consider the parallel careers of other intellectuals of Greater Mexico, such as Jovita González, J. Frank Dobie, and Aurelio M. Espinosa.

Much has now been written about Américo Paredes and the work he produced for a good portion of the twentieth century. He deserves every bit of it and more. In the six chapters that follow, it is my hope that the reader will obtain an alternate and, I trust, fresh and illuminating sense of Paredes's contributions to a host of significant intellectual, political, and cultural issues. Indeed, I hope it may also have the effect of stimulating even more assessments of the important work of this scholar, writer, and intellectual who spoke so substantially to Greater Mexico with erudition, eloquence, and passion.

ONE

Radical Hope

According to literary historian John-Michael Rivera, in 1845, on the eve of a momentous shift in the histories of both Mexico and the United States, John O'Sullivan, the American editor and founder of the *Democratic Review*, broached what he called "the Mexican question." O'Sullivan used the phrase to label the debate concerning the imminent expansion of the United States westward into Mexican territory, an expansion he certainly favored since he also invented the phrase "Manifest Destiny." For him there was indeed no question that mixed-race Mexicans were neither racially nor culturally fit to possess such a western dominion, and therefore it was providentially intended to belong to the United States—a generalized American opinion that provided a cultural grounding for the coming war against Mexico in 1846.

The phrase continued to be used to name the issue of annexing *all* of Mexico into the United States after the American victory and occupation in 1847, and before the issue was settled in 1848 with the Treaty of Guadalupe-Hidalgo. Yet, along with other influentials, O'Sullivan was opposed to the annexation of most of what is now the Republic of Mexico. Senator John C. Calhoun, for example, also opposed such a total incorporation on racial-cultural grounds similar to those of O'Sullivan, saying, "Are we to associate with ourselves as equals, companions, and fellow citizens, the Indians and mixed race of Mexico? . . . I should consider such a thing as fatal to our institutions" (Rivera 2006: 58–70). In this fashion "the Mexican question" was historically defined as a still discernible U.S. attitude toward Mexicans in general, but perhaps more so toward Mexicans living in the United States, in much closer proximity to white America. The toxic residue of such xenophobia can be traced to the present. The raging debate on Mexican immigration and views such as those articulated nightly on Fox News is one very recent, and very public, example, as is the only somewhat more benign recent exclusion of Latinos by Ken Burns in his PBS documentary on World War II.

Yet, against such racism and other forms of social marginalization, Mexican Americans have also broached our own "Mexican question," which is: "How are *we* to define ourselves and make our way in such an American society?" Over time these two intimately related questions have been addressed within this community in different ways; indeed, one such public answer may be seen in the recent nationwide demonstrations by Mexican immigrants and their supporters, the latter including many Mexican Americans, now U.S. citizens, but also in the strong critical reaction that Ken Burns received from the Latino intelligentsia. Both reactions, it should be noted, are premised on the decisive contributions that Mexicans and other Latinos have made to this country. But the question has also been addressed by a historical and present-day lineage of Mexican-American intellectuals and artists. Among the latter, no figure is more important than the late Américo Paredes, especially in his early novelistic writing.

AMÉRICO PAREDES AS NOVELIST

Until recently, Paredes's most important work was thought to be *"With His Pistol in His Hand": A Border Ballad and Its Hero,* his study of the heroic *corrido,* a Mexican-American balladry of resistance to Anglo America, and the subject of Chapter 3. In terms of critical commentary and influence, that work may now be superseded by his novel *George Washington Gómez: A Mexico-Texan Novel,* recovered and published in 1990. The latter has become, in Marco Portales's words, "the master . . . narrative produced by a Mexican-American writer so far" (2000: 82). Though written in the 1930s and '40s, the novel was not published until 1990. This long hiatus was itself possibly a racist effect of O'Sullivan's version of the "Mexican question." Through its many different and complex characters, the novel articulates different and compelling positions on the Mexican question(s), positions that continue to be efficacious in the present moment.

This capacious work has drawn significant critical commentary, principally from Mexican-American literary intellectuals, but others as well. Acts of cultural interpretation are themselves acts of culture and politics, and so the readings of these critics—their varying points of view on this novel—must themselves be seen as responses to the Mexican question interpretively intertwined with the text of the novel.

Very understandably, these commentaries have focused on the novel's central protagonist, George Washington Gómez, the Mexican American from whom the book takes its title, and his coming-of-age development from 1915 through the Second World War. In the novel this character is more often than not known by his nickname "Guálinto," and I shall therefore mostly use this name as well, later changing it to "George," as the character himself does toward the end of the story.

After reviewing the Guálinto/George-centered criticism, I will offer an alternative view of the character Guálinto, but also focus on the largely overlooked figure of Guálinto's uncle Feliciano, whose character, in my estimation, offers a far more nuanced, complex, and far-reaching response to the Mexican question(s). The work of Anne Anlin Cheng (2001) on racial mourning and melancholia will be of the greatest assistance in making this distinctive case, as will philosopher Jonathan Lear's (2006) concept of "radical hope." Let us first review the novel and its extant critical commentary to chart its different responses to the Mexican questions.

Set in what today we would call the Lower Rio Grande Valley (hereafter "the Valley"), which is also to say the most southern border between the United States and Mexico, *George Washington Gómez* (hereafter GWG) begins in 1915, at the moment of Guálinto's birth. In the novel's opening scene we also meet his mother, María, his grandmother and sisters, as well as his father, Gumersindo, and his uncle Feliciano García, Maria's brother, all living in a rural area of the Valley. Gumersindo has brought an Anglo doctor from town to assist in the birth.

All of the novel's critics almost necessarily pay close attention to this scene. After debating on a proper name for this child, the family finally decides on "George Washington Gómez" because his parents, at least, believe the name of a great American leader is very appropriate for a son whom they hope will be a "leader of his people." The Spanish-speaking grandmother, however, cannot pronounce "Washington," saying instead "Guálinto," which then turns out to be the boy's very Mexican-sounding nickname, although he will still be known by "George." Thus we have the named beginning of what will become the central issue in the boy's development: Will he be "Mexican" or "American"? Even with this possible nickname, Uncle Feliciano, a proud Mexican American and anti–Anglo American, is very unhappy with the name "George" and wanders off, quietly singing a *corrido* as if in protest. Later Feliciano will foreground the name "Guálinto," although in the end the name will not prevail.

Feliciano has fought the Americans in armed conflict in the 1915 violent revolt of the *sediciosos* against racist and vicious Anglo-American authority in the Valley. Indeed, in the novel's first sentence we meet the Texas Rangers, who "at first sight one might have taken . . . for cutthroats. And one might not have been wrong" (9). At the same time, for national Mexicans in northeastern Mexico, life is also being violently defined by the Mexican Revolution, during which many Mexican nationals crossed over into nearby Texas to escape the violence and Porfirio Diaz's oppression. Guálinto's father, Gumersindo, is one such figure who has come to the United States, eventually marrying into the García family. By contrast, Feliciano traces his origins not to recent immigration, but to the older Spanish/Mexican ranching culture of the Valley, which is why he participates in the *sediciosos* revolt. He survives the insurrectionist war, but in reprisals against all Mexican-origin civilians, the Texas Rangers kill Guálinto's noncombatant father, Gumersindo. The loss of his father and the post-1915 Anglo-American dominance of the area play pivotal roles in the formation of our young protagonist.

After Gumersindo's death, Feliciano moves the family to the nearby town of Jonesville for their safety and stability. In the city, Guálinto's formation will occur as a necessarily antagonistic dialogue in his consciousness between his Mexican cultural origins and the now competing cultural force of Anglo-American dominance that is rapidly becoming institutionalized in the Valley, especially in the educational system.

The novel takes several twists and turns, and adds many more characters, but after Guálinto comes to maturity in Jonesville, he eventually becomes a seemingly fully assimilated American subject after attending the University of Texas at Austin, becoming a lawyer, marrying an Anglo-American woman, and securing employment in Washington, DC. By then he is going by the name "George," and as a climax to this seeming track of assimilation, he seems to develop a classical ethnic self-hatred, which he freely voices in one of his infrequent returns to the Valley, even as he has a recurring dream upholding this very ethnic identification.

On what appears to be his final trip to the Valley, he learns that some of his old friends and high school classmates, led by an outspoken woman named Elodia, are organizing to contest Anglo-American political and social dominance in the Valley. At a dinner party in a restaurant, they attempt to persuade Guálinto/George to stay in the Valley and join their cause. He refuses, later saying to his uncle, "They're a bunch of clowns playing at politics. And they're trying to organize yokels who don't know anything but getting drunk and yelling and fighting. . . . Mexicans will always be Mexicans" (300). During this trip we also discover that he is a covert agent for the United States, gathering intelligence on possible seditious activities. The novel ends with a bitter parting between Guálinto and his uncle as Guálinto, now firmly "George," leaves the Valley for what appears to be the last time.

THE NOVEL AND ITS CRITICS

Even though George seems to have become the assimilated subject exemplar, two major critics appear to reject total assimilation as the novel's final outcome as they attempt to retrieve some form of a left-critical, culturally resistive, and emancipatory possibility in Guálinto's fraught life.

For José Davíd Saldívar (1997), all of Paredes's work is "a critique of the cultures of U.S. imperialism" (38). It is, he continues, a "counter-discourse to the homemade nativist discourses of U.S. imperialism" as "[Paredes] articulates the experiences, the aspirations, and the vision of a people under occupation" (49). GWG is central to this critique, which Saldívar locates exclusively within the character of Guálinto. One evening, right before the teenaged Guálinto goes away to college, he happens upon and is invited into a domestic, working-class Mexican-American party with dancing to *conjunto* music, often identified as the quintessential, deeply border Mexican, working-class music and dance (Peña 1985). It is a moment that Saldívar reads as one of cultural resistance. For this critic, in this "wonderful scene . . . young Guálinto relishes his mestizo/a working class culture by dancing to the local accordion-driven music of South Texas." He continues:

> Here Paredes dramatizes that, for Chicanos, *norteño* music is synonymous with a vernacular working-class consciousness. In Guálinto's embrace of *conjunto*, he subtly shows how his hero's place (late in the novel) was with his local mestizo/a working class. . . . In the novel, *conjunto* polka music becomes a political ideology by stressing local characteristics, by representing vernacular music, and by confirming everywhere the multiple dynamics of Chicano/a identity and nonidentity. (Saldívar 1997: 46–47)

I disagree. The "wonderful" dance scene is much more an affirmation that Guálinto is, indeed, *not* relishing a local cultural identity. Rather, it seems a prelude to his decisive assimilation once he leaves for the university. A more careful reading of the scene reveals that Guálinto, emulating Peter, *thrice* turns down the invitation to join the dancing, first saying, "I—I can't dance" (243), then protesting, "But, I can't dance" (246), and finally saying, "I really must go" (246). And leave he does, refusing "all exhortations to dance," as John Moran González (2009) has also noted. Moreover, as González further notes, a more comprehensive reading of this "wonderful" scene clearly indicates that for Paredes, "the working class culture out of which *conjunto* emerged offered no vision of communal resistance, but only leisure-oriented entertainment that fostered unfocused male violence and unregulated female sexuality" (33). When the working-class crowd—especially a dark, sexually attractive young woman named Mercedes—invites him to come back any time, Guálinto replies, "I must go . . . but I will come back." Later that night, safely in his bed, he thinks,

> Yes, he would go back to her. These were his people, the real people he belonged with. His place was among them. . . . He would marry Mercedes and live on the farm. He would go back. Tomorrow night he would go back. He never did. (242–247)

While conceding the obvious—namely, that at the novel's end Guálinto has acquired a manifest, assimilated and colonized, "solid bourgeois and modernist identity," Saldívar (1997) critically continues to try to save the novel as "resistance literature" by way of a now infamous dream recurrent in George's mature life.[1] Saldívar then only partially quotes George's fantasy/dream, which I quote here in full because it is so central for all of these critics.

> He would imagine he was living in his great-grandfather's time, when the Americans first began to encroach on the northern provinces of the new Republic of Mexico. Reacting against the central government's inefficiency and corruption, he would organize *rancheros* into a fighting militia and train them by using them to exterminate the Comanches. Then, with the aid of generals like Urrea, he would extend his influence to the Mexican army. He would discover the revolver before Samuel Colt, as well as the hand grenade and a modern style of portable mortar. In his daydream he built a modern arms factory at Laredo, doing it all in great detail, until he had an enormous well-trained army that included Irishmen and escaped American Negro slaves. Finally he would defeat not only the army of the United States but its navy as well. He would recover all of the territory west of the Mississippi River and recover Florida

as well. At that point he would end up with a feeling of emptiness, of futility. Somehow, he was not comfortable with the way things ended. There was something missing that made any kind of ending fail to satisfy. And he would stop there, to begin from the beginning a few days later. But he had outgrown those childish daydreams long ago. Lately, however, now that he was a grown man, married and with a successful career before him, scenes from the silly imaginings from his youth kept popping up when he was asleep. He always woke with a feeling of irritation. "Why?" he would ask himself. Why do I keep doing this? Why do I keep fighting battles that were won and lost a long time ago. Lost by me and by me too. They have no meaning now. (282)

It is, Saldívar (1997: 46) says, "precisely at this stage . . . that we realize Paredes's cultural deconstruction. For his recommendation in the narrative is not to solve the crisis of the hero's identity politics but to proliferate and intensify the crisis by having George's 'I' dissimulated through a recurring fantasy and daydream." Thus this critic seems intent on locating and stressing the moments of Guálinto's seeming resistance, one response to the Mexican question, but based on a misreading of the dance scene and in his understanding of Guálinto's dream states as a "political 'phantasmatic' of the U.S.-Mexico borderlands" that "continually haunts and contests the borders that circumscribe George's construction of a stable identity."

Like José Saldívar, Ramón Saldívar also finds critical potential in Guálinto's dream crisis, but in a more complex manner. As we have already noted, from the outset—which is to say, from the moment of Guálinto's birth—this protagonist is a figure interpolated initially into traditional Mexican culture, but more specifically for Saldívar, Mexican-American folklore, and principally the *corrido*, the Mexican-American ballad of resistance, with its warrior-hero protagonist in violent conflict with the Anglo oppressor (2006: 163–165). Guálinto's dreams, says Ramón Saldívar, constitute "alternative public spheres"; though "latent and repressed," "the fact of their continued existence, even if only in the attenuated forms of daydream and fantasy signals the possibility of their emergence as critique in other, more opportune historical eras" (175).

Such a future emergence, however, presupposes a paradoxical negation as this critic offers a gendered and feminist analysis. Guálinto's dreams are of armed resistance, textually best represented by the *corrido* and its heroic, male, warrior-hero protagonists, now "filtered through the related but diminished form of *corrido*-inspired narratives" (Saldívar 2006: 177), presumably such as the dream. However, both the *corrido* and any such subsequent forms "could not but be proscribed by ethical and political limitations" (177). The *corrido* "identifies the community and represents it in monologically male terms" and therefore, "to the extent" that such forms of resistance "continue to be articulated within uncritical, male-dominant, gendered discursive systems, and hence with the limits of such systems, their own viability as enunciations of liberation will remain, inevitably equally in doubt" (177–178). Thus, if I understand this argument correctly, Guálinto's dream recollections of the now-attenuated *corrido* tradition paradoxically represent a now gendered, progressive step forward, though articulated "poignantly" in the "failed utopian vision at the end of the narrative" (177). Ramón Saldívar further argues that "the sublimation of the possibility of historical agency into the political unconscious does not represent the end of praxis, but only its transference into an unspecifiable future"; though George now appears as an almost wholly assimilated subject, "social categories are not static; they are conditions that people may traverse. But traverse to what end? *George Washington Gómez* concludes with that open question and its horizon of unresolved possibilities" (187–188).

As critic, however, Ramón Saldívar does not leave this novel historicized as it is with its chosen plot and open, fraught ending. He wishes to imagine a kind of "future" closure to the "open question." Such a closure, he seems to say, is provided by the Chicano movement, beginning in the 1960s, although he is clearly more interested in its later phase, "at the end of the twentieth century," when the questions of gender and sexuality became much more salient (186). Although, he admits, that while

> we are not able to specify in satisfyingly concrete and definitive terms the nature of a completed Chicano and Chicana subject position through the figure of George Washington Gómez . . . the Mexican-American subject Paredes imagines in *George Washington Gómez* exists on an unstable ground of double negations. Yet through these self-negating subject-effects, we can glimpse the future of the past through which Chicana and Chicano subjectivities would one day emerge into real history . . . (188)

If I am understanding this formulation correctly, Saldívar seems to be saying that the "Chicano" and "Chicana" identity that emerged out of the cultural politics of the sixties is the better—indeed, almost ultimate—response to the Mexican question. Although it receives no articulation in the novel itself, in the character of George, or, more precisely, in George's dream, Paredes provides the negating staging ground for a future and positive Chicano and Chicana identity, a kind of "always darker before the dawn" argument.

A later critic also reads this story of youthful development and its assimilated ending as a structural outcome that indeed paradoxically completes the traditional structural development of the bildungsroman. In such a completion, the subject is brought into harmony with a new and also developing history of Mexican-American culture change and assimilation (Johannssen 2008: 81–99); however, in agreement with both Saldívars, and also with most of the other critics, Johannessen too turns to the famous dream sequence as "the only thing left of Guálinto, and it persists as a reminder of his cultural past . . . a kernel of hope in an otherwise profoundly pessimistic tale of cultural destruction" (99).

In disagreement with such a "kernel of hope" reading, Mendoza (2001) does not see any utopian progressive politics somehow emanating from Guálinto's vexed life into our own time, the so-called future in the present. Rather, he thinks that Ramón Saldívar does not pay full attention to the perhaps utopian but positive possibilities that are actually present in the text. Anticipated by Garza-Falcón, Mendoza shares Ramón Saldívar's feminist preoccupation, though in a far more specific manner as he focuses on the resistive stance taken by Elodia and her friends in the restaurant scene toward the end of the novel when they, and especially Elodia, denounce George's assimilated stance, calling him a *vendido sanavaviche* (sellout sonofabitch). That, as a woman of that time and place, Elodia uses such an expression further marks her rebelliousness.

For Mendoza, "the emerging, organic model represented by Elodia offers an alternative vision that has its analog in the labor movements of South Texas and their examples of collective action and female leadership" (2001: 156). He continues to lend emphasis to the female leadership of such collective action: "Through [Elodia's] active pursuit of change in political social relations, we are reminded of that which Paredes does not name but we know to be nonetheless true: that in this era there were many women who were organizing and speaking on behalf of other women and for all the residents of Greater Mexico" (167).

Women are also of central concern to a later critic. Focusing on Guálinto's mother and sisters, and also somewhat anticipated by Garza-Falcón (1998: 194–196), González (2009) much more fully examines this novel's gender representations, concluding that "Paredes's public sphere interpretation of the *corrido*'s anticolonial value rests upon the removal of *tejanas* from the anticolonial struggle altogether . . . a process repeated by the absence of gender analysis . . . in . . . *George Washington Gómez* . . ." (39). Somewhat qualifying his criticism of Paredes, however, González also valorizes Elodia "as a postcolonial alternative to outright capitulation, either politically or culturally," noting that she and her husband, Antonio Prieto, have established a Mexican restaurant "as a counter-representational enterprise and safe haven for political organizing." Moreover, in a particularly astute observation, González notes that it is Elodia who runs the business while Antonio, who plays guitar and sings, is relegated to entertaining the customers by singing "old *corridos*," a musical genre thus now "fallen from its heroic heights" (40). González goes even further: "Elodia figures the repressed utopian possibilities for anticolonial resistance by Texas-Mexican women not otherwise acknowledged by the narrative" (41).

Both Mendoza and González may be overestimating the scene in the interest of extracting an "alternative" politics, be it a collectivist, feminist, radical or "counter-representational" politics, even by analogy. First, it needs to be carefully noted that the scene does take place in a restaurant that Elodia and her husband Antonio Prieto *own*; that is, since growing up with Guálinto, they have become members of the Mexican-American petite bourgeoisie, "raking the money in," as Paredes has one of their friends say (287). Second, they and other of George's old friends have invited him to the meeting to persuade him to speak on behalf of one of their candidates for political office—indeed, a city council race. That is, they are engaged in the most conventional, if necessary, electoral politics within the prevailing party system governing the political fortunes of the very small town of Jonesville, but certainly not anything approaching radical labor action, as Mendoza implies, nor, in González's case, does such an electoral action seem encompassing enough to be "a post-colonial alternative to outright capitulation, either politically or culturally." And yet, these two critics, preceded by Garza-Falcón, do remind us of the way in which Mexican-American women have taken a decisive role in contemporary U.S. politics as yet another response to the Mexican question, some such as Secretary of Labor Hilda Solís on the Democratic left; others such as New Mexican governor Susana Martinez on the Republican right; neither, however, radical, although Solís might be construable as a "postcolonial alternative."

For Mendoza and González, a certain Mexican-American left radical alternative is at least intimated by Elodia and the restaurant scene, namely the activities of the radical Mexican-American Communist Party activist Emma Tenayuca. In 1930s San Antonio, Texas, she truly did propose a radical, labor-centered path for the then mostly working-class Mexican Americans, many of them women. Tenayuca also makes an appearance in another commentary on *George Washington Gómez* by John-Michael Rivera (2006). Rivera evokes Tenayuca not in relationship to Elodia, but through the figure of a little girl named Chonita in another of Paredes's fictions, a short story called "The Hammon and the Beans," where Chonita offers a mocking, childish verbal "resistance" to Anglo Americans. Rivera argues, however, that Chonita and, by extension, Tenayuca fail to communicate with the greater Mexican community, and therefore concludes that "the only language Mexicans can understand by the end of the story is that radicalism in South Texas is, in fact, a loose signifier that holds no real meaning for their peoplehood" (153). But a young boy in the story does admire Chonita. Though she "dies in the story, her radical spirit lives within the memory of one individual, a young boy whose nostalgic consciousness desires Chonita to lead the Mexican people out of economic and racial oppression in South Texas" (154). Rivera then links this story to *George Washington Gómez*, for like George, "brown radicalism haunts only the individual boy, in his dreams . . ." such that in the end, for both the boy and for George, "Mexican peoplehood . . . is fleeting and partial, only realized in the dreams of the unconscious individual, not the collective" (154).[2]

Paredes himself tells us that the novel gestures toward yet another position on the Mexican question, that associated with the League of United Latin American Citizens (LULAC) and, after World War II, the American GI Forum. Formed in 1927–1929, and restricting membership to U.S. citizens, LULAC stressed educational attainment, learning English, and civic participation in U.S. culture, politics, and the legal system as the best means for bringing about social equality for Mexicans in the United States, while eschewing radical or nationalist programs. Yet many have criticized LULAC as favoring blind, patriotic, U.S. political integration and total assimilation, including distancing itself from Mexican culture, especially the speaking of Spanish, a criticism of LULAC voiced by Américo Paredes himself. Indeed, Paredes explicitly points to LULAC as one of his models for his negative construction of George as an assimilated subject—that is, a potential member of LULAC (R. Saldívar 2006: 123–125). As I will argue in Chapter 6, the record, however, suggests otherwise, and I think Paredes erred with respect to this organization, as some later critics of this group continue to do.

MEXICAN QUESTIONS, MEXICAN-AMERICAN ANSWERS

Viewed through these various critical prisms, *George Washington Gómez* becomes a kind of compendium of the different positions taken historically and contemporaneously by Mexican Americans on the Mexican question.

We may recall that Paredes's novel opens with a radical possibility— the insurrectionist, ethnonationalist violence of the *sediciosos*—but then forecloses such violent insurgencies and their presumed aftermath as a viable option after 1915. In similar fashion, as seen through the implied figure of Emma Tenayuca, a radical labor option is also not viable after the 1930s, and certainly not after World War II, although trade-unionist activity will always have some strong presence, as evidenced most prominently by César Chávez, but by others before him as well. As Emilio Zamora (1994) has eloquently shown, older and more encompassing forms of radical labor activity among Mexican Americans in Texas did speak directly to the Mexican question with strong cultural affirmation. Yet, though they occurred during the historical period of GWG and in the Valley, the novel does not admit of these, including no representations of such activity—an odd omission.

Thus, beyond the conservative, conflicted George, the novel seems to leave us with only Elodia and George's other classmates as a materially evident alternative possibility. As I have noted, I think Mendoza, González, and others overread these characters in the direction of radicalism and protofeminism, although González (2009: 41) does offer a more tempered understanding of Elodia and her friends as also akin to members of LULAC. Such an identification would certainly represent a historically consistent and very productive alterative, as I suggested in my earlier discussion of LULAC, but only if Paredes had developed her more fully and made this LULAC identity much more explicit, which he does not except insofar as he has extratextually (and wrongly) identified George as a kind of LULAC figure.

As we have seen, Ramón Saldívar creatively extracts yet another and utopian position on the Mexican question, namely that of an imagined ethno-nationalist Chicano and Chicana movement in a future beyond the novel, especially in its feminist dimensions. It is a generous and creative reading of George's dreams, but in my view the novel itself simply does not offer any warrant for such a "progressive" projection. Moreover, even if we were to accept such a projection from a dream into the future, here too there are potentially serious limitations. While the movement made substantial contributions, principally in academia and the arts, its primary influence has remained there—especially when we recall that even at its height, its general influence beyond academia and the arts was minimal.[3] In California, where the movement was strongest, David Hayes-Bautista (2004: 49) estimates there were "fewer than thirty thousand . . . in the movement, out of a Latino population of close to two million. . . . The vast majority of Latinos at that time did not even wish to be called Chicano." I know of no such estimate for Texas, but based on my personal experience in the movement there, I would estimate an even wider disparity in participation, with an even stronger mass unpopularity of the term *Chicano* (Limón 1981). Ethnonationalism of the sort imagined by the Chicano movement—including its "postnationalist," gender-progressive stages, as imagined by Saldívar—simply has not resonated within Mexican America as a whole.

Thus to the degree that we concentrate on George in his mostly manifest waking moments, the novel still leaves us with an overall reading of political pessimism. For Hector Perez (1998: 44), "this novel's overall vision . . . seems to be that major, significant social change is unaccomplishable. . . . For Chicanos, then, there is no way out of this labyrinthine social construction according to this novel's naturalistic scheme of things." Perez clearly is not including George's assimilation as a form of "significant social change." In similar fashion, and also ruling out George as an acceptable option, González concludes that "ultimately, the historical tragedy of Paredes's work is precisely his inability to imagine an anticolonial paradigm that would address questions of social justice within the Texas-Mexican community as well as between that community and Anglo-Texans" (41).

Therefore, with his centrality, it appears that George, even with his vexing dreams, seems to offer the one narratively foregrounded option for Mexican Americans, which appears to be a total political, structural, and cultural assimilation—a choice that, as Ramón Saldívar says, "one could reasonably make" (187). Obviously such totalistic assimilation is not at all a popular option with many of the novel's younger readers, and none of its Mexican-American critics, yet a form of social change is undeniably one response to the Mexican question, perverse though it may be for many.

MOURNING AND MELANCHOLIA

Before leaving George to this seemingly assimilated fate in which is embedded "a kernel of hope," one senses an alternative possibility for him in which the dream sequence and other aspects of his life are more what they seem manifestly to be: psychoanalytically revealed symptoms of what Cheng (2001) has called the "melancholy of race," and less "kernels" or launching points for what are really the political/cultural ideological hopes of the novel's critics. It is clear that the dominant critical view of George is, in Cheng's language, one of grievance rather than grief. Without exception, the critics' disavowal of George is based on his failure to become a true leader of his people in the arena of politics and civil rights, articulating and seeking redress for his people's grievances. But drawing on Freud's work on mourning and melancholia, Cheng encourages us to take a closer look at George's more complicated psychological existence as one of grief which culminates not in mourning, but in racial melancholia.

For Cheng (after Freud), melancholia, unlike healthy mourning, is the condition of losing a source—a love object—of potentially sustaining affirmative identity, but one not achieved because said object also disappoints in some profound sense. The obligatory love for the object and its loss overwhelm the subject who cannot express his/her profound resentment, leading to an internalization of this resentment so as to define the subject's ego with consequences of depression, but also aggressive symptomatic behavior. Cheng correlates this relationship to the sense of loss incurred by racialized communities subjected to racial injuries great and small in their history and everyday existence. But "loss" here must also have reference not to materiality, but to the loss of self-esteem, to failure, and to the cultural transmission of such loss generationally.

While Cheng recognizes the dangers of focusing on racialized psychological loss rather than material grievances and redress, she thinks it important—and I agree—to explore the resulting complicated psychical dynamics of such loss. Only by such exploration and "working through" can such subjects move toward a greater and healthier maturity, both the individual subject and the racialized community. This is not the utopian "future in the present," but a long-term project of analysis and introspectively focused development of racial subjects even as they also address their racialized materiality in the realm of grievance.

By such measure then, is it possible to see George as a melancholic subject? We may be able to improve upon Cheng's fascinating effort to move Freud into U.S. racial relations if we recall that Freud was principally concerned with the individual subject, especially in relation to the "family romance." In this instance, it is possible to trace the conjoined vectors of family and race but also nation in the emergence of George's melancholia by recalling scenes of instruction in the novel that have escaped careful attention.

Early on, George's most manifest loss is his father, Gumersindo, an agricultural laborer, who has drawn critical attention principally in his role as the person who does not wish George to be told the circumstances of his death, which produces the conflict and resolution in George's relationship with his uncle. But the novel tells us more about him. From the beginning he is foregrounded as a different and lesser racial and national species-being. When a Mormon missionary comes to the Valley preaching the "brotherhood of men," Feliciano has this critical thought: "It was all very well for Gumersindo, who came from the interior of Mexico to be taken in by such talk. But a Border Mexican knew there was no brotherhood of men" (19).

Feliciano's caustic comment underscores the perception that what he calls the "Border Mexican" has of Mexicans from the interior—which is also to say Mexican immigrants. Elsewhere Paredes labeled such immigrants *fuereños* (foreigners), and not just to the United States, but to the native Spanish-Mexican population of south Texas—the Border Mexicans—with their long-standing presence in the area. Echoing Feliciano, in his scholarship Paredes suggests that the Border Mexicans saw these new immigrants as transients and outsiders because they had no historical roots in the land and no stake in the ongoing struggle with the gringos (1958: 13). Adding to this negating perception, the novel describes Gumersindo as someone who is trying to learn English (13), who is like a "sheep" (19), who likes his Anglo bosses (20), and who came from Mexico to "find work and peace" (21). Of course, ironically, he is killed by the Texas Rangers not fighting with his pistol in his hand, but as a coldly executed prisoner. Until the very end, George does not know how his father was killed, but he surely knows that Gumersindo was from the interior of Mexico and not a border Mexican. "When you were little," Feliciano tells him, "you used to ask about him, and we would tell you stories" (262–263).

Other than George's experience with the educational system (in the realm of grievance), the critics have paid little attention to the more foundational and precise source of George's unsettled, conflicted, psychological condition, which feeds into a continual questioning of his Mexican identity. I suggest that George's melancholia is set in motion by his awareness of his father's sociocultural status, an awareness probably reinforced during his childhood by seeing thousands of poor immigrants entering the area after the Mexican Revolution began in 1910. It is an awareness of one's father now gone, but also of a non–border Mexican who disappoints George, even though he is gone, and through this awareness passes on to George a sense of racial stigma. In the predominantly Mexican-American Brownsville of that time (and today), Guálinto's "Mexican-ness" should not be a source of anxiety unless, of course, it is the stigmatized Mexican-ness of the poor, laboring, and probably darker *fuereño*, the outsider both to border Mexicans and Anglos.

There are more than hints of this condition during George's early years, although they recur throughout, perhaps climaxing in the famous dream, but not beginning there. In one telling scene, the young boy thinks his home is an enchanted place, especially a lush banana grove in their backyard. Yet we are told immediately that "night changed the world," and ghostly apparitions, fear, and death abound (50). The novel then vividly describes a world of social violence surrounding the little boy as Mexicans kill each other in "a vomit of murders and gun battles." The violence is attributed to the town's "stormy politics," but there were undoubtedly other causes as well, premised on a new and difficult social reality.

Young George is coming to consciousness specifically at a time in the 1920s when Jonesville, right across from Mexico, fills with new and impoverished Mexicans leaving the ravages of the Mexican Revolution (50). The boy is exposed to such people and such violence. When his mother tells him that before his birth he was in heaven with the angels, he reacts in a style and scene anticipating Tomás Rivera's *. . . y no se lo tragó la tierra* (1992). The boy

> . . . was silent, thinking. Thinking, thinking. If I was up there, I ought to remember, just like I remember I was in the banana grove yesterday because I was. I was born but I don't remember that either. And she says I was up there. Was it me? . . . Maybe it wasn't me at all. Maybe it was somebody else. Maybe I'm somebody else! A cold emptiness settled into his stomach. Familiar objects suddenly looked strange to him, as though he were out of his body and looking at himself and all other things at a distance. Strange, terrible questions surged inside of him, questions for which he had no words, no concrete form, so that they floated around in his head like little clouds. Why am I? Why am I not somebody else? . . . A numbing loneliness seized him and he felt like crying out. Then, for a moment he almost grasped and put into solid thought the vague and desolating questions which floated inside his head. But as his mind reached out to hold onto them they dissolved like spots before his eyes. (51–52)

What, one needs to ask, occasions such manner of emotion and thought in an otherwise seemingly happy, nurtured child? Placed where this internal monologue occurs, in the immediate narrative context of endemic Mexican violence, I suggest that George is experiencing a displaced and unnamed psychic disequilibrium; that he is being haunted by his father—both loved as a father and repulsed as a poor, passive, and stigmatized Mexican immigrant now represented by thousands like him now entering Jonesville, the Valley, and the United States. In short order they will give the United States its own racial sense of the "Mexican," but also haunt all Mexican Americans. "Why am I not somebody else?" the boy asks.

Later, as a teenager, in a moment of anger, the melancholia becomes manifest as Guálinto blurts out: "My father was just an ignorant Mexican!" (193). As he incorporates his father's identity into his own still weak ego, the result for this individual subject at this moment of childhood is the onset of "a wide range of complicated, conflictual, interlocking emotions: desire and doubt, affirmation and rejection, projections and identification, management and dysfunction" that will perdure (Cheng 2001: 15). Such a condition is itself a response to the Mexican question for so many Mexican Americans in the twentieth century and today as walls against immigrants become mirrors for "natives" (Gutiérrez 1995). To paraphrase young Guálinto, as we reach "out to hold onto them they dissolved like spots before" our eyes.

For this subject the melancholia continues into adulthood. Even his lashing out against "Mexican yokels" is itself a telling overstatement of the condition that is more often than not expressed as depression: "Somehow, he was not comfortable with the way things ended. There was something missing that made any kind of ending fail to satisfy" (282). Or, as Schedler suggests, George is less a wholly assimilated subject and more a modernist Mexican-American figure, "divided between outer mask and inner consciousness, producing a pluralistic representation of identity divided along multiple axes" (2000: 167). But racial melancholia is a double-edged sword and can also target the dominant authority, hence the "dream" of resistance deferred, as well as, more interestingly for me, his relationship to his Anglo wife. As he gazes at her asleep in bed, he thinks not in romantic idioms of love for a lovely wife. Instead, "she was rather plain, and some of her lower teeth were crooked, but she had beautiful hair . . . blond hair . . . naturally straight and lank and she had a long Anglo-Saxon face. A horse's face his mother once said . . ." (282–283). Such melancholia worked through over time may give way to a healthier state of affairs, though that is never achieved in this novel. Paredes did, however, hint at a different ending that perhaps would envision such a state (Saldívar 2006: 124).

In all of this, we must not forget that George is not the only principal character in the story. All of these conclusions—assimilationist, ethnonationalist, radical leftist, utopian "future" Chicano, feminist, naturalistic, tragic, LULAC, or melancholia—markedly overlook another key figure in the novel who might furnish a totally different alternative to the Mexican question, a figure also in grief, but one who chooses mourning over melancholia and thus offers a kind of radical hope.

At the very end of the novel, the now assimilated though psychologically fraught George sees his uncle Feliciano for what might be the last time. As he gets ready to leave the Valley, George fully acknowledges his complicity, not only with the U.S. government, as a secret agent spying on border Mexicans, but with American culture as a whole and his disdain for all things Mexican. Feliciano's reaction is both wry and bitter.

> "I'll tell you," his uncle said. "This is one of those when I wish I believe in another life, in a life after death."
> "It is?"
> "Yes. Then I could look forward to seeing your father in purgatory or limbo or wherever it is that Mexican yokels go. We could sit down and have a good long talk about you."
> George smiled. "I didn't know you had a sense of humor," he said.
> "I don't," his uncle said. (Paredes 1990: 302)

Thus, Feliciano literally and symbolically has the last word in the novel. George has become a big success, yet Feliciano's disappointment knows no depth, a disappointment possible only because he himself continues to be a repository—neither a dream, nor a brief restaurant scene—but a narratively living, breathing, well-developed, yet flexible repository of a different set of values.

FELICIANO GARCÍA

Present from the beginning at Guálinto's birth and naming, Feliciano, his maternal uncle, has a clear and major role in his nephew's already well examined development. As Guálinto's father, Gumersindo, is dying after being shot by the Texas Rangers in the 1915 uprisings, he makes Feliciano promise that he will never reveal the circumstances of his death to the boy because he does not wish him to become bitter toward Anglo-America and thus not succeed within that world to become a "leader of his people."

After Gumersindo dies, one of Feliciano's two principal, well-developed, and intertwined roles in the narrative will be to assure Guálinto's success, beginning with moving the family to safety in the town of Jonesville. The move will also bring him into much closer proximity to the cultural forces of capitalist modernity that are coming to the Valley, including an Americanizing educational system that will ironically contribute both negatively and positively toward making Guálinto a "leader of his people." But moving to a predominantly Mexican-American town has another outcome, giving Feliciano access to the economic, political, and cultural resources he needs to provide for his family's general well-being, even as these same resources produce a second distinct signification for Feliciano.

Withdrawing from his insurgent past and creating a new public persona, Feliciano initially takes a job as a bartender in a saloon, but from there he makes great socioeconomic progress, including owning a grocery store and buying a home and rental properties as well as some farmland. In addition to his own hard work, entrepreneurship, and financial astuteness, his progress is also assisted by forging connections with the local political machine and engaging in some contraband smuggling from and to nearby Mexico. Finally, although he has sexual liaisons, he does not marry—as one might think he could—so as to provide maximum support to his immediate family and, centrally, Guálinto.[4]

Feliciano's success has been treated with keen skepticism by some critics. According to Mendoza (2001),

> In his need to protect his family and provide the economic and social stability that will facilitate George's emergence as an intellectual and leader, Feliciano secures the way by functioning as a power broker between Anglos and Mexicans and participating as an elite in the capitalist economy. . . . Feliciano exercises privilege and authority over other Mexicans; he becomes a functionary of the new economic and political order. Feliciano's privilege is further evident in his ability to reacquire land in the period that closely follows the deterritorialization of Mexicans from their land . . .

And, indeed, Mendoza further accuses Feliciano of acting as a model for his assimilating nephew. "George's ultimate emergence as a traditional intellectual of the hegemonic order . . . follows a pattern set for him by his uncle and is symptomatic of the problem of individualism and leadership that characterizes this period of an emergent middle class in the Mexican-descent community" (153–154). Mendoza is fairly alone in this negative assessment, yet while other critics see Feliciano in a more positive light, none seem to give him his full due in his response to the Mexican question. Schedler (2000) concludes that "by the end of the novel, Feliciano has become a fairly well-off, middle-class landowner with two houses and his own farm" (159). But earlier, he also notes that Feliciano "takes on the character of the *corrido* hero, at least at the beginning of the novel" (157), clearly implying that at the end Feliciano is no longer heroic. Following Schedler, Ramón Saldívar (2007: 161) also notes that Feliciano is "the true inheritor of the warrior tradition," but he does not significantly explore Feliciano's role after the defeat of 1915.

A more sustained exploration would clearly suggest that Feliciano could be reasonably construed as a warrior, although he becomes such in what Gramsci (1985) famously called the "war of position," and no longer the literal "war of maneuver" of 1915. Johnson (2005: 204) notes that during the 1915 insurgency Feliciano refused to kill innocent civilians, and "whereas . . . Guálinto ultimately turns his back on his own people, Feliciano survives as a respected small businessman and farm owner" who is "ultimately the most admirable character in the book . . ." For his part, Perez (1998: 34) concludes that Feliciano "learns to function in the community's economic and political system while maintaining his 'Mexican' sense of self" such that, "to the extent that Feliciano counters assimilation into the new 'Anglo' culture by cultivating his organic borderlands roots, he lives out the spirit of the *corrido* tradition." Thus, "Feliciano seems an intelligent, rational, forward-thinking, practical person if not an outright admirable figure" (36).

Garza-Falcón (1998) comes closest to my developing argument. For her, Feliciano "represents *Mexicanos* who formed part of the resistance, either overtly or by maintaining their identity and culture despite the hostile surroundings," as he goes "to great lengths to maintain even inner resistance, making accommodations to preserve his life and that of his family" (176). Such a seeming and yet resistive accommodation is in the name of a larger and historical interest. Indeed, Feliciano "learns to manipulate the system for his own benefit and perhaps even to wear a different public face in order to fulfill hopes dreamed long before the Anglo occupation. . . . Fulfilling that dream requires money, education, hard work, and cunning" (177). As Garza-Falcón astutely notes, quoting from the novel, "There were many factors in Feliciano's increasing prosperity—hard work, luck, Judge

Norris and the Blue Party, Santos de la Vega. That, and his mother's fierce determination to regain for her children something of what had been lost to her grandparents when the Gringos came." Thus we also now learn that history, memory, and social practice stemming from Feliciano's mother were very instrumental in the formation of his being, even as we are led to appreciate Paredes's protofeminism:

> Her parents had only dim memories of their own as to what life was like before the Delta became part of Texas, but they passed their parents' memories down to her generation. This is why her children had learned to read, write, and figure at the *escuelita* in San Pedrito and why she had saved what little money she could throughout her life, a nickel or a quarter at a time. (Paredes 1990: 155)

An *escuelita* was a small, informal school often created and sustained by Mexican-American parents who wanted their children to learn formal Spanish and at least some math and penmanship, although they also offered cultural and historical instruction on Greater Mexico. They were often taught by educated locals or teachers brought in from Mexico. Although the children might attend the formal Anglo-American public schools, their parents wanted them to have this additional training, especially since the segregated public schools too often were inadequate, and certainly did not teach formal Spanish, indeed discouraged it. By the late 1950s these schools were fast disappearing as parents gained more confidence in the public schools or enrolled their children in Catholic schools.[5]

Such an *escuelita* would likely have been available in 1920s Jonesville, but Guálinto's family, with Feliciano in the lead, decides to enroll him in public school. The town and the schools, after all, were predominantly Mexican American, and it is as if even the strongly ethno-nationalist Feliciano recognizes that his nephew should have the best education possible if he is to succeed in the new world coming, including learning English well. Some critics point to this schooling as the source of Guálinto's eventual assimilation and thereby hold Feliciano complicit. I would contest the point. For all of its flaws, the local educational system prepared the boy to attend a major university, but it also fostered a critical outlook on society with enabling teachers such as Mr. Darwin, who admired students like Guálinto "who do not always agree with the textbooks" (Paredes 1990: 280).

As Guálinto gets ready to leave for Austin on the eve of his high school graduation, he is angry because he wrongly believes that his uncle ran away to Mexico during the 1915 insurgency rather than fight the Rangers. Together with his own bad experiences with racist Anglos in the nearby Anglo-dominated town of Harlanburg who refuse to let them attend a graduation party, Guálinto is actually in a fever pitch of angry cultural pride and resistance reinforced by having to sit through a racist commencement speech by a professor from the University of Texas at Austin, a man named "K. Hank Harvey" (more on the latter in Chapter 6). In high anger he initially resolves *not* to go away to UT-Austin, as he had been planning to do, as if that was the ultimate way to reject the Anglos (273–275). He later changes his mind, but we can only conclude that the school system in itself has done little to attenuate his sense of ethnicity.

Feliciano deserves a large measure of credit for fostering his nephew's formal education, but he can also be credited for Guálinto's sense of native cultural pride. His cultural upbringing also succeeds in retaining his loyalty—occasionally fraught though it may be—to his people. As most critics note, such pride is fostered by a vernacular, folkloric culture based on the heroic *corrido*, but they are also correct that it is Feliciano who has inculcated such border folklore into Guálinto's formation. When Guálinto and his friends are turned away from the graduation party because they are Mexican, they drive home while singing a heroic *corrido* led by a boy named Antonio Prieto who plays the guitar. Yet, there is another kind of education that Feliciano is also well-equipped to provide, one that critics have wholly overlooked. Guálinto himself observes that "the parlor was full of books, newspapers, and magazines all in Spanish. They were his uncle's reading matter . . . his uncle read a lot. Through each and every volume of books famous and books unknown . . . Feliciano had read with the grim resolution of educating himself" (189–190).

Thus, up to the moment he leaves for Austin, Guálinto has not gone over to the other side, and Feliciano has everything to do with the boy's continuing cultural loyalty. The unwelcome transformation into the assimilated, though fraught being he becomes occurs in Austin, far away from Feliciano and his ancestral culture.

His concern for Guálinto's education does not exhaust the whole of Feliciano's narrative being, for we can grasp his full alternative plenitude only if we put him in deep relationship to other significant facets of culture: family, region, history, and political economy. Feliciano is a man who never loses his *psychological* connection to a past of resistance, although such a path is no longer practically nor politically possible, and he has the wisdom to recognize this reality. He is also prudent and wise enough to recognize that an Anglo-driven, racist, and economically exploitative modernity has come to the Valley and all of South Texas, and that the only serious task for Mexicans now is to figure out how to live and prosper under such conditions. Conventional politics may be part of the answer, but by no means is it central. Indeed, it is far more telling that Feliciano has the wisdom to purchase land and start a small subsistence farm precisely in critical counterpoint to the massive Anglo-driven agribusiness that is starting to envelop the Valley. Yet Feliciano's virtues, forged in history by people like his mother, become far more socially meaningful and collective when they are viewed in intimate relationship to his region and community in the present. That is, he forges his admirable significance in relation to what Raymond Williams might call his "effective" community. Williams is referring to a modernizing yet still rural England, where communities of "a local kind" can "survive in older terms, where small free-holders, tenants, craftsmen and labourers can succeed in being neighbors first and social classes only second." Such an effective community "must never be idealized, for at the points of decision, now as then, the class realities show through. But, in many intervals, many periods of settlement," continues Williams, "there is a kindness, a mutuality, that still manages to flow" (106).

Such, I think, was and is the case within the Mexican-origin community in Jonesville-on-the River, in the Valley, indeed in South Texas, "now as then," even while living within and coming to terms with an Anglo-driven and racist modernization, and often precisely *because* of it. For again, I insist with Williams that one must not idealize, for "it is a matter of degree, as it was in the villages before and after enclosure. When the pressure of a system is great and is increasing, it matters to find a breathing-space, a marginal day-to-day independence, for many thousands of people." As the new economic system "was now in explicit and assertive control . . . community, to survive, had then to change its terms" (106–107). Nowhere is this community affiliation more evident than in Feliciano's close relationship to his field hand Juan Rubio, to whom he will bequeath half of the farm after George disowns his future inheritance.

As we have seen, in response to the Mexican question that initiated our efforts, *George Washington Gómez* and its critics offer us several possibilities, and we have noted their pros and cons. But the critics invariably construe such possibilities within overtly political, collective, and public groups and programs, such as *los sediciosos*, LULAC, labor radicalism, the Chicano movement, and so on. Johnson (2005), for example, links Feliciano with LULAC as if to give him greater social significance, even though LULAC never appears in the novel (204). In our politically narrow criticism, we overlook the possibility of a mode of critical existence that need not be tied to a political position and agenda, but yet may turn out to be the most fundamentally political in the ancient Greek sense of the *polis*.

Who, then, is this man for whom the term "admirable" recurs among most critics, now including myself? Nothing more or less than an *exemplary* socially and economically competent, well-educated, deeply cultural Valley Mexicano who, though now having to live within and make use of "Anglo" modernity, nevertheless always remembers his essential opposition to the racism and exploitation of *some*—indeed, many— Anglos. For he has also discerned that not all are such, beginning with Judge Norris, who initially provides him with support when he decides to move his family to town. Feliciano becomes a constellation of alternative and resistive lower border Mexican social, psychological, and cultural values, willing to bend but not break, a flexible repository that is able to live well within the storm of modernity—admirably well—by himself partaking of its benefits, reminding one of Manet's *Steamboat Leaving Boulogne* (1864).[6] Indeed he occupies the most resilient, creative, and encompassing "political" position of all, perhaps another example of what philosopher Jonathan Lear might call a figure of "radical hope."

RADICAL HOPE

In his book *Radical Hope: Ethics in the Face of Cultural Devastation* (2008), Lear focuses on the life of a man named Plenty Coups, the last great chief of the Crow Nation, who lived through the second half of the nineteenth century and into the twentieth beyond the First World War. As such, Plenty Coups was witness to monumental events in the life of his nation, of which two were especially critical: the disappearance of the buffalo and the end of Crow warfare, especially against the Sioux, both having everything to do with the inexorable advance of the United States. These endings, particularly that of warfare, precipitated a fundamental cultural crisis, for it meant not merely some sort of material attenuation but the loss of the very deep cultural concepts that gave life meaning for the Crow people. While hunting was important, much, if not all, of Crow life centered on the warriors in battle, particularly the practice of counting coup, or striking an enemy with a coup stick before actually fighting him. So fundamental was this loss that Plenty Coups would say that after they lost their hunting and warring lifestyle, for the Crow, "nothing happened."

Yet, in a marvelous, subtle analysis combining Aristotle and Freud, Lear shows us that something did indeed happen for the Crow beyond mere physical survival. Although obviously no longer the continuation of the old culture, in another sense the Crow culture continued to be efficacious through a process and symbolism wholly unlike that of the warrior. As if in anticipation of the crisis, at a young age Plenty Coups had a vision. This was not an ordinary, individual, Western kind of dream, for the Crow "had an established practice for pushing the limits of their understanding: they encouraged the younger members of the tribe (typically boys) to go off into nature and dream. For the Crow, the visions one had in a dream could provide access to the order of the world beyond anything available to ordinary conscious understanding" (2008: 66).

In Plenty Coups's dream, this cultural process gives forth imagery foretelling the demise of the buffalo and their replacement by American grazing cattle, even as a fierce Four Winds knock down all of the trees. But one tree is left standing, and in it is a key Crow cultural symbol—a chickadee—who provides Plenty Coups with a model for dealing with the coming crisis. At the furthest remove from the image of the strong and fierce warrior, the little bird is interpreted by a strong voice in the dream as being

> least in strength but strongest of mind among his kind. He is willing to work for wisdom . . . is a good listener. . . . Whenever others are talking together of their successes and failures, there you will find the chickadee listening to their words. But in all of his listening he tends to his own business and yet never misses a chance to learn from others. He gains successes and avoids failure by learning how others succeeded or failed, and without great trouble to himself . . .

As this scene of instruction concludes, the voice says,

> The lodges of countless Bird-people were in the forest when the Four Winds charged it. Only one person is left unharmed, the lodge of the Chickadee person. Develop your body, but do not neglect your mind, Plenty-coups. It is the mind that leads a man to power, not strength of body. (70–71)

Thus Plenty Coups begins to imagine and think his way through the crisis in full knowledge that after the Four Winds, life for the Crow will never be the same, and it is precisely under these conditions that a new way must be imagined. And, lest the reader take this to be an individualistic solution, Plenty Coups "recounted his dream in public," and the tribe "incorporated the dream into its own self-understanding . . . as the Crow used dreams cooperatively" (71). Lear argues that the Crow then held to what he calls "radical hope," by which he means having the deep hope that, even among the wreckage, something good will come for the Crow because of their cultural ideals. More specifically, it is "the hope that if they followed the wisdom of the chickadee (whatever that would come to mean) they would survive (whatever that would come to mean) and hold onto their lands (whatever that would come to mean)." They would do so in ways that would allow the Crow to flourish, remain together, and articulate their identity in new ways (141).

Above all, radical hope resides in believing that goodness awaits even when the present does not at all guarantee it. But how did Plenty Coups's culturally sanctioned vision lead into cultural practice, and in what forms? The Crow could not totally imagine their future either short or long term, but under Plenty Coups's leadership, and over time, certain steps were taken to assure the ultimate good for the tribe. Even though they could no longer be warriors, through astute politics in the U.S. Congress they managed to hold on to a sizeable portion of their ancestral lands. Some, including Plenty Coups, adopted Catholicism. They also turned to farming, learned English, built a college, fought in the U.S. military, produced a cadre of lawyers, and even became entertainers. Lear notes that "in 2005 the Crow hip-hop group Rezawrecktion won the Native American Music Award in Los Angeles" (98–99).[7]

Feliciano had his own chickadee, but she was not a bird. Recall "his mother's fierce determination to regain for her children something of what had been lost to her grandparents when the Gringos came." Though her parents had only dim memories of what life was like before the Delta became part of Texas, they had passed their parents' memories down to her generation. This is why her children had learned to read, write, and figure at the *escuelita* in San Pedrito, and why she had saved what little money she could throughout her life, a nickel or a quarter at a time." Note that Feliciano's mother was determined to regain "something," not an idealistic *everything*, and also that this regaining was to be done out of memory, indeed, but practically, by reading and writing and figuring "a nickel and quarter at a time," all lessons learned by Feliciano.

Amidst the early-twentieth-century wreckage that the Anglos—as well as a corrupt Mexican state across the river—brought to the Valley, we may see Feliciano, like Plenty Coups, as another figure of radical hope. Both

men may be said to be in mourning over the loss of their respective racialized traditional communities, but as Cheng (2001: 7) reminds us, after
Freud, "mourning is a healthy response to loss; it is finite in character and
accepts substitution (that is the lost object can be relinquished and eventually replaced)." Initially, almost nothing assures Feliciano of success in
the new environment, but he eventually succeeds, even as we know that
he remains Mexican-American through and through, and intimately loyal
to his Valley community. Like Plenty Coups, he too becomes an exemplary figure for his community, as indicated by his acquiring the honorific
"Don" (268).[8] He reminds us of Grandpapa in Carson McCullers's *The
Heart Is a Lonely Hunter*, the critically overlooked, successful, and honorable black farmer who holds his own in the 1930s racist South while most
of the other alienated characters are floundering about for a "solution" to
racism and exploitation. In all of this, of course, Feliciano is the most fundamental of foils to the errant George. As Paredes says, "Once I started
writing, Feliciano, Guálinto's uncle, for example, became more and more
important. Toward the end of the story, I think, he's a much more appealing character than Guálinto Gómez" (quoted in Saldívar 2006: 120).

In my estimation, Feliciano's "appealing character" is an alternative to
the other paradigmatic ways of responding to the Mexican question. Some
might argue that his very age makes him such a figure only for the past,
but I would propose that he can also be seen as an exemplary figure for
ongoing social life for Mexican Americans, certainly in the Valley but possibly everywhere. Indeed, there is considerable evidence that Feliciano's example has been emulated by many Mexican Americans in the Valley and
elsewhere as well. As Ramon Saldívar acknowledges for the real, present-
day Valley, "Only in the last generation or so, at the end of the twentieth
century, have Mexican-Americans regained control of some of the civic,
social, and educational institutions of the region that they lost after 1848"
(5). I would respectfully disagree, only to replace his "some" with "most, if
not all." For even though they may not have read this novel, its wise author,
in crafting Feliciano, may have been projecting his own radical hope that
his people—in the Valley and elsewhere—would be capable of producing
many such figures, and that over time a community's radical hope would
take on greater reality if Feliciano's example was followed and expanded,
as it has been. Critics of this novel have paid too much attention to George
and conventional politics, including trying to extract a political "future"
out of that morass. Feliciano and the vibrant regional culture and radical
hope that he signifies offer a much better focal point for understanding
how to continue to be Mexican in America.

TWO

Asian Américo

Having written *George Washington Gómez*, and somewhat like Guálinto, Américo Paredes left the Lower Rio Grande Valley in late 1944 to serve in the U.S. Army during World War II. By the time his training was over, the war was drawing to a close, and he wound up in Japan during the occupation after August 1945. That September 3, he turned thirty. With some experience as a journalist in the Valley, he served out his tour working for the U.S. Army newspaper *Stars and Stripes*, covering and filing stories on a myriad of small and large events happening in postwar Japan. After his discharge in 1946, Paredes remained in Asia for four more years during which he worked for the Red Cross but also as a journalist. He also continued to produce creative writing as he had done in South Texas before the war, the latter principally *George Washington Gómez*, with its critique of Anglo-Mexican relations in South Texas, as we have seen.[1]

Indeed, in *The Borderlands of Culture*, Ramón Saldívar argues for continuities and parallels between Paredes's critical understanding of the conflict in his native South Texas Mexican community and his view of the occupied Japanese relative to their respective and oppressive Anglo-American occupiers. Further yet, Saldívar argues that Paredes's Asian experience was vital to the latter's postwar intellectual work, which we will take up in subsequent chapters.

In what follows, I want to question the manner in which Saldívar, and perhaps Paredes himself, too easily establish a commonality between border Mexicans and the Japanese, even as I also wish to question Saldívar's understanding of the relationship of Asia to Paredes's postwar work. But in a second section I also wish to return to some key instances in Paredes's Asian fiction — interesting paradoxical moments — when Paredes appears to break down the binary between "Anglos" on the one oppressive hand, and on the other, the allegedly subaltern pairing of Mexicans and Japanese created by critic Saldívar, seemingly after Paredes. Put another way, I am proposing that Saldívar offers a particular rendering of Paredes as a vital, dynamic, and critically postcolonial transnational cultural critic, whose transnationalism extended beyond the United States and Mexico, and their border. While Paredes does occasionally lend himself to such a reading, other evidence suggests a more complex and ultimately national and regional figure.

THE PROBLEM OF "ASIA"

Paredes's creative writing before the war certainly focused largely on Anglo-Mexican relations in South Texas. Perhaps surprisingly, the prewar Paredes also addressed Asian countries, if briefly, in his major work from that period: the already discussed novel *George Washington Gómez*, with its young protagonist, Guálinto. At one later point in the novel, Guálinto and some of his high school friends are conversing with two Japanese-American classmates, brothers and children of Japanese farmers who came to South Texas in the earlier part of the century.

> Jimmy and Bob Shigemara were the sons of a prosperous Japanese truck farmer . . . fat, well-fed boys who talked a glib, smooth English and were much liked by all their schoolmates. . . . Jimmy Shigemara was saying, "Of course we're not the same race as the Chinese. We're much more civilized." . . . The group talked a little longer about the relative merits of the Chinese and the Japanese, and [George] agreed enthusiastically with Jimmy and Bob Shigemara that the Japanese were a very wonderful people. (170)

Given George's eventual development into an assimilated, if psychologically fraught, American, one cannot help but imagine that Paredes is suggesting, in wry irony, that as part of that fraught development, George is also learning certain ethnocentric attitudes even as, in adolescent fashion, he plays up to the prosperous and well-liked Shigemara boys. Yet, as we shall see, perhaps this encounter is less than ironical and oddly more predictive of Américo Paredes's later encounter with these same two Asian peoples during the immediate post–World War II period that he spent in Asia.[2]

With very few exceptions, Paredes took very well to the Japanese during the occupation period, in both cultural/aesthetic and political terms, and Saldívar quite accurately records this perspective. In cultural/aesthetic terms, Paredes reports,

> It was eerie and wonderful to be in Tokyo in those days. . . . When I arrived it was still a half-ruined city. But what struck me most was the poetry of politeness of the Japanese. . . . Really, the peacefulness of the Japanese bewildered us when we remembered Pearl Harbor, the many atrocity stories that were circulating, and the recent bitter fighting in the Pacific. (Saldívar 2006: 97)

Only in this and two other passing instances that I know of does Paredes specifically refer to Japanese atrocities during the war, as he gave himself much more over to Japanese sociocultural poetics and postwar politics. For Saldívar these poetics seem to emerge around women, who, as he says, "were in everyone's mind during the occupation, in Paredes's mind no less than in anyone else's" (360). But these were women largely within one sexualized universe, one that will eventually lead us back to both politics and atrocities. Saldívar tells us of one particular evening when

> the similarities between Mexican and Japanese women were also on Paredes's mind, as he describes how the geishas . . . served the guests dressed in "colorful kimonos reminiscent of the costumes of our Tehuanas," an indigenous people of Oaxaca and southern Mexico. More than the geisha's sensuous apparel, he writes, their "dark complexions and oblique eyes with long lashes" could have allowed them to pass for Mexican women. (361)

The geishas also play music and sing, and Paredes, once a professional singer, is carried away when one geisha sings an old Mexican song translated into Japanese: "I listened to the geisha as she finished her song with great satisfaction, like that of one who encounters a veiled woman, lifts her veil and encounters a former lover" (361–362).

Women are also a central part in a larger social sphere. According to Saldívar, "Paredes represents in one magnificent *Stars and Stripes* Sunday feature spread the sex industry as it 'blossomed forth from the ruins' of bombed-out Tokyo to provide night-life and 'comfort' to the occupying quarter-million-man American army." The Tokyo entertainment district known as the Ginza, "reports Paredes, has become a 'Japanese cross between Broadway and a Mexican market place,'" a scene centered on nightclubs, taxi dancing to American music, and prostitution (353). "The appeal of this glittering scene of commercial and entertainment nightlife in the context of the torched desolation of metropolitan Tokyo," says Saldívar, "can hardly be overestimated," for the Japanese but, one senses, for Paredes as well (355).

Yet even as they approach the Ginza with a certain enchanted admiration, both Paredes and Saldívar also want to underscore that the prostitution within the Ginza had much to do with the immediate postwar chaos and literal hunger resulting from the destructive effects of the war on Japan: principally the infamous B-29 raids on its major cities, but also the difficulties for the Americans in administering food distribution and other forms of social support to such a large population even while providing for the army of occupation (356–359). Although Paredes and Saldívar don't say so, these difficulties were severely compounded by the relatively sudden and unanticipated end to the war following Hiroshima and Nagasaki rather than its anticipated and prolonged continuation. Yet even over the short term, and certainly by the mid-1950s, Japan would be doing very well, due in no small part to substantial U.S. support for the new Japan, especially as a developing partner in the Cold War against the Soviet Union (Dower 1999).

Paredes also wrote a great deal concerning postwar Japanese political and legal affairs, including the major trials of Japanese military leaders charged with various war crimes. Hideki Tojo was the best-known of these, having served as prime minister during most of the war with the United States. He had previously served as a primary military leader, including service as a field general and later chief of staff of the army in the war that Japan conducted against China and Korea in the 1930s. Along with war crimes, principally the maltreatment of prisoners, Tojo, along with other Japanese leaders, was also charged with waging aggressive war (Dower 1999: 456). Paredes was permitted a brief interview with Tojo that proved to be inconsequential in terms of a full story, but says much of what Paredes thought of Tojo and his evaluation of Tojo's war crimes. The general thrust of Paredes's journalism (as well as a poem) is to defend Tojo against various charges of war crimes, principally atrocities by the Japanese army allegedly committed in its various theatres of war. "There was Tojo, the great statesman and warrior, a taciturn man, trying to retain as much dignity as he could under the circumstances. . . . I felt sorry for him because I knew that he was being accused of 'war crimes' that had in fact been committed by both sides" (385–386). Paredes's sympathetic view of Tojo is then further underscored by what Saldívar calls "Hideki Tojo's iconic gravitas and dignity being played out under the bright lights of history's judgment" (389).

Together with his positive assessments of Japan's poetic politeness and the Ginza in all of its sexualized ramifications, Paredes's devotion to postwar Japan is borne out even more by his seeming admiration of Tojo coupled with his continuing critique of American power. In a later interview, Paredes expresses his admiration for Japanese culture as he again spends more time criticizing the American treatment of Tojo (Calderón and López-Morín 2000: 210–211).

Paredes also traveled and worked for the Red Cross in China as a public relations man, but he was also involved in overseeing the distribution of relief supplies in that beleaguered country. He was there substantially from October 1946 to May 1947, although he appears to have returned to China from Japan intermittently until 1948, even as he also made a short visit to Korea (Saldívar 2006: 102). In this capacity he also filed reports to his Red Cross superiors on which he comments on the overall situation in China, often in a literary mode.[3]

While in Japan, he had already taken journalistic advantage of this Asian opportunity. Citing his previous newspaper work in Brownsville and being fluent in Spanish, he had offered his services as a foreign correspondent to the famous Mexico City newspaper, *El Universal*. It was happy to take up his offer, especially when Paredes suggested that Mexico and Japan were similar, and that there was much in Japan that would "escape the attention of an Anglo-Saxon but that a Mexican would see, but more so, feel."[4] In this capacity he also filed several articles for *El Universal* from China.

His pronounced admiration for Japan and its aesthetic sensibility did not carry over to China, then still largely under Chiang Kai-shek's control, although the civil war with Mao Tse-tung's Communists was in progress, with the latter gaining. In sharp contrast to Japan, Paredes, in a letter to his brother back in the Valley, wrote, "No. China is not beautiful."[5] In China, according to Saldívar, he takes a sympathetic and politically aware note of the extreme poverty, poor health, and alienation of most of the population, describing "faces horribly disfigured by smallpox," while others "were hard even in repose, and they all seemed to hate the foreign barbarian" (100–101). Hong Kong, he says, is "really rough" (101). "Housing was awful in Shanghai," where "as winter set in, things got worse. More unrest, more stealing" (102–103). The original letter elaborates: the city's "sickness shows. . . . It is sick economically; it is politically sick, loaded with corruption . . . and sick physically," with extremely high rates of tuberculosis.[6]

Yet, on occasion, China did offer some aesthetic relief. The same letter that speaks of China's sickness also mentions flower shops and grocery
shops "where the fruit is arranged like a modernistic painting" and the
canned goods "are placed with an eye for color and composition," while
"the pastry shops look like a child's Hansel and Gretel dream." According to
Saldívar, Paredes saw a play with "weird, wailing songs" and heard a street
vendor's "queer musical cries." The actors in the play did have "gorgeous
costumes," and the street vendor's cries remind him of "those heavy orien-
tal songs of the gypsies of southern Spain" (102); elsewhere in his letters he
concludes that "Japanese music is Western and modern compared to this."[7]

As with Japan, Paredes also speaks of women in this Chinese context,
and here too there is difference. In China there are no geishas. In a personal letter to his male friends back in Japan, Paredes wrote,

> It was really romantic to go with a Chinese woman, following her down
> the street with all those Chinese men staring at me with hate in their
> eyes and finally going into this place where she lived and not knowing
> whether the papers would say the next day that a Red Cross man had
> been found in an alley with his throat cut. The Chinese seemed to lose
> no sleep loving their brothers from across the sea. (quoted in Saldívar
> 2006: 100–101)

But in an immediately preceding part of the same letter, not quoted by
Saldívar, we hear a young Paredes evincing such a sexually grounded view
of Chinese women articulated in a jocular tone, though with a measure of
continuing political awareness. Unfortunately, he speaks of such women
in the masculinist idioms characteristic of young men in that time and
circumstance.

> Dinner, my friends, is at 9 p.m. every day, with great formality and
> cooks, butlers and houseboys cluttering up the place. It will take a great
> time in China for me to get used to being waked up in the morning by
> a boy who calls me "Master." I see what the communist armies in the
> North are fighting for. Things are really high over here. A bottle of beer
> in one of the foreign joints will cost as much as 4500 Chinese dollars —
> merely a $1.25 U.S. Got myself a bit of "Paredes delight" the second day
> I was here — all on my own too — and it cost me 32,000 dollars CNC.[8]

Paredes then reviews the different nationalities of women in China —
British, Russians, Poles, and others; there are, after all, mostly Chinese

women, "which I don't like," and who don't "appeal" to him, he says, though they are "cheap."[9] In all, Paredes says, "In China, I was homesick for Tokyo and everything that went with it" (Saldívar 2006: 102).

We thus see Paredes making clear distinctions between his two major Asian experiences, but also Korea, as he clearly privileges Japan. Or, as he says in a personal letter, "China has its foreign population— boy that's good—and Japan has the Japanese. Korea—god forbid—has the Koreans."[10]

Saldívar, however, sees another Paredes, one who considers Japan a victim of American imperialism, but now also China—both now understood as "Asia"—a victimhood shared by Greater Mexico. This view is most vividly expressed in one of his poems from this experience, "Pro Patria," where Chinese, Japanese, Mexicans, and even poor white folks in the United States, "even if their eyes are blue," are said to be his "fatherland," "my people," presumably over against another form of dominating *patria*, the Western imperialist powers, especially the United States (1991: 84). Indeed, Saldívar proposes that Paredes's "fatherland" expresses "the kinship of affiliation with other races and ethnic groups that already existed in Paredes's experience of the transnational borderlands of Greater Mexico" (343). Moreover, "with reference to China, Korea and Japan, [Paredes] came to understand the possibility of a shared Asian culture, bonded by differences and similarities" (392). And women, always much on Paredes's mind, are also thus subsumed by Saldívar as a central locus of this kinship: "From Tokyo and from China, moreover, we get disconcerting insight to the place of the Asian woman's body as a site on which new subjective identities and social imaginaries were being negotiated, possessed and occupied" (393). Thus, to judge from the word "new," it would seem then that it is the new American presence—including the discriminating American Paredes—that is now negotiating, possessing, and occupying, for Saldívar, a now *homogeneous* female "Asian" body in a "shared" Asian culture.

Yet we have also heard Paredes's own unpoetic words on the differences between China and Japan, especially in terms of the female body, and Japan consistently gets pride of place. If, indeed, Paredes believed that such a kinship existed between Greater Mexico and an "Asia," for Saldívar (2006: 343) such a Paredes vision "accelerates to fruition *in Japan* under the consciousness created by a sense of *shared* oppression and injustice, as *mutual* recipients of race prejudice, and of having experienced the catastrophe of imperial conquest" (emphasis added).

What both Paredes and Saldívar seem to elide is the "catastrophe of imperial conquest" that befell China at the hands of a profoundly racist, sexist, imperialistic Japan at that historical moment. Indeed, as Paredes said earlier, the faces of the Chinese were "hard" as they eked out an existence in 1946–1948 amidst total social disruption, mostly as a result of a major sociopolitical event that is often ignored in conventional accounts of Japan in Word War II, which tend to focus heavily on the war in the Pacific.

I refer to the total war, the hyperaggression, that Japan initiated against China beginning with an early and erratic phase from 1932 to 1937 but massively accelerating and focusing on China's total destruction between 1937 and 1945, four years longer than the war with the United States. I am not saying that Paredes was unaware of the war, only that he does not foreground it as a major cause of the sick China that he has seen, perhaps because he is conflicted in his keen admiration for Japan.

In one Red Cross report Paredes briefly tells of "punitive" Japanese military expeditions where "houses were burned, furniture destroyed, livestock and food resources lost. The people were left almost totally destitute."[11] In another such report, he recounts meeting a British "lady" who tells him of being "starved all the time" when she was held in a Japanese concentration camp."[12] Even these brief, only occasional, and passing reports are balanced, as it were, by others that seem tangentially admiring of the Japanese during their occupation of China, especially Manchuria. The Manchurian city of Changchun, for example, "was planned by the Japanese as a copy of modern European cities . . . its buildings are well-built and modern, its streets wide."[13] Paredes was in Changchun during Christmas of 1946 and attended a Christmas party for American Red Cross workers held at the Yamato Hotel, named after the Yamato, he tells us, the dominant ethnic group of Japan: "after the mighty race of Yamato, whose descendants conquered Manchuria, overran the Pacific and were to have taken the world with fire and sword." Even as he acknowledges that "the mighty have fallen" at the end, the admiration seems to me unmistakable.[14]

There is one other instance when Paredes notes, again briefly, the Japanese armed intervention in China. He sent El Universal an article that mostly describes the passing scene—a travelogue—as he journeys from Shanghai to Nanking, but he does identify Nanking as the "site of the famous 'rape' of which the Japanese army was guilty."[15] Given that this "famous 'rape'" may have been the central moment in the long Sino-Japanese war, might he have said more?

No other moment in this war better exemplifies a pattern of state and *culturally* sanctioned focused, programmatic, and extended Japanese atrocities than the events known as "the rape of Nanking," with horrific consequences for Chinese women. In support of his argument on Tojo's behalf, Saldívar cites one book by coauthors Meirion and Susie Harries (1987), whom he considers authorities on Japan. Yet in another book that he does not reference (Harries and Harries 1991), they also write authoritatively on this appalling subject, as did journalist Iris Chang in her stunning book, *The Rape of Nanking* (1997).

On December 10, 1937, with Peking already in their hands, the Japanese military in China, known as the Kwantung Army, launched a major attack on the new Chinese capital of Nanking. After defeating the Chinese, with many casualties on both sides, the real horror began to unfold as the Japanese entered the city. "There was order of a brutal kind when they first arrived. The official priorities were to secure the city, to find food, fuel and shelter from the cold, to destroy the industrial and commercial sectors of Nanking, and to kill any Chinese soldiers remaining in the city" (Harries and Harries 1991: 223). But the "Chinese soldiers" killed soon also included prisoners, and soon thereafter many members of the population as a whole, such that "the total number of [Chinese] corpses amounted to a staggering 377,400—a figure that surpasses the death toll for the atomic blasts at Hiroshima and Nagasaki combined," all over a period of *several* weeks (Chang 1997: 101).

According to Harries and Harries, this "official Rape [as metaphor] continued unabated but soon . . . moved from center stage to become the backdrop to a worse horror as gangs of [Japanese] soldiers drunk and out of control began roaming the streets. . . . the first [real] rapes were reported on the sixteenth. During the previous night an estimated thousand women had been raped" (224). A German official representative (in 1937, presumably a Nazi) "estimated that twenty thousand women had been raped in the first two weeks" (224). "But," they continue, "the bare statistics, grotesque though they are, convey little of the terror that must have possessed women trapped with nowhere to hide within Nanking's walls. The norm was gang rape" (225). In excruciating detail that even the word "horrific" fails to capture, Chang tells us not only of the rapes as such, but of the varied *manner* of raping and often accompanying murder that the Japanese committed upon these women (89–99). In time there were also other kinds of casualties.

> . . . not a single Chinese woman has to this day come forward to admit that her child was the result of rape. Many such children were secretly

killed. . . . One can only guess at the guilt, shame and self-loathing
that Chinese women endured when they faced the choice of raising
a child. . . . a German diplomat reported that "uncounted" Chinese
women were taking their own lives by flinging themselves into the
Yangtze River. (Harries and Harries 1991: 89–90)

Lest we think such rapes were a passing aberration of war, Harries and
Harries remind us of the culture at that time: "these young [Japanese] men
came from a cultural background in which women were considered lesser
beings, their thoughts and feelings totally disregarded, their rights not even
conceived of" (230). As for Japanese culture at that moment,

> there were far too many atrocities all to be the product of madness.
> More influential was a lack of moral sense, in Western eyes. Japanese
> war criminals rarely expressed guilt . . . the Japanese soldier admitted no
> higher authority than the Emperor, represented in practical terms by
> his superior officers. . . . In part this was military conditioning, but it was
> paralleled in civilian society by a similar lack of a transcendent moral
> authority comparable to God in the Judeo-Christian system—to guide
> the individuals' actions, to which he could appeal, by which he could
> be judged. There were no absolute moral values . . . the lack of an over-
> riding moral authority meant that there was little resistance to orders to
> commit atrocities . . . (Harries and Harries 1991: 478)

They also warn us that "too close a focus on the Rape of Nanking ob-
scures the fact that it was only one tidemark left by a sea of atrocities in-
flicted by the Imperial Army on the Chinese," an "army guilty of both controlled and indiscriminate war crimes all over China" (227).[16]

I submit that awful historical particularities such as this put China at
utter cross-purposes with Japan and thwarted any efforts to subsume both
under some common "Asia" lest it be that of imperialist nation versus the
grossly exploited, but especially through the latter's women. With these
Chinese women, we are a considerable distance from the land of the poetically sensual geishas and the erotic Ginza. As Paredes accompanied a Chinese woman to her place, he noticed "those Chinese men staring at me
with hate in their eyes" and wonders "whether the papers would say the
next day that a Red Cross man had been found in an alley with his throat
cut." We can only wonder if they might have been remembering Nanking.
In contrast to his feelings about China, Paredes was obviously enchanted
with Japan beginning with its code of politeness. By coincidence, Chang

also speaks of Japanese manners, asking how one can "reconcile the barbarism of Nanking with the exquisite politeness and good manners for which the Japanese are renowned." But with greater Freudian psychological insight than Paredes had, she also suggests "that these two seemingly separate behaviors are in reality entwined" (54).

Moreover, John Dower (1999: 510), the eminent historian of the war with Japan and its aftermath, reminds us that Hideki Tojo, he of the "iconic gravitas and dignity," had come "out of the Kwantung Army" and "played a major role in prosecuting the war in Asia." Indeed, Tojo was the Kwantung Army's chief of staff in 1937, and in that capacity, as the Chinese war unfolded, he argued for a "blow first of all upon the Nanking regime to get rid of the menace at our back" (Harries and Harries 1991: 207). The blow was indeed given, and it defies even the most sympathetic imagination that the Kwantung Army's chief of staff would *not* have been aware of the rape of Nanking as it unfolded over a period of several weeks. No orders were ever issued to stop it.

The American military authorities who put Tojo on trial focused on atrocities committed principally upon American troops and took great pains to overlook his Chinese victims, in large part because China was on the verge of becoming a Communist power, while Japan had been enlisted as a U.S. ally in the developing Cold War (Dower 1999: 504–513). A few months before Pearl Harbor, Tojo was appointed prime minister, and in that capacity he was in command of all Japanese forces almost to the end of the war in 1945. As prime minister, he might or might not have shared some responsibility for the atrocities committed against Americans—the record is unclear—but the Chinese experience is very different, and perhaps that should have been the focus of the international tribunal that tried him. In China it is difficult to see the simple moral equation that Paredes suggests—namely, that Tojo "was being accused of 'war crimes' that had in fact been committed by both sides." But even in the Pacific such a simple moral equation simply does not hold. There is no doubt that individual U.S. troops shot Japanese trying to surrender and too often committed depravities such as extracting the teeth of dead Japanese. Yet I see no evidence that such crimes were widespread, nor that they were institutionally sanctioned or directed by the U.S. military.

By sharp contrast, among the several sanctioned and extended atrocities committed against American troops by the Japanese, we need only recall the most infamous of these, especially as it involved another Asian people, the Filipinos, but in direct proximity to another part of the U.S.–Mexico borderland. I refer to the fate of the American and Filipino prisoners—military and civilian—taken by the Japanese after their invasion of the Philippines in 1941 and the fall of Corregidor and the Bataan Peninsula. The Allied troops had fought off superior Japanese forces from December 8, 1941, to May 6, 1942, with no support from the mainland United States, then too busy recovering from Pearl Harbor and concerned about potential Japanese attacks on the California coast.

After their surrender, and in very poor condition, these prisoners were force-marched some sixty-five miles to a prison camp, Camp O'Donnell, on what has now come to be known as the Bataan death march. Again, according to Harries and Harries (1991: 316), "at several points along the way there were bloody motiveless massacres. Almost 11,000 American and Filipino prisoners died on the road . . . thousands more died after reaching Camp O'Donnell, where the captives were forced to exist in indescribable squalor." However, among the American prisoners—as well as among the dead in the battle—names such as Barela, Chávez, García, González, Gómez, Madrid, Montoya, Rodríguez abounded. They were members of two New Mexico National Guard units—the 200th and the 515th—which had been posted to the Philippines in part because so many of them spoke Spanish. The 200th and the 515th were the first units to engage the Japanese in ground combat and the last to surrender alongside their Filipino brothers and sisters.[17] This too is a "transnational" relationship that oddly—given that Mexican Americans were at its center—receives no mention by either Paredes or Saldívar. In the always grim record of random and unsystemic atrocities carried out by Americans and the Allies against the Japanese, there is nothing even remotely comparable to Bataan, and certainly not to Nanking and the Japanese record in China (Dower 1986: 33–73).

What has gone awry here is the linking of two very different sociocultural and political experiences, Japan and the Lower Rio Grande border, and the elision of another, China, with much greater relevance to the lower border, although the Lower Rio Grande never experienced a Nanking. The effort to produce this nexus between South Texas Mexicans and an imperial Japan that has yet to own up to its war record seems to me to be seriously skewed. If anything, and given their quick rapprochement after the war, the white, capitalist, dominant United States may be far more directly comparable to Japan as *fellow* racist imperialist powers relative to subaltern Chinese and Mexicans.

In a perceptive essay on the novelist Winnifred Eaton, Gretchen Murphy (2007) reminds us of the way in which U.S. influentials, political and scientific, made a case for the Japanese as a "white" race "at the beginning of the twentieth century," when "both Americans and Japanese represented Japan to U.S. audiences as uniquely allied with the United States' new overseas mission to spread commerce, freedom and enlightenment in Asia" (36). And González (2009) tells us that in the mid-1930s, the State of Texas issued a "style guide" to be used by those preparing publications, advertisements, and festivities for the celebration of the Texas centennial in 1936. In a largely failed effort to control anti-Mexican imagery and writing referencing the conflicts leading up to Texas independence in 1836, the guide for 1936 reminded its readers that "from Mexico's point of view . . . the Texas Revolution of 1836 and the U.S.-Mexico War of 1846 appear akin to the creation of the puppet state of Manchuria and the Japanese invasion of North China" (69). And in the cruelest ironical conjunction for Mexicans in Texas: "In 1914 Japanese geographer Shigetaka Shiga erected a monument at the Alamo in San Antonio and a similar one in Okazaki, Japan, to draw parallels between the battle of the Alamo and similar battles in Japanese and Chinese history."[18]

Contrary to the Paredes/Saldívar understanding of Mexicans and Japanese as common victims of "Anglo" imperialists, it may have been the Anglos who had much more in common with the Japanese as fellow "white" imperialists relative to Mexicans and Chinese.

TOWARD A CRITICAL TRANSNATIONALISM

Ramón Saldívar (2009) has replied to an earlier version of my commentary (Limón 2008) suggesting that my critique of the Japanese/ Mexican-American nexus is a "banal" concern relative to what he sees as far more important issues in Paredes's relation to Asia. For him, Paredes perfectly fits the current cultural studies interest in vital transnational connections, and he thinks that my objections show me to be a mere "national regionalist." First, he objects at length to my suggestion that thinking about Asia as a potentially singular, unified, anti-Western imperialist sphere is misguided at best. He thinks me to be "simply wrong," adducing the Chinese cultural theorist SUN Ge in support as well as various unnamed other Asian intellectuals to argue that Asia as a totality is very much on the minds of many such intellectuals and constitutes a "community of knowledge" that Paredes presumably also joined through his occupation-era writings (Saldívar 2009).

In her exhaustive review SUN Ge does indeed show us that there has been much discussion as to the meaning of Asia and that this concern is in large part in reaction to the West. (By the way, she does not explicitly name the United States, although one assumes it is subsumed under "the West.") However, what she also shows is that much of this discussion is idealistically abstract, indeed a community of academic perspectives and ideational knowledges, many literary, with the interesting exception of Umesawa Tadeo, a historian and cultural ecologist in close proximity to anthropology. Based on his empirical researches, for him this articulation of abstracted ideas about Asia, "the symbolization of Asia," is conducted in a manner that, according to SUN Ge (2009: 37), "ignores the multifarious facets of Asia, which is not acceptable to his academic training. For him, the pluralistic nature of civilization does not need to be articulated through setting up the binary opposition Asia versus Europe. Just dissolving the presupposition of a unifying Asia will do the job." Thus Umesawa Tadeo would seem to be one Asian who would dissent from SUN Ge's perhaps overstated proposition, quoted with approval by Saldívar: "For Asians, the Asia question is primarily a question of the sense of solidarity, a sense that arises in the midst of aggression and expansion perpetrated by the West" (27).

Saldívar also refers to a collection of unnamed "Chinese, Japanese, not to mention Taiwanese and Korean scholars," engaged with this question (9–10). What he does not tell us, but SUN Ge clearly shows us, is that this community of knowledge and its concern with "Asia" has been and continues to be largely a *Japanese* affair, occasioned in large part by Japan's contradictory impulses to, on the one had, identify with Asia, and on the other, to identify with and emulate the imperialist modernity of the West, even though in racial difference. It is largely the Japanese who are acutely anxious about this issue with Professor SUN Ge—Chinese—now in the position of a cool and comprehensive observer of their dilemma.

For one horrible moment in World War II, the Japanese "resolved" this dilemma through the perfidious formulation and ugly implementation of the "Greater East Asia Co-prosperity Sphere," attempting to forcibly create an "East Asia" (at least) by mimicking and even exceeding the West's worst racist, sexist imperialism, toward the West but also to the other East Asian countries. As Christian Caryl (2008) notes in a recent review of Ian Buruma's *The China Lover*:

Early-twentieth-century Japan was both a latecomer and an outsider to the game of imperialism, the first non-Western nation to compete with the European countries that had already been in the business for centuries. As a beginning of this imperialist project, the Japanese militarily established the pseudo state in China they called "Manchukuo" (in Manchuria) which . . . became the proving ground of Pan-Asianism, an ideology that (in the form propagated by the Japanese) revolved around the notion that Tokyo's version of colonialism was actually enlightened and progressive, one in which Asians were their own "masters" rather than the subjects of cynically racist Westerners. Japanese-occupied Manchuria, in this reading, was a modernizing laboratory of inter-ethnic harmony among the "native peoples" of the region (the Han Chinese, the Koreans, the Mongols, the Manchus, the Japanese). The reality, of course, was quite different. (56)

In this context, and in general agreement with Umesawa Tadeo, I do not therefore see what is so wrong in suggesting, as I did, that any efforts to think an Asian totality are at cross-purposes with the hard political and nationally based realties such as the Sino-Japanese wars, but also, beyond China, many others such as the India-Pakistan nuclear-armed tension. I fully acknowledge that such "Asia" thinking obviously goes on, but I do question its practical political reality, as does SUN Ge from her perhaps more Chinese perspective as it concerns Japan. As she says, the question of Asia "remains undecided today and why, whenever opinions regarding the question of Asia are put forward, the aggression committed by Japan is always raised" (27), indeed as I do now. As Edward Said (1994: 43) also notes, the issue of Japan's war culpability and its choice between "Japanese imperial history" versus an "acceptance of the West's aesthetic and intel-lectual predominance" continue to occupy Japanese intellectuals to the present day. To raise such a question is not to be "simply wrong" but only to ask how and to what practical effect is "Asia" possible after Nanking and the other protracted histories of endemic conflict between other Asian nations which seem to me to overwhelm "Asia"?

But all of the above has another and larger significance for Saldívar, which is the point of his principal argument that he says I miss in my con-cern with the merely banal; it has to do with his central understanding of Paredes's work as a transnational formation, a "transnational imaginary" between Asia and the U.S.-Mexico borderlands. In pure chronological terms, we should first begin with the relationship that Saldívar sees be-tween Paredes's *prewar* borderlands (really South Texas) experience and his later writings in Asia: "Here in these newspaper articles, as in a handful of poems written between 1945 and 1949, we find Paredes's *first full expres-*

sion of the necessity of linking the anti-imperial struggles of the peoples of the United States–Mexico borderlands with those of the people of Asia, and historically with the fates of conquered nations globally" (Saldívar 2006: 388, emphasis added).

I fully grant that such a linking expression does occur in the "handful of poems"—really one, "Pro Patria"—although I have also already noted the difficulty and irony of including the Japanese among the "people of Asia" who struggle against imperialism like the "peoples of the United States-Mexico borderlands" (Saldívar's use of the singular "people" of Asia is revealing here). But this specific anti-imperial linkage is simply not at all evident in the journalistic writings that Saldívar discusses. As he notes, "Paredes's articles for *Stars and Stripes* are not about Texas but about the economic, political, social and cultural turmoil in postwar Japan . . ." (350). I agree.

Such was also the content of the Spanish-language articles that he wrote for *El Universal*, the Mexico City newspaper. He reported the pleasures of meeting other Mexicans in Japan and China, hearing Mexican music while visiting the Mexican Embassy with its Mexican décor, and eating food with *picante*. But, as he was writing in Spanish for a major Mexico City newspaper, for a Mexican audience, in an always nationalist posture toward the United States, one is struck by the total *absence* of any political analysis linking Greater Mexico, Japan, and China against the United States.

The only substantive connections that Paredes makes have to do with women and music (Saldívar 2006: 361–368). Nowhere in the journalism that Saldívar reports, or that I have independently examined, is anything said about a common anti-imperialist struggle. Nor does Paredes make any such extended linkage either in his interviews with Saldívar nor, as far as I know, anywhere else in his earlier and later writings or other interviews, such as with Calderón and López-Morín (2000).

Saldívar is far more emphatic concerning the second phase of this relationship between Asia and the borderlands *after* the war, his central argument. Referring to Paredes's journalistic work in Asia, he says, ". . . there can be no doubt that Paredes formed an idea of Asia that he later transported to his work in the American borderlands" (2009: 584–585). And, more specifically, ". . . his years in Asia were crucial for Paredes's later formulation of the idea of 'Greater Mexico,' which on his return to the US in the early 1950s, he would use as a core feature of his magisterial studies of the borderlands" (584). Later in his reply, Saldívar (2009) says,

... what Paredes learned during his years in postwar Japan, China and Korea ... would lead him to his own work on the border during the 1950s and later to understand the cultural and political conflict in more richly textured terms than he had before the war. (590)

But there is even more:

The "border" would become a transnational space that extended beyond the geopolitical line separating Mexico and the US to encompass a larger sphere of engagement and response extending across the Americas, north and south. And, what is more, it is crucial that he learned this in Asia, not in the U.S.-Mexico borderlands. (590)

It was not that I missed this central argument as Saldívar suggests, opting instead for the "banal"; I simply chose not to address it since at the moment of my original writing, I simply had not decided what precisely I thought about this core argument. I now have more definitive thoughts, subject to counter-evidence not yet available.

I find Saldívar's argument ultimately unpersuasive; one based on creative conjecture; an imagined imaginary about which there can be some considerable doubt. Let us consider these questions:

1. *Was Asia responsible—"crucial"—for Paredes's famous "core" formulation of "Greater Mexico"?*

I see no evidence anywhere to support this contention although some may have been had if Saldívar had simply asked the question of Paredes. Nor does Saldívar say when and where Paredes uses the concept for the first time, odd lapses considering that it is such a "core" idea. Had he asked, he probably would have gotten the same response that I did when I asked Paredes many years ago where he got the idea: simply, that it came to him when he was working on *"With His Pistol in His Hand,"* where as far as I know, he uses it for the first time. No mention of Asia. There is one ironical possibility—a cruel one—namely that Paredes was led to the very fruitful "Greater Mexico" by way of the Japanese "Greater East Asia Co-Prosperity Sphere." I can only hope not. Other than such a startling, unlikely linkage, I see no evidence to support Saldívar's assertive proposition.[19]

2. *Is there textual or autobiographical evidence that Asia continued to play an explicit and substantive role in Paredes's postwar work, especially "With His Pistol in His Hand"?*

I submit there is no such evidence and much counter-evidence. Saldí-var himself says, ". . . it is telling that while his writings after 1950 focus explicitly on Asia in only *one* instance, the marks of Asia are visible throughout 'With His Pistol in His Hand,' and especially in Paredes's final novel, *The Shadow*" (12) (emphasis added). I believe that Saldí-var is thinking of an explicit footnote in *"With His Pistol in His Hand,"* but other than that, I certainly see no "marks" in content, style, or per-spective that connect these texts to Asia, nor does Saldívar demonstrate these in close textual readings. One looks for a connection such as that Paredes explicitly makes to Scottish balladry, but there is none.[20] Un-less, of course, Saldívar is saying something like Paredes was inspired to examine folk cultural resistance to Anglo Americans by Japanese "resis-tance" to American occupation. He would then have to explain (away) Paredes's published interest in the ballad of Gregorio Cortez *before* the war. Here, I believe that Saldívar's argument is on the shakiest of grounds.

Paredes had established the core of his future scholarly work in his *prewar* "The Mexico-Texan *Corrido*," requiring only a higher education in folklore studies to bring it to its final fruition (1942). Yet nowhere in his book does Saldívar discuss or even reference this first of Paredes's scholarly publications. The article clearly demonstrates that in his later work on the Cortez *corridos*, Paredes was *returning* to an old and con-tinuing interest that had really nothing to do with Asia. As Paredes him-self said to Saldívar (2006: 117): ". . . the anger that I felt in the 1930s in the creative writings, I was now venting in the scholarly work on the Cortez book in the 1950s." No reference to an intermediating Asia whatsoever.

Nor, in his own commentary on the novel, does Paredes ever con-nect Asia to *The Shadow* (Saldívar 2006: 106–116). In his own detailed analysis of the novel, Saldívar himself can say only that we see "versions of the story in Paredes's . . . reporting from Japan, which redefine ethics, politics, and aesthetics as belonging to related domains of knowledge" (426). This is a far too general proposition for my taste.

> 3. As a result of Asia, did Paredes come to "understand the cultural and political conflict [in the U.S.-Mexico borderlands] in more richly textured terms than he had before the war"?

Here we move beyond the banal questions of factual evidence and into aesthetic judgment. I agree that Paredes's postwar work became more richly textured, but in *scholarly* terms, that was reasonably the result of academic training and not Asia. However, I offer the counter-suggestion that Paredes's later work became *less* richly textured in its understanding of cultural and political conflict. That is, we are looking at the primary postwar example, *"With His Pistol in His Hand,"* with its fulsome scholarly apparatus, as we shall see in the next chapter. Yet its relatively uncomplicated model of masculine Mexican-American folk resistance against the Anglo stands in contrast to the prewar *George Washington Gómez* with, as Saldívar himself shows us, its richly textured universe of waning folk resistance, economic mobility, education, assimilation, cross-border intrigue, intra-*mexicano* political and racial differences, gender and women, the country and the city, "good" Anglos, "bad" Mexicans, and even a bit of Asian America, all of this without leaving Brownsville. In short, a postwar brown and white world versus a prewar "checkerboard of consciousness" (Saldívar 2006: 145–189).

> 4. *Did Paredes substantially shift his focus from Greater Mexico "to encompass a large sphere of engagement and response extending across the Americas, north and south"? And, Saldívar also adds, "what is more, it is crucial that he learned this in Asia, not in the U.S.-Mexico Borderlands" (emphasis added).*

Again, no factual autobiographical or textual evidence is provided for this alleged major, Asian-inspired impetus toward a larger Latin American sphere, but the statement is misleading in another way. The *prewar* Paredes had *already* demonstrated considerable interest in Latin America beyond Mexico. Saldívar seems not to have heard Paredes when the latter told him: "The 1930s were the period of Sandino's revolution in Nicaragua, and we in South Texas were very attuned to the political struggles of Latin America" (Saldívar 2006: 350). After the war the factual evidence clearly indicates that Paredes's activity regarding Latin America beyond Greater Mexico was comparatively minimal. He did correspond with and hosted Latin American folklorists, attended a major conference in Argentina, and published two major, non-fieldwork papers that, in part, addressed non-Mexican, Latin American folklore (1963, 1969).[21] He included Latin America materials in one of the several seminars I took with him as a graduate student, but the others were principally focused on folklore theory and method or Greater Mexico. He also occasionally reviewed other-than-Mexico Latin American publications.

We measure a scholar's encompassing interests by his or her primary scholarship. In hard quantitative fact, Paredes's most substantial work, *Folklore and Culture on the Texas-Mexican Border* (1993a), finally dealt not even with Mexico, but with the United States and, more so, South Texas. At no point did he offer any book-length treatment of Latin America beyond Mexico. His most important such work is his 1969 article, "Concepts about Folklore in Latin America and the United States."

In the early 1950s Asia became part of Paredes's very interesting past, but as his commentary to academic interviewers clearly shows, Asia ceased to play any significant role in his new work at hand, which was fully now a much more learned continuation of his prewar focus on Greater Mexico (Calderón and López-Morín 2000). Finally, one may ask, if Asia and its close comparative relationship to Greater Mexico was of such importance to Paredes, why did he not write something, even a short essay, on the subject after 1950 with some such title as "On Asia and Greater Mexico"?

None of this is to diminish Paredes's journalistic achievement in Asia; indeed, I may have been the first to bring this Asian moment to the awareness of the general public as I summarized his much better known work on Greater Mexico (Limón 1980). Asia also surely affected him in important ways, including greater maturation. As he told his wife, he came back from Asia a "different person," but in his new work there was a difference of substantial degree from before the war though not of kind.[22] One may even grant what still seems to me to be a generalized overstatement, namely that his Asian journalism "offered Paredes an education in rhetoric and language consciousness that would serve him to great effect when he returned to the American borderlands in the era of cold war and uncompromising segregation" (Saldívar 2006: 388). *George Washington Gómez* and his other prewar writings amply demonstrate that the prewar Paredes already had such talents in abundance before Asia, although more writing and thinking experience always helps, as did the G.I. Bill.[23] Put another way (and leaving aside the G.I. Bill), could Américo Paredes have accomplished what he did on Greater Mexico without the Asian interlude? I leave it to each reader to decide after a careful reading of all the evidence.[24]

Saldívar has written a very long book, but perhaps he might have considered adding at least a paragraph on another American literary intellectual of color — W. E. B. DuBois — who chronologically overlapped with Paredes, and who consistently, substantially, and explicitly connected Asia to African Americans, Africa, and anticolonialism, a fascinating comparative baseline from which to measure Paredes's own career (Mullen 2004: 1–42; Mullen and Watson 2005). Seemingly intent on aligning Paredes into the current trend of "transnationalism," Saldívar seems too determined to create such a substantial East-West, truly transnational, Duboisian figure in Paredes. Rather, the available evidence I have seen tells us of a Mexican-American intellectual of high achievement in two relatively discrete spheres, but one who first was and finally became much more of . . . how shall I put it? . . . a critical "national regionalist" of Greater Mexico.[25]

THE FICTIONS OF POSTCOLONIALISM

I have argued, in part, that Paredes and now Saldívar both seem to fall under the spell of an eroticized, exoticized, and even sentimentalized postwar Japan rendered in feminized idioms, as did many Americans under the influence of postwar Hollywood films such as *The Bridges at Toko-ri* (1954) and *Sayonara* (1957). But more importantly, I have also criticized their shared sense of commonality between the peoples of Greater Mexico and Asia, a commonality of, again in Saldívar's (2007: 343) words, "shared oppression and injustice, as mutual recipients of race prejudice, and of having experienced the catastrophe of imperial conquest."

Saldívar also reads all of Paredes's short stories from the Asian moment in similar, if very brief terms, and indeed three of these — "Ichiro Kikuchi," "Sugamo," and "The Terribly High Cost" (Paredes 1994) — do seem to support the idea of a Japanese/Mexican commonality against the imperialist "Anglo," misleading though it may be. However, I would like to take up another possible and paradoxical result of Paredes's time in Asia. Prior to the war and even after 1950, Paredes largely viewed the U.S.-Mexico borderlands, especially Texas, as an arena of struggle between Anglo Americans and Mexican Americans. As such, much of his work explores the rich and nuanced identity of Mexican Americans in this struggle, with minimal attention given to the Anglo side except to cast them mostly as abstracted, sometimes caricatured, figurations of racist domination, such as his representations of the Texas Rangers and K. Hank Harvey in *George Washington Gómez*.[26]

In two of these stories largely written in Asia, Paredes appears to break with this binary representational strategy, instead offering more detailed and searching renderings of the "Anglo" subject, which he largely had not done before and would not do again. We obtain an alternative and much more nuanced view of the postcolonial relationship encompassing Anglos, Mexicans, and Japanese.

In "The Gift," an Anglo-American protagonist, Lt. Commander Young, is a naval officer in charge of a group of Allied prisoners in a POW camp somewhere in the South Pacific. He is billeted in a hut along with the other prisoners, including the story's narrator, who tells us that the prisoners "were all afraid," but that Young, who is regularly interrogated by the Japanese, "was afraid in a different way." The look in his eye "was like a crack in a thick wall through which you could see the scared soul of Lt. Commander Young" (Paredes 1994: 119).

Following this narrator's lead, Saldívar (2006: 323) interprets Young as a man who "is gripped by abject fear of the Japanese. His captors have completely broken his spirit . . . because of this abjection, Young regularly informs on the other American prisoners to spare himself the wrath of his jailers." In another place Saldívar (1994: xxxv–xxxvi) tells us, "the Navy officer shamelessly informs on his fellow GIs nightly to gain himself some small comforts." As a consequence of Young's information, prisoners are taken away and publicly executed. Thus, for this critic, the "Anglo" continues to occupy the stigmatized role in Paredes's imagination, although now as a traitor and a craven coward.

As Young's interrogations continue with the same reprisals, the remaining prisoners plot to kill him, and after a drawing of straws, assign the task to the narrator. "You're it, Mex," he is told (122), identifying his ethnicity with the slur "Mex," which speaks of Anglo racism among the other prisoners (122). The narrator seems to speak to this racism both here and back home: "I knew it would happen. . . . all my life, I've gotten the short end of the stick" (122).

Although "Mex" decides to lie in wait in the camp latrine to kill Young with a stolen knife, the plot is foiled when the Japanese commander whom the prisoners call "Monkeyface" shows up at the hut and begins to harass Young (323). But then, Saldívar (2006: 323) says, Young is "pushed too far," and grabs his adversary's sword and kills him. Young and the others in the hut are summarily executed. Since he was waiting to kill Young in the latrine, "Mex" is not held complicit in the killing, although he is forced to watch the executions. In a reversal of form, Young, the treacherous, craven coward, is said to be the "the calmest man there . . . all his starch had come back" (124). Or, as Saldívar says, he accepts his fate "calmly, maybe even heroically" (323). The young Japanese officer in charge of the executions, who "looked more like a student than a soldier" (124), decides not only to spare the narrator's life, but even gives him a small gift, presumably for not having taken part in the killing of Monkeyface. The camp is finally liberated, and the narrator, clutching his small gift, has literally lived tell the tale both to his liberators and to us.

For Saldívar, the "Mex" narrator is "granted the gift of life by circumstance and the good fortune of a young lieutenant's mercy, [but] he [the "Mex" narrator] also finds himself in the peculiar position of having been recognized as a Subject by the enemy" (1994: xxxvi). Thus, by this reading, the Japanese officer's gift of life and the small token appear to be evidence of the two men's racialized and "colonized" condition even in the midst of war. Paradoxically, it is as if they are really allies relative to Lt. Commander Young, but also to all of the other Anglo prisoners who, as the narrator says, "never cared much for me" (125). At the end, says Saldívar (324), the narrator can only wonder about his good fortune amidst so much random killing.

My own inquiry flows from a singular perplexity about this story that then leads to other issues with Saldívar's reading. I could not help but wonder why Young shows some heroism in the end when everything else that we know about him would suggest that he would go to his death not in calmness but in absolute screaming terror? Nothing in his behavior, as interpreted by the prisoners and now Saldívar, prepares us in any way for such heroism in the end.

Since we are dealing here, in effect, with Young's treason—an egregious military offense subject to an American court martial had he lived, and therefore his possible execution—the contradiction allows me to be Young's lawyer and to plead his case by retrieving an alternative narrative against Saldívar's that would then clear up my perplexity.

The prisoners, the narrator, and now critic Saldívar believe that Young has been informing on the prisoners "shamelessly," as Saldívar (1994: xxxvi) says, in return for "small comforts." To begin with, the story does not mention *any* "small comforts" given to Young by the Japanese unless this critic is thinking of a certain peach in the story. Yet the "big juicy peach" (119) is not the small comfort. Saldívar does not mention that Young's mistreatment appears to begin when he *steals* a peach "that was sitting on the military commander's windowsill." Only "that evening," the narrator says, after Young stole the peach, do the Japanese come for him and the series of interrogations begins (119). That is, there is an odd time lapse between the peach incident and the beginning of the torture sessions, as if the theft is an unnoticed irrelevancy. Yet the whole incident is rather odd. Why would a commanding office go around stealing peaches? More on this later.

We are then told that Young is periodically taken away and then returned to the hut. We are not told what the Japanese and Young say to each
other, nor does Young say anything to his men. Indeed, Young says not a
word during the entire story. The narrator reports only that after these sessions, Young "would come back shaking" (121). Because some of the men
are tortured or executed after Young's sessions with the Japanese, the narrator, the prisoners—and critic Saldívar—draw the not unreasonable conclusion that Young is a traitor—that he is divulging escape plans—and
begin to plot his killing, which they fail to execute because Monkeyface
shows up.

As noted, Saldívar tells us that finally Young is "pushed too far" and
kills Monkeyface, but he does not tell us the specific reason, namely, that
Monkeyface forcibly tried to take from Young an object described as "a
dirty little bag . . . with a drawstring around the mouth" (123). In his later
recitation to his liberators, we also learn that this is the gift that the young
Japanese officer gives to "Mex" when he spares his life—the little bag
which oddly enough gets no mention from Saldívar even though it is the
literal "gift" that gives the story its title. But the way "Mex" reacts to the
gift/bag and the revelation of its contents is wholly instructive for the alternative narrative that I am offering:

> I took the bag and squeezed it. It felt like a diamond was inside. Or a
> gold nugget. But I didn't open it until I was alone. You'd never guess
> what was in it. A kid's tooth, the kind you lose when you grow up. I kept
> it as a good-luck charm. After all, I felt lucky. I should have, shouldn't I?
> (124)

This gift from the Japanese turns the other prisoners against "Mex,"
as they also imagine the bag's contents as precious stones, a misidentifica-
tion that probably prompted Monkeyface to try to take the bag in the first
place. In the end it turns out to be a toddler's tooth, in all probability from
Young's child. Facing regular torture and an uncertain future, this little
tooth has perhaps become his one source of comfort and stability, and a
symbol of the possibility that he might yet see his family. The loss of his
child's tooth is significant, but in and of itself, it is difficult to see its loss
as sufficient reason to kill his adversary and throw his life away, thereby
utterly assuring that he will never see this child again. After all, he has been
allegedly cooperating with the Japanese. I believe there is a larger motive,
which takes us back to my initial perplexity: Young's calmness and "maybe
even" heroism at his execution.

How do we explain such heroism when everyone—the narrator, the prisoners, and Saldívar himself—have made such a case of craven treachery against the American commanding officer? And how do we explain the sudden killing of Monkeyface, ostensibly over a child's tooth? I am not persuaded that such heroism and courage can emerge so quickly out of the moral/ethical degenerate imagined by the prisoners and now Saldívar.

Young is indeed "pushed too far," but that obviously suggests that he has already been pushed a great deal through the interrogation sessions, but not in the manner one might easily assume. In truth he is not being physically tortured anywhere close to what the Japanese could inflict on their prisoners. As the narrator tells us, "They had roughed him up, that was all. He had a puffed eye and a fat lip, and he limped a little, but he wasn't hurt bad" (119). It is not the sheer physicality of the interrogations that create such an intensity of emotion that he finally must kill his adversary, ostensibly over a child's tooth. I suggest that the child's tooth is simply, but importantly, the final straw in what has been a covert narrative of grave injustice, together with a hidden narrative of honor and courage that Young cannot reveal to his men.

I submit that Lt. Commander Young's heroic conduct at the end is consistent with his conduct from the very beginning, although the narrative is hidden from us precisely because Young wishes to hide it from the prisoners. Once he knows he is going to be executed, paradoxically he has the freedom to offer a minimal display of that honor and courage. To fully grasp this alternative narrative, we first need to recognize why a relatively high-ranking officer (indeed, the only Allied officer in the entire camp)— and not one of the enlisted or drafted men—has been selected for interrogation. If what the Japanese want is information as to what is going on in the hut, then torturing enlisted men—presumably less committed to the military way of life—would seem to yield quicker results.

I offer another possible reason for torturing a ranking officer, especially a naval officer in a Pacific war fought largely by naval forces. Young is being tortured for military intelligence and not for the much less important information about the daily doings of the prisoners in one hut.[27] He is a disciplined officer who "wouldn't let us forget he was an officer and in charge of things" (118). If such is the case, then his duty-bound, honorable refusal to provide such military intelligence results not so much in his physical but rather his *mental* torture as his men are tortured and executed until he divulges the information. Like terrorist kidnappers, the Japanese torture and kill their hostages one by one until they get what they want.

It is precisely because officers will lose their people either in combat or under such circumstances that they should not get emotionally close to their men, today also women. "He never joked with us or joined in the griping when the guards weren't around" (118).

Of course, the narrator and the other prisoners do not understand what is really going on. Given what they think they know, the rest of the prisoners take the not too surprising route of drawing the easier conclusion, with Saldívar, and initiating their plot, in critical effect joining the cabal against this *gringo* officer, this representative of "imperialism." He, of course, cannot divulge his choice, for his men likely would not tolerate it and indeed kill him. With this profound moral and psychological dilemma, Young is deliberately sent back to the hut so he can see and hear the living men who will pay the consequences of his refusal. Thus it is that he is in something more like a state of continuous shock and inner torture rather than "abject fear" as he is torn between the well-being of his men and his duty. Rightly or wrongly, he chooses duty, and his agony is the price of command.

There is a figurative oddity in the story that also bears addressing if only because it is so odd. If military intelligence is the issue, why does Paredes choose a peach and its theft as the seeming starting point for a story of interrogation, torture, executions, injustice, and honor? I suggest that the fruit has nothing to do with his interrogations. Surprisingly Saldívar does not even mention the peach, which the narrative tells us is "from China" (119), thereby linking this story of Japanese cruelty to their far worse atrocities, *ad nauseum*, in that country, as noted earlier. But let me propose that the peach may yet tell us more as we are reminded of that other far more famous peach in American literature, but also of a certain peach in Japanese folklore. The erudite Américo Paredes had read T. S. Eliot before the war (Calderón and López-Morín 2000: 214). Is he suggesting that here we have a man who wishes to survive for his child and, in his hunger and heroism, will dare to eat a truly significant peach in contrast to that of the failed Prufrock?

Moreover, long before he became a renowned folklorist, Paredes was deeply interested in folklore and had made it the topic of some early journalistic articles (Saldívar 2006: 92). Given this interest, his extended period of residence in Japan, and his kinship ties to the Japanese, it is nearly impossible that he would not have come to know one of the most important stories in Japanese folklore, that of Momotaro, the peach boy. (It would be like a cultural citizen of Greater Mexico not knowing about the legend of La Llorona, the wailing woman.)[28] The Japanese story is one of youthful heroism that begins with a magical peach giving birth to Momotaro so that he may be a child to an elderly couple without children of their own. When he is older, Momotaro sets forth on a heroic military mission to vanquish the evil ogres who seek to dominate the world from a distant island. Along the way he is assisted by a dog, a monkey, and a pheasant (Sakade 1958).

This children's fairy tale gained a central political importance in the early twentieth century within the Japanese educational program, meant to instill in children a spirit of militarist nationalism leading up to World War II. Within this program, but also in popular propaganda films, the story was transformed so that the distant island of the ogres was conflated with those islands controlled by the white, imperialist United States and Great Britain at the outbreak of the war (such as the Philippines and Hawaii). The animals that help Momotaro were then represented as the "fellow" Asian nations of the Greater East Asia Co-Prosperity Sphere, although we have already seen what Asian "co-prosperity" really meant to the Japanese imperialists (Dower 1986: 255; Antoni 1991).

I suggest that Paredes has fashioned a Lt. Commander Young who, in effect, appropriates the symbol of the peach from vicious nationalist militarism to a worthier cause. In its own small way the peach serves to give him life in his heroic cause against adversity, against those who seek to dominate the world, indeed from a distant island, as it did for Momotaro.[29] Certainly it may be objected that the peach may be neither Prufrockian nor folkloric, but merely a peach that happens to appear in a Japanese prison camp, but as Paredes said about this period of his writing, "I was trying to dabble in symbolism" (Saldívar 2007: 131).

Paredes challenges current postcolonial theory by showing us that in a complicated world a complicated heroism can reside within the psyche of the alleged colonizer and that, in the end, Anglo "whiteness," along with military rank, can say both everything and nothing. But if I am correct, then this Anglo heroism is also marked by a foil, namely the Mexican-American narrator, who now appears to us as the most ordinary of human beings, indeed, subordinary. We come to know him as a certain Mexican-American figure—a *rascuache* (a low-life or rascal) who is initially marked by his inferior grammar, as he says of Young, "he didn't give us no trouble, and so we let him be" (118); who so easily joins with the cabal; who has let his racial circumstances defeat him as he whines, "all my life, I've got the short end of the stick"; who so easily imagines the gift in the little bag to be precious stones; who does not ask any overwhelming questions. Indeed, he is the most unreliable of narrators. In the end, with no moral empathy or imagination, he gives the little bag to his liberators, telling them, "Here. You can have the damn thing. A fine good-luck charm it was. See? Inside the little bag it feels like a diamond. Or a gold nugget, at least. It would fool anybody" (124–125).

I submit that in this alternative and skillfully embedded narrative, Américo Paredes offers a nuanced, beautiful, and intelligently penetrating assessment of two fictive representational lives shaped by Japanese oppression: a sympathetic, sensitive perspective of critical generosity toward the Anglo-American "colonial" subject who emerges as a quiet, enduring hero, like Gregorio Cortez; and a Mexican-American "colonized" subject who is a far cry from Gregorio Cortez, and more like a lower-class version of George Washington Gómez.

If the "Anglo" and the "Mexican" are thus reversed in this fiction, another of Paredes's stories from this period seems to join the two into one figure as he continues to explore the contradictions of the postcolonial condition in a way that escapes easy categorization.

A secret is at the center of his short story "When It Snowed in Kitabamba," a secret whose ultimate disclosure offers the central thematic argument of the story. The story provides further evidence of Paredes's prescient critical exploration of the realm of patriarchy and sexuality, but as these are encoded in transnational relationships, including the phenomenon of extreme assimilation.

The post–World War II American military occupation of Japan is the general setting of the story, specifically an American military installation in the fictive village of Kitabamba. The entire story occurs on the last day of the year, leading up to New Year's Eve. Captain Meniscus, the camp commander, is the story's central protagonist. Modeling himself on General Douglas MacArthur, the supreme commander of the occupation, Captain Meniscus sees it as his mission to run his assigned area with utmost discipline, precision, and strictly guided direction "toward the making of a better world" (127), a world clearly modeled on the United States. Indeed, in the words of Ramón Saldívar (2006: 325), "Meniscus understands that his duty as the military governor of Kitabamba is to transform the Japanese into straightforward Americans," emulating his idol, MacArthur, and what MacArthur represents to him: order and control. He repeats the saying attributed to the supreme commander: "The shortest distance between two points is a straight line." And, indeed, Meniscus demands cleanliness and orderliness from all under his management and works hard to impress his seemingly model behavior upon others.

His own men mostly resent him, but these others also include the

Japanese who now work at the camp. Racism and neocolonialism are the order of the day, evident in the way Meniscus treats Akamata, a Japanese servant whom he badgers and belittles, specifically demoralizing the man for his lack of communication skills. Meniscus's anger and cruelty grow as he shouts, "Don't loll before me like that, you bastard! . . . You are a fool. . . . Just look at you. Little better than an animal. . . . You'll never get anywhere in life" (133). Meniscus continues to harass Akamata without mercy until the pious man trembles with fear.

The story reaches its seemingly climactic moment when the captain's dominant sense of order is disrupted. As one of his orderly rituals, each day Meniscus performs a pompous walk from his office to retrieve the mail from the train that comes from Tokyo, in full view of the Japanese natives and the men in his command. On this particular day, Meniscus is very worried, indeed angered, that it might snow in Kitibamba on New Year's Day, and he expresses his anger several times (130–131, 136–137, 138). If over the top, his anger turns out to be justified. As he begins his ritual walk to the accompaniment of martial band music, he slips and falls in the snow, and slips yet again and again when he tries to get up.

For Saldívar, this is one of two key moments in the story. He first argues that what he sees as the ensuing laughter from the gathered company— Americans and Japanese alike—ultimately has a very different significa-tion. Drawing on Baudelaire's famous essay "On the Essence of Laughter," he offers an extended and sophisticated argument that distinguishes be-tween the laughter of the American soldiers and that of the Japanese at the fall of Meniscus. The former laugh to "disdain his posturing and mark their distance from him with their laughter," while "the laughter of the Japanese comes closer to the moment of Baudelairian comic *dédoublement*," which is to say a laughter of sympathetic recognition that they, like other human beings, could suffer his fate. The Japanese are ironically much better posi-tioned for such empathetic laughter because they feel sympathy toward the fall of a fellow human being as they identify him with "their own fallen state as a vanquished people" (328). Thus, for Saldívar, through their laugh-ter, the Japanese emerge from the war in a "position of philosophic wis-dom"—those present at Kitabamba and, by symbolic implication, Japan as a whole.

There is, however, a central difficulty with this otherwise beautiful ar-gument, and it is simply this: in the scene where Meniscus falls repeatedly, *nobody* laughs, neither the Americans nor the Japanese. A close reading of the scene clearly demonstrates this total absence of laughter, Baudelairian or otherwise, an absence underscored by Meniscus himself. As he sits in the snow, "he would dare anyone to laugh" (146). Later, back in his office, "he looked out at them angrily, in the way he had wanted to look at them in the square minutes before, staring them down, daring anyone to laugh. But they did not laugh, they did not smile. They just looked at him with sadness in their eyes" (147). And, even later, angry and fighting back tears and cursing, "he thought how much easier it would have been if they had laughed. But they had not laughed" (148).

Yet even though there is no laughter, Saldívar's essential point remains concerning the Japanese, as "the sadness in their eyes," an "old and patient sadness that went far beyond Meniscus himself" (147), does serve to connect them to Meniscus in their mutual fallen state and thus grant the "colonized" Japanese greater philosophic wisdom than their white Western colonizers. Paredes's empathy for the former and his critique of the latter continue.

Laughter, or rather its partial suppression, does bring us to the second key moment in this tale. After the fall in the snow, Meniscus momentarily assumes his office duties, even as two of his staff, both noncommissioned officers, are in an adjacent office talking about what just happened . . . and more. Meniscus hears them and moves closer to the connecting closed door. One of them, Fatt, with a "rumbling chuckle," is taking perverse pleasure in the moment as he "choked back a laugh" (148–149). But the other, named Hogg, offers the following thoughts about Meniscus as their back and forth conversation continues.

"Anyway, it serves him right, putting on those silly airs. I guess he doesn't know I'm on to him."

"You sure?"

"Sure I'm sure. He must have changed his name when he left town. I was just a kid, but I remember him. His sisters and brothers too, must have been ten of them. Or fifteen, I never counted them all."

Fatt replies: "He'll never make colonel now." Hogg lowers the possibilities: "He'll never make major, for that matter. When this shit hits GHQ he won't be going anywhere. Might be busted, for all we know." Fatt laughed. "He'd make a good company clerk," he said. And then the narrator tells us, "Meniscus moved away from the window trembling. Hogg and Fatt heard the muffled shot, and when they came into Meniscus' office the little pistol was still in the captain's mouth. His head was among his papers" (148–149).

So what is this "shit," this secret that might get the captain busted and thus leads to his suicide? One immediate possibility is evident but ludicrous on its face: Meniscus will be busted simply for falling in the snow, a possibility too ridiculous even for the U.S. Army. The issue substantially lies elsewhere, namely in the captain's sexual identity. Hogg tells us that Meniscus changed his name when he left their mutual hometown. Although we never know his original name, the implication is that he now has a new surname, Meniscus. For Saldívar the name change is deeply and psychoanalytically symbolic, for it refers to a curving figure "of crescent shape formed by the juncture of concave and convex surfaces" (1994: xxxviii). Through his choice of this name, he names that which is non-straight in his identity—that which is hidden and subverts his manifest obsession with the straight and orderly. At that time, and even today, one popular meaning of being "straight" is to not be homosexual. Thus, in addition to its postcolonial critique of the American occupation, the story "is an extended investigation of what it means and costs to be 'straight' in 1945" (328–329).

Captain Meniscus, U.S. Army, is gay, and being gay in the American military of the 1940s is a whole lot of shit and will get you busted. I agree with this finding, but as Saldívar offers it, it is conjecturally based solely on the name Meniscus and what it might mean. Meniscus is gay in repression, but Paredes develops this theme in other ways both before and after the suicide. Something more should be said about the manner in which he shapes Meniscus in his now sexualized, neocolonialist task, if only to appreciate his developing artistry as a writer, but also a certain limitation by today's critical culture.

The noncommissioned officers are useful foils in this effort, beginning with their names: Fatt and Hogg, allegorical efforts, heavy-handed, perhaps, to suggest a dominant heterosexual military world that contrasts with another body type, that of Meniscus himself, who early in the story is introduced as a man with a "neat little profile" (126). Paredes also tells us that Meniscus makes corrections to official documents in an "almost feminine hand" (128–129). He is said to have "a small-featured face" (148). And we also learn of Meniscus's anger at the sexual interest his men show in the local Japanese women. Finally, after Meniscus commits suicide, it falls to the Japanese servant, Akamata, and his wife to dress the body, and we are offered yet another possible stereotypic signifier of male difference. "As [Akamata] was about to draw the pink trousers over the Captain's legs, he stopped and looked toward his wife. 'Come,' he said softly. 'Look.' She came . . . and looked at the captain's hairless shins . . ." (150).

His awareness of the captain's homosexuality no doubt accounts for

Hogg's disrespectful manner, his mocking gestures and "jeering eyes" (128). The captain's disdain for Hogg, but also his discomfort, is evidenced when he avoids eye contact with the corporal as he speaks to him about some papers that were not in the captain's office in a timely fashion.[30]

I say "seeming" because I now want to raise the possibility that Meniscus, the arch colonialist, is himself a colonized subject, but of a different order of colonization. Meniscus has wholly internalized the Freudian but also socially hegemonic construction of gay sexuality as neurosis, perversity, deviance—the acceptance of the closet if you will. But there may be an additional layer of repression tightly fused with this one.

We are by now only too familiar with Américo Paredes's dominant intellectual interests in matters Anglo vs. Mexican, but now also Japanese. Yet, oddly enough, here is a story with three central Anglo characters—Meniscus, Fatt, and Hogg—a few Japanese, but no Mexicans. . . . Or are there no Mexicans? As with Lt. Commander Young's late heroism, a certain perplexity about a particular point in the story encourages additional questions. In this case, why has Meniscus changed his name, presumably his surname, and what was it originally? Clearly Hogg knows about his homosexuality, probably from rumors back in their hometown. But one's past identity as a gay person would not be hidden by a name change, as Hogg himself shows in his knowledge of the captain's past.

Without insistence, I want to offer the possibility that Meniscus's secret is that he is gay and also Mexican-American—a hidden identity *also* symbolized by his name. Hogg knew Meniscus back in their hometown, but Hogg also tells us that this hometown was in West Texas—to be sure, an area particularly well known for its anti-Mexican racism (143). Fatt is also from Texas (137). What is Paredes's point in having the officers and Meniscus be from Texas if the latter is only a sexually repressed white man? They need not be identified regionally at all, as no doubt homophobia was very deep and nationally widespread at that time, with limited exceptions such as Greenwich Village. Moreover, according to Hogg, Meniscus comes from a Texas family of ten to fifteen children (149), suggesting the large families characteristic of Mexicans at that time.

We do not know what his original name was—perhaps Limón, or even Saldívar—but he has now changed it to the more American-sounding "Meniscus." But in a manner parallel to the way that his chosen new name symbolically replays and symbolically reveals his hidden gay identity, it also names his ethnicity. At the level of a racialized phonetics, "Meniscus" might also resonate as a tortured expression of the word "Mexican" as twisted by a racist Anglo-Texan tongue into "Meskin." Paredes himself comments on this kind of racist phonetic rendering of the word "Mexican" in an angrily sarcastic passage in *George Washington Gómez* (209). In his name change, any Mexican American will instantly recognize the assimilating tactic (for too many of us) of changing our Spanish-language names to others in English, or Anglicizing their pronunciation. We already have the evident case of Guálinto becoming George.

Meniscus's obsession with orderliness is also tied to this repression of Mexican ethnicity if the latter is viewed stereotypically as a site of disorder: drinking, music, dancing, fighting, spicy food, loud colors, and so on—as we saw in Paredes's rendition of the Mexican-American working-class dance scene in *George Washington Gómez*. In a parallel manner, his ethnic self-hatred is also being displaced in his racist, vitriolic contempt for the Japanese. Five pages of a twenty-four-page story are devoted to such a racist display against the Japanese servant, Akamata. The captain's obsession with order, his racism, and his name thus perform a double symbolization. His Mexican identity is also a "secret," which the West Texan Hogg knows, and it fuels his resentment and his jeering eyes. For this West Texan to take orders from a gay man is already insufferable, but to take orders from a "Mes'kin" *queer* takes it to a whole other level.

Yet the potential revelation of his ethnicity is not inherently what drives Meniscus to suicide. In and of itself this particular ethnicity at this time cannot be such a powerful secret, indeed no secret at all. For all the racism then prevalent, a Mexican-origin identity would not have been *so* stigmatized by the time of World War II, nor would it totally stand in the way of being an officer.[31] But for Meniscus, the external perceptions of his ethnicity may not be the issue. Rather, it is that racial internal dynamic powerfully joined to homosexuality that is the overpowering secret. If we assume that Meniscus grew up as a Mexican-American boy in West Texas, then he may also be suffering in the knowledge that a revelation of his homosexuality would be an enormous violation of his deeply internalized societal notions of *Mexican* male identity, as it surely would have been then, and perhaps even now. If any of this is so, then the creative Paredes fashioned the perfect behavior and the perfect name to both express and distort both of his character's non-straight identities, as if he cannot yet quite let go of either: Meniscus, the curved, gay Mes'kin.

In his survey of the ethnographic construction of male-male sexual behavior, Bleys (1996: 3–4) notes how the repressive construction of non-Western gay sexuality across the emerging modern world was also deeply correlated with the colonial project. Such was this correlation that even anticolonial and African critics such as Frantz Fanon attack gay sexuality both as another victimization of blacks by sexually "perverse" colonial-ist and touristic whites, but also as an inherent perversion among blacks, according to this Freudian-oriented psychiatrist. Thus his focus is on the colonized.

Paredes may have been involved in a more complicated and ambi-tious project, especially for a male heterosexual from 1930s Brownsville, Texas. What Paredes—this young Mexican-American writer from South Texas—provocatively beckons us to contemplate is the internal workings of the wholly Anglicized colonialist subject, yet one internally still "colo-nized" by the demons of his societally disparaged ethnicity and sexuality. Meniscus thus struggles with his repressions but in a socially regressive way, and does so in his obsessive orderliness, his too-insistent hygiene, his hatred of women, his displaced, racist anger against the Japanese—all of which are symbolized by his obsessive identification with the rule of male but also *Anglo* patriarchy in the symbolic form of General MacArthur. For to be a culturally assimilated Mexican American, as well as a repressed gay, may also mean taking on many of these behaviors, forms of cultural hyper-correction (Labov 1966).

Yet it is also the case that the dominant order responsible for such re-pression can itself be the object of the subject's resentment, although it too cannot be directly expressed. We have already seen what his name might represent, but his choice of the awkward, unpoetic English name "Menis-cus," with its hard consonants, may also be a statement about the ugliness of the Anglo culture he has adopted. Such repressed resentment toward authority—white MacArthurian authority—is perhaps most evident in the snow that falls on Kitibamba and gives the tale its title. Symbolically, it is precisely in his fall in the cold whiteness of snow that initiates the lethal unraveling of his repressions, as if to realize that such cold and treacher-ous whiteness will never accept him. The otherwise absurd, irrational cor-relation between the fall in the snow and suicide can thus be more fully reconciled.

Thus Meniscus dies—indeed, with his pistol in his mouth, at the hands of the racialized, homophobic, patriarchy on New Year's Eve as Hogg and Fatt take advantage of the absence of authority to raid the supply room and engage in drunken debauchery with Japanese women who sing "You Are My Sunshine," testimony to Japan's own turn to American culture. And it is as if Paredes, in cold realism, is suggesting that the perversion of patri-archy has triumphed completely, and that the new year will not be new at all. A truly new year of racial and sexual equality remains to be realized in some future time . . . if ever.

As Sandra Soto (2010) has recently and brilliantly demonstrated, Paredes was exploring and questioning masculinized, racialized sexuality in other work, including the short story "Over the Waves Is Out," also written during his Asian period. Indeed such a concern may even be relevant to Guálinto, whose own assimilation in *George Washington Gómez* may also be marked by such sexual ambivalence, although at that point Paredes was more hesitant in exploring this theme. If George is in racial melancholia, Meniscus is even more so in his loss — his repression — of his racial and sexual objects of desire, but he also experiences shame. In "When It Snowed in Kitabamba" we can detect an even more provocative and paradoxical effort from Paredes to decenter the world of Anglo but also Mexican patriarchy, and to criticize its victimization of men caught within its perverse racist and homophobic logic. The story is indeed "an extended investigation of what it means and costs to be 'straight' in 1945" (Saldívar 2006: 329). But with meticulous craft, Américo Paredes may have really been suggesting that the not-so-disguised curvature may stem from being both gay and Mexican, a prescient contribution to contemporary discussions on racialized sexuality.

DESDE BROWNSVILLE AL JAPÓN

Américo Paredes undeniably had a great deal to say about Asia, specifically China and Japan, and obviously he would have even more to say later about Greater Mexico, as he had before the war. However, I largely reject the idea that Asia was crucial for Paredes's later work on Greater Mexico, putting at issue what Saldívar has called his "transnational imaginary." At issue also is the manner in which Paredes, but perhaps more so Saldívar, lends great emphasis to creating a pairing of postwar Japan and Greater Mexico as subaltern societies under the dominance of an oppressive United States, one in which women figure centrally. Such a pairing, and its attendant politics, evades what I have called the problem of China, and especially its women during the Japanese onslaught on that country, even as it also bypasses parallel Japanese conduct in the Pacific, especially, ironically, against citizens of Greater Mexico.

Yet, in his war fictions a different Paredes seems to emerge. Here we find a Paredes much more willing to explore the internal complexities of the alleged American oppressor and, conversely, the internal contradictions of the alleged subaltern, both Mexican and Japanese. This paradoxical effort leads me to suggest that Paredes's experience in the mili-

tary and in Asia broadened his postwar perspective, but not in the manner
that Saldívar suggests—that is, by linking Asian peoples to the borderland struggles of Mexican Americans against oppressive Anglos. Rather,
his time in Asia, away from the U.S.-Mexico borderland and its repressions, allowed Paredes to explore the internal world of "Anglo" subjects
but also Mexican-American queerness in a subtle, nuanced, though sustained manner that he had not really done before and would not really do
again.[32] After 1950 he returned instead to an almost singular concern with
largely heterosexual Mexican Americans and their continuing struggle
with Anglo America, although in the production of this localized project,
he paradoxically became a folklorist of transnational significance, as we
shall see next.

THREE

The Folklorist

After his years in Asia, Américo Paredes returned to the United States in 1950, principally to resume a college career that he had left off after two years of community college in Brownsville, Texas, before the war. He enrolled at the University of Texas at Austin to resume and professionalize a career that he had initiated before the war, that of folklorist. It is important to underscore again that in addition to several journalistic articles on the Mexican-American folklore of the Lower Rio Grande Valley, he had already had his first truly professional publication in this field in the *Southwest Review* in 1942. In an impressive surge of academic energy, by 1956 he had completed his BA, MA, and PhD—all in English literature—including his doctoral dissertation, titled "El Corrido de Gregorio Cortez: A Ballad of Border Conflict" (1956). In a second burst of such energy, in two years the dissertation was transformed into a book, his now classic *"With His Pistol in His Hand": A Border Ballad and Its Hero* (1958). This was followed by a prodigious output of other books and scholarly articles, mostly in the new, developing field of folklore and on Greater Mexico. These undergirded his rapid rise through the academic ranks as a faculty member in the English department at UT-Austin, where he would spend the rest of his academic career.

It is likely that the late discovery and publication of his creative writing has now overshadowed his scholarly work in folklore. That is, the critical scholarship on his creative writing, and now his journalism, simply overwhelms any parallel, focused commentary on his scholarly work in folklore, and what little exists I find unsatisfactory for reasons I will address later.

What follows is, first, a closely focused and extended exploration of the central texts in this corpus of folklore scholarship that continues and expands upon my earlier assessments (1983, 1984, 1992, 1994). I argue, first, that in his studies of Mexican-American balladry, Paredes joined the ranks of the leading international ballad scholars, and indeed surpassed them. However, his second most important body of work—his studies of the Mexican-American joke form in the 1960s—opened an intriguing area of inquiry that, given the limited theoretical resources and time available to him, was not as fully exploited analytically as one might do now with the benefit of new thinking in this area.

BALLAD SCHOLAR

Américo Paredes's central contribution to ballad scholarship is *"With His Pistol in His Hand": A Border Ballad and Its Hero*. Published by the University of Texas Press in 1958 and reprinted in 1971, it is a comprehensive study of the Mexican-origin ballad, or *corrido*, as developed by the Mexican-American people of the lower Texas-Mexican border, or South Texas. The study focuses on one such ballad and its folk hero, a man named Gregorio Cortez. *"With His Pistol"* has been, and will always be, at the center of discussions of Paredes's work, but such discussions take us in one particular direction—that of contemporary cultural studies, the principal subject of the next chapter.

One of my intentions in this chapter is to explore an almost wholly overlooked aspect of the book and its author. I wish to closely examine the book in its most manifest terms, as a ballad study, and its author as a ballad scholar. We need to see Paredes not as the alleged "transnational" scholar between Asia and Greater Mexico, but as a true transnational of another kind, one who in a few short years took command of international scholarship on the ballad and transformed it.

"With His Pistol" is the scholarly and intellectual apogee of ballad scholarship of its historical moment. In it Paredes synthesized and applied, in a wholly unprecedented manner, the four main conceptual approaches to folklore at the time: the literary/aesthetic, the comparativist, the historic-geographic, and the so-called "rationalist" perspectives, all derived from European sources. Moreover, Paredes offers a fifth approach that would become much more salient after the 1960s: the leftist school of "resistance." Yet from the date of its publication to the present, ballad scholars and intellectual historians of folklore have mostly failed to recognize the singular importance and place of the book and its author. What follows charts this lack of recognition and offers a partial explanation of it.

Possibly more than other genres of folklore, folk song, especially the ballad form, has always furnished the occasion for strong scholarly controversy, no doubt having something to do with what seems to be folk song's, especially balladry's, seemingly more proximate thematic engagement with human conflict either within humanity itself and/or with the forces of nature. Folk song's movement across time and space, and its relationship to written poetic narrative have also fostered controversy and debate, as has its relationship with history, especially with issues of nationalism, authenticity, and historical origins (Bendix 1997). More specifically, Bendix observes that within such issues, "the ballad in particular has preoccupied collectors and theorists over the centuries" (142).

Historically, the scholars involved in such debate often gave little or no quarter. In the early sixties, for example, Tristam Coffin (1964), a preeminent folklorist of his time, had this to say about the scholarship of the eminent Phillips Barry:

> At the end of his serial on the ballad, "Springfield Mountain" in the *Bulletin of the Folk Song Society of the Northeast*, Phillips Barry presents the hypothesis that the original Myrick version of the ballad was not written before "the second quarter of the last century" or nearly sixty-five years after the event. G. Malcolm Laws, Jr., among other scholars, has found this statement hard to believe—and, actually, in light of the text of the Myrick "Springfield Mountain" itself, Barry's thesis is preposterous. (202)

Preposterous! How's that for an assessment rather than, let us say, "problematic," seemingly the critical term of choice among today's younger scholars? And Coffin is not yet done with Barry and other ballad scholars: "It might be worthwhile," he continues, "to prove Barry's dating of the ballad incorrect and leave things at that. However, Barry's disregard of narrative obituary tradition is typical of ballad scholars in general" (205). Coffin, now elder statesman of the discipline of folklore, will resurface in our discussion.

My remarks are offered as an engagement in debate and possible controversy about balladry, and they concern another ballad scholar, Américo Paredes, although to name him a ballad scholar is immediately to be involved in this debate, for it is precisely Paredes's full definition as a ballad scholar that is at issue in what follows. It is not an issue for me—quite the contrary, and I hope to demonstrate exactly this definition—but it seemed to be an at least tacit question for the discipline of folklore. There are compelling reasons for thinking of Paredes in this manner, as there are reasons for understanding his unwarranted absence in the history of folklore scholarship, particularly ballad studies. Let me begin with a marked moment of such an absence, one that will then lead us into a reexamination of Paredes's book and, in my view, its considerable merits as a synthesizing and unprecedented model of ballad scholarship in its historical moment.

In 2004 I presented a first version of this chapter to the American Folklore Society, which gathered in Salt Lake City over a period of four days. Forty-three years earlier this same but much smaller society held its annual meetings on one day, December 28, 1961, in the then smallish town of Austin, Texas. The meeting featured one special panel titled "Folksong and Folksong Scholarship: Changing Approaches and Attitudes." The panel was principally organized by Frances Gilmore, John Q. Anderson, and Roger D. Abrahams, with Abrahams providing the introductory remarks for the panel and for its subsequent publication by the Texas Folklore Society three years later in a volume called *A Good Tale and a Bonnie Tune* (1964), edited by Mody C. Boatright, Wilson M. Hudson, and Allen Maxwell.

As a new assistant professor at UT-Austin, Abrahams was just beginning his illustrious career in folklore. Indeed, together with its organizers, the panel was a real who's who and who's going to be who of folklore scholarship. Abrahams and his fellow organizers were, in his own words, "trying to stir controversy" (1964: 199) by bringing together four papers with "widely divergent" views on the question of folk balladry, for although the panel's title speaks of folk song, the papers were all focused on the ballad form.

Coffin (1964: 201) spoke on behalf of the "literary and aesthetic approach," saying, "I can think of a dozen books on the ballad as a literary and aesthetic form that desperately seek for their author." John Greenway (1964: 213) offered, or better yet, asserted the "anthropological approach," complaining, with Coffin seated next to him, that folk song, especially balladry, has been "left to the aesthetes—song, which has no real function except to communicate the immaterial culture of its singers: attitudes, emotions, prejudices, biases, ideals, vices, virtues and occasionally art."[1] W. Edson Richmond (1964) defended the "comparative approach," which by its nature and its distance from us might require a longer summary. For Richmond,

... the comparativist is a student of the history of individual ballads. Given an indefinite number of texts of a particular folksong, he attempts

(1) to establish lines of development, (2) to show how each text is related to every other text, (3) to suggest what the major early form or forms of any particular ballad must have been. In doing so, he sometimes finds it possible (1) to indicate relationships between two or more distinct songs, (2) to suggest certain probable relationships between various bodies of song, and (3) to comment on the relationship between ballads and history. (219–220)

Moreover, the comparativist approach is closely linked to the historic-geographic method, which "consists of four principal steps."

(1) all possible texts of a ballad are collected; (2) the collected texts are grouped according to the geographic area whence they came and arranged chronologically within each area; (3) the individual texts are analyzed and broken down into the motifs which they include; and (4) by a comparison of the grouped and analyzed texts, by a collation if you will, the life history of a ballad, and thus the probable relationship of each text to every other, is reconstructed. (Richmond 1964: 221)

The application of this method is quite complicated, so Richmond (1964: 218) cites with approval Archer Taylor's recommendation that "it is wiser to stay nearer at home and determine as well as may be, the life history of a single ballad."[2] Finally, says Richmond, the comparativist

does not deny that the aesthetics and (cultural) functions of ballads are worthy of study, that to study both aesthetics and function can contribute to our knowledge of the ballad and ballad singers; but for him, neither aesthetics nor function has any special significance. He is interested in texts as texts, as specimens in the historical development of a song. (219)

The fourth paper, by D. K. Wilgus, did not fit easily into any particular school but came to be called "the rationalistic approach," although in the paper itself, Wilgus disowns "rationalistic," preferring the term "rational," which Abrahams (1964: 200) tells us is not meant to imply that the other papers are not rational. As Wilgus also explains, by "rational" he means not romantic (228), which I think he means to refer to free-form literary renderings of folklore. Such literary practices were not represented on this professionalizing panel, an irony of medium magnitude given that the proceedings were published by the Texas Folklore Society, and the two lead pieces in the total volume were by Riley Aiken and J. Frank Dobie, exemplars of such "creative" literary treatments of folklore.

Strongly argued, the various perspectives offered in this folk song forum were persuasive in their own terms, but necessarily partial. If we had been in the audience, and perhaps even now, could we not agree with Greenway that the study of folk song as a "mirror of culture" is surely a valid approach, while also lending appreciation to Richmond's contention that we should have some sense of a folk song's movement and change over time and space as well as knowing something of its cross-cultural comparability? And, in agreement with Coffin, isn't it surely the case that a folk song does achieve artistic and therefore thematic effect as a result of its well-performed formal properties, which is to say its poetics? In summary, rather than supporting only one of these partial positions, did not each have something to contribute to the developing understanding of folklore at that historical moment and, with some greater theoretical and methodological subtlety, perhaps even today? Or, as stated in the fourth paper in this forum, by D. K. Wilgus (1964: 237) — as once again he offers his perspective — "the approach to folksong must be rational, not rationalistic or absolutist in any form. I have yet to find an approach to folksong from which I have not learned something; I have yet to find one whose dominance is not dangerous."

So there you have it: a 1961 meeting of the AFS in which major emerging figures in the discipline were brought together in a special panel to discuss the state of scholarship on folk song, especially folk balladry—a panel in which we hear of three very different approaches to the study of balladry, but in which we also note clear sectarian partiality. Only Wilgus evoked the possibility of something like a folkloristic unified field theory that would simultaneously bring all or most of these seemingly mutually exclusive perspectives to bear on a corpus of ballads, preferably a single ballad, as Taylor suggested. An ideal ballad study called for a synthetic approach, if you will, by an open-minded, generous, and intertheoretical, intermethodological folklorist who, at that moment, might deploy all or most of these approaches and perhaps yet others—the available folkloristic intellectual currency at that moment in 1961—into a full analytical understanding of balladry.

We have reason to believe that such a folklorist may have been present in the audience at that session in 1961, and one has to wonder what his thoughts were and whether or not he was experiencing a sense of irony as he listened to these various scholars. Indeed, this folklorist, Américo Paredes, was a still relatively new assistant professor at UT-Austin. Three years earlier, in 1958, he had produced just such a synthesizing model of folklore scholarship on the ballad in *"With His Pistol."* Yet, oddly enough, this comprehensive study of a single ballad "nearer to home," in Taylor's words, gets only a brief, passing footnote mention in these papers. One senses that either (a) these leading scholars had not read it, or (b) had read it and thought it unrelated to their concerns, or (c) simply overlooked the obvious.[3]

If one places *"With His Pistol"* within the historical trajectories of folklore scholarship up to but also beyond 1958, I submit that it is the folkloristic equivalent of "the perfect storm," where the different and powerful scholarly traditions discussed above come together, becoming greater than the sum of their parts because their very congruence generates another force to expand their energy. It is a critically cogent condensation but also a critical expansion of the key folkloristic traditions that Paredes inherited.

Keeping the aforementioned scholarly traditions in mind, let me now attend to the particulars of the book to make my case for why *"With His Pistol"* is such a synthesizing work on the ballad, even as it also opens a new critical dimension in the interpretation of folk song.

First to be noted in such an analysis is the division of the book into two parts. Let me speak of these as history/legend on the one hand and balladry on the other. Part 1, Chapter 1, "The Country," opens with a history of the folkloric area and its culture. By itself, this accounting of historical context might strike us today as rather conventional until we stop to consider how sociocultural history was so utterly set aside in the folklore scholarship of the 1950s, by all the perspectives I have discussed above — literary, anthropological, or comparativist. History, then, and its exclusion from folklore scholarship as an explanatory ground for the object of folklore are wholly innovative here. In Paredes's work, moreover, this is no mere history of the "background" variety, for it succinctly narrates a history of social oppression in South Texas as, after 1848, newly arriving Anglo Americans came to racially and economically dominate the Mexicans of the region even as, in prelude to the ballad, it places folklore and folk life in general as an efficacious practice within such an arena of social conflict.

Chapter 2, "The Legend," places Paredes's work within another dominant tradition of the time, literary renderings of folklore, a practice keyed on the rewriting of traditional folklore, or items perceived as such, into literary form in an accessible language, and, as I have noted, a perspective deemed unprofessional and thereby excluded from the AFS panel of 1961. For, indeed, in this chapter Paredes offers a literary condensation of the legends of Gregorio Cortez, who begins to emerge as the "hero" of the book's subtitle, legends which tell of Cortez as a good, decent, hard-working man wronged by the Anglo-American legal authorities. However, the "charm" and "quaintness" often attributed to such retellings is obviously not the rhetorical and thematic objective here, for this literary rendition is employed to tell, once again, of social conflict between decent, hard-working Mexicans and mostly dominant and racist Anglos in early-twentieth-century Texas.

In Chapter 3, "The Man," Paredes counterposes biography to literary legend as he draws on archival and oral history resources to tell us of Gregorio Cortez, the man, a figure not at great variance from the legend. It is also here that we obtain a factual recounting of the actual events that on June 12, 1901, led Cortez, with his pistol in his hand, to defend himself and his brother against false arrest and possible lynching for alleged horse thievery. Now a wanted man, Cortez rides for the Mexican border, and Chapter 4, "The Hero's Progress," concludes Part 1 by offering an illuminating comparison of the factual versus the legendary history so as to foreground the way the latter draws on the former to create a hero larger (but not that much larger) than life, which in the Texas of 1901 was already dramatic enough.

Part 1 thus offers a rich ethnography of the history and legendry of Gregorio Cortez, but the book's subtitle is *A Border Ballad and Its Hero*, and the native Mexican-American balladry that was generated by the Cortez matter is clearly Paredes's principal interest, which is dealt with in Part 2 of the book, and opens with a sequential Chapter 5, "The *Corrido* on the Border." This chapter traces in detail the history of the *corrido* along the lower Texas-Mexican border, demonstrating its historical presence from the mid-eighteenth century, when the Spanish settled in the area, bringing with them a precursory form of the *corrido* called the *romance*. Trained in Spanish as well as English, Paredes carefully notes that the *romance* itself dates back to Spanish culture in the medieval period.

In South Texas, by the mid-nineteenth century, the more thematically and aesthetically stringent form of the *corrido* emerged and began to take one predominant form and one thematic concern, becoming what Paredes calls the "heroic" *corrido* that largely depicts social conflict with the newly arriving Anglo Americans. The balladry of Gregorio Cortez that began to appear after the 1901 incident became the most well articulated and best-known of these heroic *corridos*.

Paredes might well have chosen to organize his book in a different manner, eschewing the two-part division and writing instead a treatment ending with Chapter 5. I submit that had he done so, he would have responded more than adequately to John Greenway's methodological and interpretive preferences for folklore study, lending emphasis to the role of folklore as a representational instrument of culture and society. But Paredes chose to add three more chapters to Part 2, chapters that likely would not interest Greenway, but rather are written as if in response to, but really anticipating, Richmond and Coffin.

Chapter 6, "Variants of 'Gregorio Cortez,'" is an example of the pre-liminary basic step in the historic-geographic method as it is solely comprised of eleven variant texts of the ballad, eight of these field collected from folk performers by Paredes himself. But he also included one printed broadside and one commercial recording, as if anticipating another point that Wilgus made in his 1961 article, namely that field collectors should not turn aside from commercial recordings as interventions in or even the beginnings of strictly oral transmission (235–237). And he also offers what he calls variant X, a version neither commercial, printed, nor field recorded, but rather representing Paredes's sense of an original or *ur*-form of the ballad, although he frankly acknowledges that it is his imagined version and that no such version was found in the field. His method for this reconstruction is worth noting for the way it adheres to the tenets of the historic-geographic method even as he does not hesitate to add a salutary dose of restrained imagination.

> I have not assumed a single line of variant X, every line that appears there coming from oral tradition. X is made up entirely of quatrains from Variants A to I, with the exception of a few variations within lines, coming from versions with which I have been familiar for thirty-five years or so. The elements that make up variant X have been selected and put together in accordance with definite and consistent rules, based on the assumption (which the traditional variants support) that the original ballad was intended to inform and that it was therefore more detailed and factual than its later variants. (Paredes 1971: 180)

In Chapter 7, "Gregorio Cortez, A Study," Paredes subjects these eleven variants to a close, careful, cautious, and detailed examination to determine the earliest of his collected versions and the geographical distribution of the song as well as his argument for Variant X, "without too many apologies as a point of departure for the study of other variants . . . a fairly accurate idea of *El Corrido de Gregorio Cortez* before singers began to develop their own variants" (181). As he traces changes in these variants, Paredes is also careful not to lapse into any notion of degeneracy and de-evolution, implicit in the historic-geographic method and in much folklore scholarship (Dundes 1969).

> In these variants of *El Corrido de Gregorio Cortez* one has a contemporary example of the process which ballads go through in developing from comparatively long and detailed originals into shorter works which are sometimes true works of art, and which continue to live after the events that gave them birth are forgotten or have been turned into legend. (203)

Now we see Paredes also invoking the category of *art*, as if responding to (but, again, really anticipating) Coffin. The remainder of Chapter 7 is devoted to just such an analysis of the poetics of the balladry of Gregorio Cortez but with implications for all ballad composition. Indeed, the chapter's final section carries the subhead "Versification, Rhythm and Structure," as Paredes takes us through a close reading of the compositional details and poetic devices employed by the tradition as a whole as well as by individual folk composers. But artfulness here goes beyond poetic devices such as imagery, rhyme, and meter. Paredes also has something to say about the ballad's *musicality*, about the *singing* of ballads. An accomplished musician on the piano and guitar as well as a singer of ballads, Paredes, in a passage worth quoting at length, tell us:

> If one disregards the opening note, the current tune of *Gregorio Cortez* has a range of only six semitones. Even considering the first note, the range is still less than an octave by two semitones. The short range allows the *corrido* to be sung at the top of the singer's voice, an essential part of the *corrido* style. Though the whole melody can be and sometimes is accompanied with the two basic chords on the guitar (the major chord formed on the tonic and the dominant seventh), it is customary to end the second line of the quatrain with the major chord formed on the subdominant, the *tercera* in the language of the *guitarreros* [guitarists]. (209)

In Paredes's otherwise technical analysis, musical form can also become a politics of style, as he concludes, "Together with the high-register singing and the counterpointing of rhythms, this adds a great deal of vigor, almost defiant vigor, to the delivery of the *corrido* when it is sung by a good singer" (209). The sheer music of balladry, by the way, was an aspect of ballad study wholly missing from the 1961 panel in Austin.[4] It is an expansive part of Paredes's ballad scholarship, one that surely would have pleased Phillips Barry if he had ever read *"With His Pistol in His Hand."*

The book ends with a brief Chapter 8 simply called "A Last Word," which one might expect to be a conventional conclusion, "I have argued thus and such . . ." Paredes does some of this, but then he also takes this opportunity to go beyond the perspectives broached in the 1961 panel by offering a further comparison — not between variants of "Gregorio Cortez," as he already did in Chapter 7, but cross-culturally, between Mexican-American balladry and that of the Scots, who of course had their own Anglos to deal with.

What one looks for in the 1961 AFS panel in Austin is some recognition that the 1958 work of Américo Paredes — probably sitting right there in the audience — had, in effect, brought together the various perspectives represented on this panel into one focused treatment of one ballad tradition. As far as I can tell, no such recognition was offered.[5] This elision of *"With His Pistol"* seems particularly odd because two reviews of the book had offered at least a partial recognition of its total achievement.

In a review of *"With His Pistol,"* Austin Fife approvingly notes of Part 1 that "seldom have we encountered a study in which a manifestation of folk literature has been studied in its social and historical setting with such illuminating results," but then also says that Part 2 "may leave all but the ballad scholar by the wayside, but this much is necessary to place the entire book on a level that will encourage respect for a long time" (1960: 78–79). But perhaps even more telling and inexplicable is the seeming disparity between Coffin's 1961 lecture, where nothing is said about *"With His Pistol,"* and his review of the book in 1959, especially his commentary on Part 2. "Part II, which is a treatment of the Border *corrido* and the variants of the Cortez song, moves a bit slowly after the chase and trials of Part I. However, once the reader adjusts to being back in the library, he realizes that he has found in Part II what amounts to a handbook for a ballad type that little is known about" (244). *"With His Pistol,"* he concludes, "is as good as any of the classics, in technique, competence and readability. It is something any folklorist (and his family) will want to read, and it should satisfy the *whole discipline* from the antiquarian to the indexer" (244; emphasis added). This distinction between Parts 1 and 2 would continue to influence the reception of *"With His Pistol."*[6]

In the years that followed, Paredes's work drew little notice from the professional folklorist community, particularly ballad scholars.[7] Perhaps the exception was Richard Dorson, who did take favorable notice of *"With His Pistol."* He tells us of Paredes's excellent analytical study of the *corrido*, praising the way Paredes uses the *corrido* thematically to reveal anti-American attitudes among the Mexican-American population of Texas (1967: 168, 1971: 90). However, because he is solely interested, as Greenway was, in the use of folklore as a cultural document, Dorson necessarily focuses almost exclusively on Part 1, saying nothing about the other folkloristic theoretical and methodological features and contributions of Paredes's work that I have discussed, which is to say, he does not discuss Part 2. Thus, from a powerful position of folkloristic authority, Dorson initiated the later definition of Paredes work almost exclusively as a contribution to Mexican-American studies.[8]

The immediate moment of recognition having passed, Paredes's "With His Pistol" might well have faded into total obscurity, especially given the advent in the later sixties and early seventies of performance folkloristics with its small-group, microfocused elision of history, broader cultural concerns, and certainly the Finnish method.[9] But "With His Pistol" was paradoxically given new life by an emergent politics of culture well known to folklorists: ethno-nationalism.

I am referring, of course, to the Chicano movement of the sixties and early seventies. Initially Paredes had some interesting ambivalence about the movement, although very quickly it became evident that it furnished a substantiation of one thrust of his work, which was the valorization of Mexican folk culture in the United States, particularly in Texas. He soon wholeheartedly adopted the movement's political-cultural concerns, even as it wholeheartedly appropriated him—in the best sense of the term—as its leading intellectual and political ancestral resource, as we shall see in much more detail in the next chapter.

However, the Chicano movement's sharp and encompassing identification of Paredes as the premier Mexican-American studies scholar of our time, and perhaps forever, may have also played into the unreflective thinking among mainstream American folklorists who were perhaps also, if unconsciously, ready to bracket him solely in this singular identity, thereby erasing his contribution to the general history of ballad scholarship. I have suggested that he also lays claim, beginning in 1958, to another identity, which is simply but profoundly that of the most original, intellectually provocative, scholarly competent, and socially grounded *American* folklorist and ballad scholar.

The 1961 AFS symposium in Austin was certainly one occasion for recognizing Paredes's contribution to ballad scholarship, but yet another opportunity presented itself as the Chicano movement began to wane in the 1980s. The distinguished William Andrews Clark Memorial Library

Seminar at UCLA in 1983 might have been another prime occasion for the (belated) recognition of his work as a prime example of the kind of expansive and synoptic ballad study that Wilgus seemed to be advocating in 1961. This seminar, called "The Ballad and the Scholars: Approaches to Ballad Study," featured only two major papers—indeed, one by the same D. K. Wilgus of 1961, and the second by Barre Toelken.

For his part, Wilgus spoke on "The Comparative Approach," while Toelken's paper is titled "Context and Meaning in the Anglo-American Ballad." In a manner echoing Richardson in 1961, Wilgus is true to his title and rehearses the tenets of the comparative approach, again closely linked to the historic-geographic method. For Wilgus, the comparative method requires that "(1) the materials be interesting and valuable in and of themselves; (2) that a historical, or diachronic, study of the materials is essential to an understanding of them; and, (3) that such diachronic study begins most fruitfully with individual items, however necessary it is to relate them to similar items." (By "individual items," I believe that Wilgus, still following Richardson, means an individual ballad and each of its variants within a single cultural tradition, which are then to be compared to each other but also to similar ballads from other cultural traditions.) True to his charge of describing and defending the comparative method, Wilgus also continues with his earlier 1961 catholic approach to the ballad: "The comparativist is not one who denies the validity of other approaches and indeed can and should utilize any results that contribute to the understanding of the ballad as a product of humankind, just as the contextualist needs comparative evidence to prevent errors in interpretation" (21). He then shows us different ways that the comparativist approach has been used to study a number of ballads, although with no reference to Paredes.

For his part, like Wilgus, Toelken practices his own folkloristic catholicism. While fully acknowledging the value of a comparativist approach, Toelken argues for the added necessity of a contextualist appraisal of balladry, noting that a contextual analysis may and should incorporate human, interpersonal features such as family dynamics; social or group life, such as ethnicity, religion, and occupation; cultural-psychological dimensions; the physical/geographical settings of ballads, such as "a front porch in Hogscald, Arkansas"; and, finally, the "time context, the occasion" for ballad singing (36). Once again, there is no reference to Paredes, who had exactly followed these procedures. And, while admittedly Toelken's topic is the "Anglo-American ballad," he might have taken license to recognize Spanish-language balladry in the United States in the same way he spends time with ballads sung in Pennsylvania Dutch (47–49).

So once again, I am surprised that both of these folklorists, now in their scholarly prime, specifically addressing the ballad form, wholly overlook "With His Pistol" as the fulfillment of just such a synthesis, as they seem to be advocating some twenty-five years after the scholarly fact. Both take us through several examples of scholarly work, including their own, that exemplifies their respective positions, but neither recognizes that Paredes had fulfilled this *complete* agenda and more some twenty-five years earlier.

In 1971 Richard Dorson asked folklorists to engage their folklore collections by interpreting them in social context—the anthropological or American studies approach, if you will. But, I believe we should at least on occasion pay equally close interpretive attention to our own professional folkloristic scholarly practices as cultural texts in themselves operating in social contexts, something I tried to do with four major folklorists, including Américo Paredes, in Part 1 of my book *Dancing with the Devil* (1994).

In such reflexive analyses of the texts and practices of our profession, we should offer an accounting of their manifest thematic and stylistic features, but also of their absences, erasures, and exclusions. I have noted such an absence, exclusion, and erasure of the work of Américo Paredes in the history of ballad scholarship, but thus far I have only implied an interpretation of this exclusionary process. Let me suggest a confluence of five possible factors moving from the general to the particular.

At the most general level, I suggest that in 1958 through the mid sixties, Paredes, from South Texas, who took all three degrees at UT-Austin and whose book was published by UT Press, may simply have been cursed by Texas—that state of mind lying between the two coasts—especially if one keeps in mind that the mainstream discipline of folklore at that time came to be defined principally as a product of Penn and later UCLA and Berkeley, but also indulge me while I place Indiana on the "eastern" coast. As such, Paredes may have fallen victim to the idea that nothing of much serious or artistic/intellectual value can come from such mid and marginal places as Texas.[10] By the time this Texas intellectual marginalization began to end, which is to say with the ascendancy of John Silber to dean of the College of Arts and Sciences at Texas in the 1960s, together with the gradual development of Austin into the great city it is today, it may have been too late for Paredes's book to get the full notice it deserved. We all know that our books often have a very limited window of opportunity to get noticed before we are quickly replaced by other authors.

We can point to other possible reasons for the externally created failure of "With His Pistol" to take a more centered place in ballad scholarship, factors such as language and national identity. It has been suggested to me that Anglo-phone, especially English, balladry exerted a hegemony over ballad scholarship in the mid-twentieth century. That is, the Spanish language of the *corrido* may have led exclusively Anglo-phone American scholars to engage Paredes's work with less interest and less sympathy than otherwise, although the work is written in English by a professor of English, and all of the Spanish-language texts are carefully translated into English. Yet several of the papers I have cited from the 1961 and 1983 symposia draw on a wide range of examples from non-Anglophone, mostly European, balladry.

The question of national identity may be more critical. Of negating importance is the U.S.-sited Mexican-American identity of the materials in and the author of *"With His Pistol."* Material from national Mexico might not have been a problem in this regard. If Paredes had done his work there, he would have joined highly respected U.S. mainstream artistic, anthropological, and literary traditions focused on national Mexico south of the Rio Grande, and preferably very far south. The great Mexican muralists were, of course, well known in the United States. In anthropology the names Robert Redfield, Oscar Lewis, George Foster, Ralph Beals, Eric Wolf, among others, are only too well known to us in relation to their work in Mexico, and a list of major twentieth-century American creative writers who did *not* experience Mexico in this period would be short indeed.

From the 1920s and '30s, American intellectual and artistic life was accustomed to artists, writers, and intellectuals from national Mexico (Delpar 1992). Such a relationship continued after World War II. As it happened, in 1958, the same year *"With His Pistol"* appeared, Mexico's still best-known novelist, Carlos Fuentes, published his first novel, *La región más transparente*, and it was available almost immediately in English translation in 1960 as *Where the Air Is Clear*. And a year later, in 1961, Octavio Paz's dominating work *The Labyrinth of Solitude* appeared in English translation, just three years after *"With His Pistol"* and the same year as the AFS Austin conference.

I am suggesting that these two books all by themselves became a cultural window into things Mexican for American intellectuals, deflecting whatever attention might have been given to a folkloric study by a Mexican American from Texas. In 1958 it was a different thing to deal with Mexicans in the United States, a nomadic people in-between "real" nation-states, not marked by the particularly exotic — unless, of course, you happened to belong to that small, Mexican-distanced, "Spanish" group in northern New Mexico, in relative isolation from the modern world, blessed by mountains and cool weather, and given to weaving, wood-carving, and deeply ritualized Catholicism. In that case, folklorists, anthropologists, Mabel Dodge Lujan, D. H. Lawrence, Georgia O'Keefe, and Robert Redford came knocking on your door.

In short, in the 1950s and largely through the present moment, Mexican Americans simply did not register much in the national consciousness, nor among scholars and writers, and that too may have been unconsciously held against Paredes himself, for the national identity of the author is not a small matter here.

Paredes's work on Mexican-American balladry of South Texas almost necessarily meant that he also had to broach a fifth perspective, one based on race, that spoke to the long history of Anglo-Mexican conflict in Texas, and read folklore as an artistic instrument for contesting domination. Such a perspective anticipated a critical understanding of the politics of folklore that would later become the basis for the "resistance" school: the "weapons of the weak" and "arts of resistance" perspective later advanced by anthropologist James C. Scott and others, which also carried over into "cultural studies," the subject of the next chapter (Scott 1987, 1992). But such a political reading of folklore may not have been as welcome among professional folklorists in the 1950s.

Then there is the matter of personality in academic life, where as we all know, aggressive ambition, if somewhat nuanced, is not unknown. Paredes's personality was largely not such. I knew him much as he describes the legendary Gregorio Cortez:

> For Gregorio Cortez was not of your noisy hell-raising type. That was not his way. He always spoke low and he was always polite, whoever he was speaking to. And when he spoke to men older than himself he took off his hat and held it over his heart. A man who never raised his voice to parent or older brother, and never disobeyed. That was Gregorio Cortez, and that was the way men were in this country along the river. That was the way they were before these modern times came and God went away. (1971: 35–36)[11]

I deeply regret to say that this disavowal of the work of Américo Paredes relative to the larger discipline of folklore, and ballad study in particular, continues in the present moment. In a review of recent theoretical trends in the study of folk song in the West, Porter concludes that "the study of song must move forward by taking into account a number of key factors in modern life: identity, ideology, and practice . . . as well as the cognitive basis of music making. To do this, theory must deal with individual and social aspects, with processes of meaning formation and community value in music" (1993: 85). In meeting this standard, Porter gives pride of place to the aforementioned D. K. Wilgus, but I submit that Paredes had earlier accomplished all of this and more. His total absence in this otherwise highly admirable review is lamentable. Finally, the centennial celebration of the American Folklore Society in 1988–89 inspired the publication of not one but two histories of the discipline by well-known scholars. These two major histories lend narration and interpretive analyses to the historical course of folklore studies in the United States. But both Bronner (1986) and Zumwalt (1988) offer only very brief, largely footnote mention of Américo Paredes, and neither offers any commentary *whatsoever* on his ballad scholarship.[12] Indeed, *"With His Pistol"* appears nowhere in their bibliographies. Yet in her review of the debate between literary versus anthropological folklorists, Zumwalt approvingly quotes Melville Jacobs.

> Melville Jacobs posed another challenge for the anthropological folklorists. He asked, "Can both scientific and literary function be combined in the production of folktales and still adhere to scientific standards?" And he answered, "I believe that they can, if interpretive comments supplement the stark translations and if the additions are written so as to include, readably and pleasurably, associations and sentiments which the native audience experienced."[13]

Zumwalt continues:

> Jacobs in this statement was proposing a blending of humanities and science, a combined approach suggested by Ruth Benedict earlier. He was also anticipating the development of performance theory in folklore. The text could be combined with the context, and both could add meaning to the other. His query and response provide a tantalizing suggestion of what is to be gained through a combination of the literary and the anthropological approach to the study of folklore. (1988: 122)

But, as I have argued, the "tantalizing suggestion" Zumwalt attributes to Jacobs had, in fact, become scholarly reality in the 1958 publication of *"With His Pistol in His Hand."* Since Jacobs's words were published in 1959, we can certainly understand that he most probably would not have known of Paredes's masterful study of the ballad form published just the year before. But others—in 1961, 1983, and now—might have recognized Paredes's singular, synthesizing, and expansive contribution to ballad scholarship, but simply did not and have not.

In his introductory remarks to the 1961 AFS panel, Abrahams (1964: 201) said that the papers presented were important "because they all sound a call for folklore to enter a new era, an era of strict professionalism, involving a reconsideration of old methods of analysis and examination of possible new ones. It is a call that all folklorists must heed" (1964: 201). I submit that by 1961, Américo Paredes had already responded fully to this call in 1958, a response that has gone largely unrecognized. In the foregoing I have offered evidence and analysis as to why this recognition should have occurred and reasonable speculation as to why it did not.

ON JOKES AND THEIR RELATIONS

Other major genres of folklore that clearly interested Paredes did not receive the benefit of a sustained scholarly and fully analytical book-length treatment such as "With His Pistol," and perhaps that is one reason this other work has garnered much less critical attention. These other genres include ethnic slurs, folktale, legend, varied song forms other than *corridos*, and proverb (1961, 1970, 1971, 1976, 1982).[14] But it is his work on the Mexican-American joke form that is more sustained, more susceptible to theoretical reflection, and more relevant to Mexican-American history, and for these reasons, in what follows, I focus on his studies of this form.

Clearly Paredes intended to offer a book project on the joke form based on extensive fieldwork in 1962–1963 supported by a prestigious Guggenheim Fellowship (1993b: 12). During that time he did collect a large number of such texts and subsequently wrote a very long and presumably analytical introduction, but for reasons that are unclear, he never published this total work as a book until much later, and then with only a very short and informal introduction (1993b). However, in this short introduction he does tell us that two major analytical articles on the specific subject of jokes were derived from the original introduction (13). Therefore, I concentrate on these two studies (1966, 1968).

In comparison to "With His Pistol" and its scholarly framework, fulsome and careful historical ethnography, and embedded social analytical theory, one is struck by the relative absence of all these in Paredes's work on jokes, reflected in its relative paucity of scholarly and historical references but also in which ethnographic and historical detail are sometimes elided, skewing the full significance of this joking material.

Analytical theorizing of this material is also relatively restricted, perhaps attributable to the relatively undeveloped theoretical climate on jokes at the time he did this work. That climate might be well described with one name: Sigmund Freud. For this section, from joke theorist and folklorist Elliott Oring, I have borrowed my seemingly odd subheading with its play on the title of Freud's famous work, but I shall also deploy him in my analysis of Paredes's joke work (Freud 1905; Oring 1992).

Paredes opens his first study of joking (1966) by proposing that the Mexican-origin community may be divided into three distinct groups: the older communities such as South Texas and New Mexico, founded during the Spanish period; the largely urban post-Mexican Revolution settlements, such as those in Los Angeles, Chicago, and San Antonio; and new, semirural immigrants.[15] All of these will, of course, come into contact with Anglo America, generating a Mexican folkloric response, including joking behavior. Seemingly following Freud, Paredes keys on aggression—outward but also inward aggression—as the key to understanding this folklore, which, in turn, he also divides into three genres and themes, although whether these are homologous with the three Mexican groupings is not clear.[16] Indeed, I will argue that they are not. Rather, it will turn out that only one of these groups, the regionalist, performs this folklore. Paredes does say that genres and groups are not necessarily aligned with the historical order in which these groups appeared in the United States. As a "working hypothesis" he offers "an oversimplification which I believe useful. Mexican attitudes toward Anglo Americans from the period of the first armed clashes in the 1830s to the present time may be seen as going through three stages . . . although I do not suggest that each of these stages is strictly confined to a definite historical period" (114–115).

Yet, while not "strictly confined," clearly there is some correspondence to history because, says Paredes (1966), in numerical semi-chronological fashion:

> First there is an attitude of open hostility principally expressed in
> song and legend, especially in the *corrido*. Next there is an attitude of
> veiled—often thinly veiled—hostility, principally expressed in an escap-
> ist type of jest featuring dream situations in which the Mexican bests

the Anglo-American. Finally there is an attitude of self-satire, principally expressed in jests which are at best mildly masochistic and at worst
frankly self-degrading. (115)

The *corrido* tradition is no joke. Rather, "open hostility is most clearly
expressed in the heroic *corrido* . . . in the *corrido* the American is the
Enemy, seen in heroic terms" (115). The representation of the Anglo in
the heroic *corrido* will then function as a kind of baseline for the rest of
the argument on "jests" where the enemy is understood in different terms,
though still fundamentally those of aggression.

Paredes calls the first of these joke forms "the Stupid American joke."

The pattern is a simple one with two main characters, a stupid American
and a smart Mexican. Through the Mexican's guile or the American's
stupidity, the Mexican gets the best of the Anglo-American and makes
the Anglo look ridiculous, beats him, relieves him of his money, seduces
his wife, or uses the American himself as the passive partner in sexual
intercourse. (118)

For Paredes, this kind of joke continues the war waged in the *corrido* by
other means because the open warfare correlated with the *corrido* "no
longer is possible with the Mexican finding himself in a disadvantageous
economic and social position." The Freudian perspective is again evident:
"The dream situations of this kind of jest serve as compensation for a strong
sense of frustration and inferiority which was not so keen when open conflict presupposed a possible victory for the Mexican" (118).

Almost necessarily, Oring critically departs from Freud in the interest of a more subtle and comprehensive conceptual framework for understanding jokes: "relations" (plural) rather than Freud's singular "relation"
to the "unconscious." For Oring, this Freudian relation is singular in an
even more specific manner, namely in its focus on *aggression*, sometimes
sexualized aggression, repressed in the unconscious, as the fundamental
motivation for jokes. As a competing theory, Oring offers what he sees as
the production of what he calls "appropriate incongruity" as the basis for
humor (1–15). Oring (1992) proposes another approach to understanding
jokes, including such "ethnic" jokes as "the Stupid American" cycle. Perhaps we can best illustrate his perspective by turning to another such example, which I collected in my own fieldwork in 1974, although Paredes
also has a variant in his collection (1993b: 94–95).

This *gringa* goes into Joe's Bakery for breakfast, sits down, and the *mexicano* waiter comes over to take her order. "Yes, *señora*, what would you like?" he asks her as she looks at the menu. She looks up at him with a smile and says in Spanish: "Quiero un ranchero con huevos."[17]

Drawing on Oring (1992: 2), we can say that the appreciation of the joke as joke lies less in the seeming aggression against the Anglo, a woman in this case, and far more in what he calls "appropriate incongruity"—that is, "the perception of an appropriate interrelationship of elements from domains that are generally regarded as incongruous," a perception usually resolved and made evident in the punch line. In this joke, everything turns on the incongruity between what the woman intended to order—*huevos rancheros*—ranch-style eggs, over easy and dressed in a hot salsa—and what she mistakenly orders—a rancher with eggs—because she is not in full command of the Spanish language. For vernacular Spanish speakers, the incongruity is, in Oring's terms, rendered linguistically appropriate and acceptable because in such Spanish the word *huevos* has an established relationship to two very different domains. It can simultaneously mean (1) literal eggs, and (2) a man's testicles, much in the same way that "balls" has two meanings in English. Thus, she mistakenly says, in transposed vernaculars, that she wants a rancher with balls, and says so to a man.[18] Oring also recognizes that such a perception is intimately linked to sociocultural contexts and the performance situation, including the narrator's identity (14–15). In this case, the narrator was a sixty-year-old, Mexican-American male attorney from South Texas, a graduate of Saint Mary's University Law School in San Antonio.

But to identify the narrator as such is also to say a great deal in the direction of history, culture, and society, and allows us to revisit and now deploy Paredes's initial tripart division of the U.S.-Mexican community, something that he doesn't really do in his essay. He leaves the impression that the three subgroups—older settlers, urban folk, and new immigrants—all perform each of the three genres since, in the essay, he does not say where and from whom he obtained these jokes. However, we may clearly infer that they were gathered largely in South Texas, where he reports he did most of his joke fieldwork (1993b: 12).

Along with Paredes, we also wish to be cautious about the historicity of these materials, yet it is clear enough that Paredes (1966: 115–118) closely associates the first genre—the *corrido*—with the first group, the eighteenth-century Spanish-Mexican settlers of South Texas who came into open conflict with Anglo America in the nineteenth century. And since he argues that the second genre, the Stupid American joke, is a kind of *continuing* aggression, it does not seem unreasonable that it is also the expressive property of this same group, but now understood as its descendants in the twentieth century rather than, let us say, recent immigrants or even the urban group which traces its origins largely to the Mexican Revolution.[19] His list of informants for most of this humor clearly suggests as much, for the great majority are not only Texas Mexicans with some long-standing presence in the Lower Rio Grande Valley but also members of the lower-middle to upper-middle class (1993: 149–153). Our attorney-narrator traces his origins to such a community although he now resides in Austin.

Rather than read his joke and the Stupid American genre as signs of aggression, Oring (1992: 17) suggests that we might better understand such jokes as correlates of aggression, with the appropriate incongruity at its center. That is, the woman is made to look stupid, but that may not be the principal or certainly the only message. Keeping our narrator and his history in mind, we might take much more seriously something that Paredes says almost off-handedly, namely that these are bilingual and bicultural jokes (125).

I would argue that the joke performance in itself resolves and makes "appropriate" another larger incongruity "beyond" the joke yet which makes it possible—that in his very joke virtuosity, the lawyer is demonstrating that although the Anglos have ostensibly "won" (they even practice culinary colonialism by coming into "our" Mexican restaurants), it is we—and not "she"—who are in command of two cultures and two languages (in the formal and the vernacular) and of the linguistic-cognitive-aesthetic ability to make appropriate the incongruous. I have heard this very well known joke narrated either almost completely in English or completely in Spanish, and in varying combinations of both. Such a well-fashioned command has not been incidental in, nor has it impeded, scoring a larger victory, namely our hard-won social effective positioning as lawyers and other professionals while remaining "Mexican," and this is perhaps the ultimate joke played upon the Anglo. Against the racist and class odds, Mexican Americans have achieved social mobility, and these jokes are part of the evidence. As another joke theorist, Mary Douglas (1968: 366), has noted, "if there is no joke in the social structure, no other joke can appear."

Then there is the third subgenre, the self-satirical jest, which can also be masochistic and self-degrading, such as one of Paredes's examples: "Several nations compete in designing the submarine which will stay longest under water, and Mexico wins. Its submarine never comes up" (1966:

125). Again, in 1966 Paredes does not identify his narrators, but they continue to be the same largely Texas-Mexican narrators of the Stupid American cycle to judge, again, from the list of informants he provides in his 1993 collection. This linkage between subgenres through the same kind of narrators is made more evident if we now move to Paredes's second major article (1968), also derived from this same fieldwork and these same informants, and which treats a particular cycle of six such self-satirical jokes.[20]

The jokes satirize and make fun of Mexican-American folk healing traditions, particularly the usually male folk healers themselves—*curanderos*—hence the name of these jests: the *curandero* joke. Here the informant/narrators are specifically identified as citizens of Brownsville, Texas, and members of a "bilingual community with an influential Mexican-American middle class including doctors, lawyers, teachers, well-to-do merchants and individuals in elective and appointive public office." Paredes then adds another critical social distinction: "These are for the most part descendants of the old Mexican settlers of the region when Brownsville was a 'Mexican' town rather than immigrants or children of immigrants from Mexico." Further, the actual narrators "speak good English and have received advanced education in American colleges and universities" (111).

By now it is also quite clear that these are also very likely the same narrators of the Stupid American joke cycle, as Paredes tells us that these six *curandero* jokes "intruded into a session of Stupid American jokes" (107), and on occasion, even these jokes can include a stupid American, namely the Anglo doctor who cannot understand Mexican-American folk illness. But for the most part, the jokes satirize the *curandero*, and as such, Paredes—now working with a more muted form of aggression theory, now also married to a functionalist approach—argues that these jests "release a complicated set of conflicting emotions ranging from exasperation to affection in respect to the unacculturated Mexican-American, coupled with a half-conscious resentment toward the Anglo-American culture" (113).

But if these middle-class informants narrate such ambivalent double-edged jokes, they do so along with those of a single edge, such as that of the submarine. The overall impression of all such jokes is one of "masochism," "self-degradation," and "it is the Mexican rather than the American who is now the protagonist and the ridiculous figure as well. It is the Mexican rather than the American who may be the victim of a bilingual pun or a bicultural situation" (1966: 125). Paredes (1968b: 113) argues that such self-degradation is occasioned by the presence of unacculturated Mexican

Americans in the social environment, no doubt, a working-class presence, probably recent immigrants. He then proposes that his middle-class narrators and Mexican Americans in general have now historically developed beyond such unacculturation and passed into a third stage beyond *corridos* and Stupid American jokes as he compares this third stage of joking to Jewish humor.

> It will be seen by even the most casual student of the jest that these self-directed Mexican tales show a strong resemblance to Jewish humor. There is the same ambivalent attitude toward the member of a more powerful group—Gringo or Goy—expressed in a comic framework approaching sophisticated wit. There is also the same suggestion of masochism, arising from mixed feelings of acceptance and protest, a passive protest that has not only gone beyond the possibility of violence but has even abandoned an imaginary aggressiveness as satisfactory compensation. (1966: 126)

This is a confusing formulation, because as we have shown, his narrators tell both kinds of jokes in the *same time frame*. How then do we explain both kinds of attitudes in what amounts to the same performance setting? Certainly one explanation is a kind of social schizophrenia, but there is another, more sociological possibility that also has comparative historical support in Jewish humor. To make this case we need to return to Paredes's earlier tripart division of the U.S.-Mexican people into long-tem settlers, urban dwellers, and ruralized immigrants. If, indeed, we can now see that all three genres largely originate with the regional Texas-Mexican middle class, then what is the role of the other two groups, who by and large may be classified as immigrants (1966: 113)?

I would suggest that these narratives of seeming self-degradation may also be linked to expanding immigration from Mexico in the first half of the twentieth century, including the massive movement of such folk into the agribusiness of the Lower Rio Grande Valley. Today we speak much of the "transnational," and surely it is in play here, but we should also keep in mind globalization's interplay with the regional and even the microregional (Peacock 2007).

Such ruralized Mexican immigrants entering the Lower Rio Grande Valley tended to concentrate themselves in the agribusiness area of Hidalgo County, thirty miles or so upriver from Brownsville, in Cameron County on the Gulf Coast. This upriver area acquired a reputation for severe racial discrimination as poor Mexicans were exploited for their labor yet kept at a marked distance in the social and civic spheres. Therefore one is surprised when Paredes, native to the Valley, says that he is not prepared to say why some of these jests "are placed in Hidalgo rather than Cameron County." He can only speculate that "it may be that Mexican Americans in Cameron County feel that their people in Hidalgo live under worse conditions than they do" (1968b: 114), which, of course, was probably true. We can also return to his novel, *George Washington Gómez*, and recall the racist restaurant scene with Guálinto and his friends and their graduation party away from Jonesville (Brownsville). Paredes sets the scene in the fictive town of Harlanburg (a composite name from the real cities of Harlingen and Edinburg in Hidalgo County, well known for their segregation practices into the 1970s). As David Gutierrez (1995) has shown, there has always been deep ambivalence and internal conflict among long-term resident Mexican Americans concerning recent Mexican immigrants. Rather than a model in which Paredes's narrators are telling self-degrading jokes about themselves, I would argue that these are really jokes about immigrants.

Oring (1992) is very useful here as well as he cautions against a too narrow interpretation of such self-degrading jokes and illustrates an alternative, also with Jewish humor, often seen as self-degrading, as Paredes does in his comparison. However, such humor often flowed from better-off Western/German Jews, for example, in jokes about Eastern European Jews, and Oring, who knows these traditions well, argues that such narrations do not include the Western/German Jews themselves as objects of the jest. The perception that such jokes speak about *all* Jews actually comes from analysts "who perceived the Eastern and Western Jews as a unity and viewed the Eastern Jews as being deserving of brotherhood and identification" (134).

I would propose a similar dynamic is at work in Paredes's material with his middle-class Texas Mexicans, now in the analogous position of German Jews. But to say that the latter narrate degrading jokes about such immigrants and not about themselves, while true, may also be simultaneously an overstatement and an understatement. For as Paredes notes, although different in many respects, they continue "to reveal a strong feeling of identification with the unacculturated Mexican" (1968b: 113). And a close examination of the jokes themselves does not reveal intense negative feelings, but rather a teasing kind of attitude toward certain understandable cultural and social constraints in the Mexican immigrant, such as in another very well known joke.

A Border Patrol officer was questioning a Mexican *mojado* about the whereabouts of another *mojado*. The first *mojado* replied that his companion was in the thick brush relieving himself. The officer then asked: "Does he have papers?" And the *mojado* replied, "No, *señor*, he cleans himself with leaves."

A *mojado* is literally a "wet one" or "wetback" (from swimming the Rio Grande)—vernacular synonyms for "illegal immigrant"—and the humor, of course, lies in the appropriate incongruity concerning the double meaning of the word "paper" (toilet and legal) but also in the immigrant's presumed ignorance of this incongruity. But my principal point here is that any degradation of the immigrant is not at all particularly mean-spirited or vicious, if it is degradation at all.

These jokes may also be understating a correlate of such immigration which we can foreground and amplify. Many of them have as their principal protagonist and object of ridicule not the Mexican immigrant, as in the joke above, but rather some aspect of the Mexican *state*, as in the earlier submarine joke. That is, such seemingly self-directed humor is not at all directed toward the "self" that is the Texas Mexican narrator, nor even to the Mexican immigrant. Rather, the real target may be the ineffectual and corrupt state that has created such immigration by its largely self-inflicted inability to become a successful and well-functioning political entity after the illusory promise of the Mexican Revolution of 1910. The current out-of-control situation with the drug cartels only adds to this feeling that Mexican society—they who also made the submarine—is on the verge of creating a failed state. Perhaps *it* is the real target of these critical though not self-degrading jokes told by Mexican Americans who still value their ancestral home and close neighbor, but also by native Mexicans who are themselves only too aware of this failure. It would explain why Paredes (1966: 126) notes but does not explain that "the self-critical jest is current throughout Mexico." As things get worse, perhaps we will see the passing of such jokes in Mexico and the return of the revolutionary *corrido*.

Paredes concludes his overview essay on the Mexican-American joke with a semi-philosophical closing assessment.

It is not only the Mexican who in these times faces a world that is more than a man can cope with, and therein lies the appeal of the self-directed jest . . . we have seen how the Mexican folk hero goes from confidence and violence to an ineffectual state . . . in a complicated and incomprehensible world . . . thus the Mexican works through a series of attitudes in regard to the inescapable actuality which the Anglo American represents for him, not only moving toward greater wit and wisdom but attaining a kind of universality as well. His humor becomes part of a general *Weltansicht* rather than a cry expressing nothing more than his own particular pain. (126–127)

In effect, Paredes is aligning the self-satirical joke with the current and modern period in 1966, historicizing even when he is reluctant to do so and implying very different narrators for each period, though I have shown otherwise. By thus historicizing, it is as if in the end, he empties the Mexican American of any distinctive cultural and political significance as he renders him/her a modernist figure of "universality."

In 1966 and today, the everyday social experience of Mexican Americans in the Lower Rio Grande Valley belies what Paredes seems to be proposing, which is a kind of end of Mexican-American history in modernist, inescapable ineffectuality relative to a triumphant Anglo America. Oring (1992: 129) counsels to take a full accounting of the narrator's sociocultural identity before assuming that the protagonists in a joke mirror the social identity of the joke's narrators; that is, before we assume that Paredes's modernist characterization of the jokes' protagonists is also true of his Texas-Mexican narrators. Based on what he himself has told us about these informants, they seem a far cry from modernist ineffectuality. Quite on the contrary, with a "wit and wisdom" not requiring universality, they are effective civic actors in English and Spanish, an organic part of the Mexican-American community in Brownsville in 1966–1968, and today, generally, in the Lower Rio Grande Valley. We might venture the further proposition that they closely resemble the very admirable Feliciano in *George Washington Gómez*. On the other hand, it would seem that the severely conflicted George, who abandoned the Valley *and* lost his sense of humor, is the only one who clearly demonstrates a modernist-inflected ineffectuality and a vacuous "universality."

The foregoing builds upon my previous work on Américo Paredes's folkloristic work, but others have also commented on this aspect of his scholarship in more or less encompassing terms. The more encompassing is offered by Ramón Saldívar (2006: 55–56) in a generalized assessment in which he places Paredes's folklore work within a Gramscian framework. Such an alignment of Gramsci and Paredes is a bit odd as it overlooks Gramsci's persistent and "enlightened" insistence on the eventual eradication of folklore. Much like colonialist nineteenth-century British evolutionary anthropologists, Gramsci did recommend the study of folklore, but only "to know what other conceptions of the world and of life are actually active in the intellectual and moral formation of young people, in order to uproot them and replace them with conceptions deemed to be superior" (Gramsci 1985: 191). As with any modern folklorist, Professor Paredes studied folklore to fully understand a people and their sociocultural milieu, but he would have never advocated that it be "uprooted" and "replaced."[21] Less encompassing is López-Morín's (2006) very brief and mostly biographical work, but one also keyed on the concepts of "performance" and "post-modern ethnography." The latter is derivative from previous readings of Paredes in this vein (Limón 1993, 1994). The former is only too self-evident as Paredes was well-identified with the performance school of folkloristics. In this very short and very biographical work, the specific instances that López-Morín offers of Paredes's application of "performance" are really too few, but he does offer original and engaging readings of certain joking scenes in *George Washington Gómez* as performances (48–54).

I have argued that Paredes's professional work in folklore has received too little attention in extended analytical terms with close attention to his texts from both Mexican-American and other scholars. For "other" scholars, the inattention is keyed on a complicated politics of culture, but for native intellectuals, it has far more to do with the compelling power of *"With His Pistol in His Hand"* as a progenitor of what has come to be called "cultural studies" as the latter intersected with the Chicano movement of the 1960s. We turn now in this direction.

FOUR

Cultural Studies

In the preceding chapter we closely examined Paredes's academic work within the professional discipline of folklore. Indeed, one can make the further argument that this body of work appeared at a historical time in the late 1950s into the late seventies when this discipline was at the apogee of its development. Vibrant PhD programs in folklore came into full stride at the University of Pennsylvania, University of Indiana, UT-Austin, UCLA, Ohio State, and UC-Berkeley, with smaller though important programs at other academic sites, such as the universities of New Mexico, Oregon, Utah, and Western Kentucky. Indeed, Paredes cofounded the UT-Austin program.

Such an extensive disciplinary programming at that historical moment clearly suggested a distinctive object of study called "folklore." But this same period also saw the beginning of another academic enterprise known as "cultural studies," beginning in England, but later and to the present becoming a large and pervasive interest in the United States, including a formidable presence within what came to be called Chicano/a studies. Yet the latter can also trace its origin back to the late fifties, or so I will argue. That cultural studies has largely replaced the erstwhile thriving discipline of folklore as it has literary studies is a bit of an irony and worthy of a larger intellectual history to which the present chapter might be taken as a small contribution.

In what follows, I argue that Paredes's work, and folklore in general, has had a particular and distinctive relationship to such a transnational cultural studies in both historical and geographical dimensions. That is, we may see his work in folklore in a historically proximate and comparatively critical relationship to the early English formation of cultural studies, even as we can also critically trace a more obvious and long-term but ultimately vexed relationship to Chicano and Chicana cultural studies (hereafter Chicano/a studies). The latter is itself a consequence of English cultural studies both directly and also as mediated through an American prism.

My more central concern is the data field that informs cultural studies and the place of folklore in that field, as well as the methodologies for apprehending such cultural studies data. Matters of theory and politics are always salient in cultural studies, and they will not be overlooked here. John Storey (1996: 1) reminds us that, as a discipline, cultural studies may be "defined by three criteria: first, there is the object of study; secondly, there are the basic assumptions which underpin the method(s) of approach to the object of study; and thirdly, there is the history of the discipline itself." Using Paredes's folklore work as a touchstone, I propose to closely examine the first two as a contribution toward the third, beginning first and comparatively with the English origins of cultural studies in relation to folklore and Paredes.

FROM BIRMINGHAM . . .

It may reasonably be said that both cultural studies projects—the English and the Chicano—have their origin point in the same exact year. "*With a Pistol in His Hand*" (*WPH*) appeared in 1958, but so did *Culture and Society: 1780–1950* by Raymond Williams (1958). We begin with the latter. In his foundational book, Williams charts and contests the evolution of the concept of culture centered on a series of largely canonical English literary texts. He closely examines a key segment of the English canonical literary intellectual tradition—Matthew Arnold, the Bronte sisters, Mill, and so on—with a view to understanding their role in the developing class divisions and conflict in British life, given his developing commitment to Marxism (O'Connor 1989: 6–38). But as he does so, Williams (1958: 319–327) must almost necessarily question the prevailing definition of culture away from the idea of culture as synonymous with great literature and other canonical artistic production. Rather, he encourages a view of culture as a more democratic and shared daily lived experience and as a whole way of life.

We could think of this expanded and democratic vision as an anthropological view of culture, although to have moved in the direction of anthropology at that particular moment would have immediately placed Williams in conjunction with the concurrent powerful forces of British social anthropology and its almost exclusive concerns with the English colonial empire and other societies on the colonized or postcolonized periphery.

Seemingly not yet ready to venture into the colonial realm, which is also to say into the realm of race, in 1958 Williams was concerned mostly with thinking through his expanded vision of culture with reference to British and, by extension, Western societies and to locating this working-class culture within these kinds of societies (Williams 1979: 117–118).

In a later formulation, in which he again reviews the history of "culture," Williams does reference anthropology as he makes important distinctions which restrict and focus the rather broad domain of all "lived experience," of a "whole way of life." In 1981 he writes as if he is familiar with new work in symbolic anthropology, where culture is now conceived in terms of a "signifying system," an order of symbolic activity (Geertz 1977). One such system is the humanistic and dominant sense of "culture" as the production, circulation, and consumption of basically canonical art and intellectual works, "through which necessarily (though among other means) a social order is communicated, reproduced, experienced and explored," thus maintaining a linkage to a "whole way of life" (Williams 1995: 13).

But, in a crucial turn, Williams (1995: 13) then expands the objects of "cultural studies" such that the earlier signifying system of a culture—its artistic and intellectual activities—now converges with another, as such activities, "are now much more broadly defined, to include not only the traditional arts and forms of intellectual production but also all of the 'signifying practices' from language through the arts and philosophy to journalism, fashion, and advertising—which now constitute this complex and necessarily extended field." He continues: "The work of the new convergence has been best and most frequently done, either in general theory and in studies in 'ideology,' or in its distinctively new areas of interest, in the 'media' and 'popular culture'" (13).

The "new convergence" is, of course, cultural studies. By "media" and "popular culture," Williams is clearly referring to "journalism, fashion, and advertising," and also, most likely, other unnamed signifying practices such as mass-mediated popular music, comedy clubs, book-of-the-month fiction, and today, reality TV, *People* magazine, ad infinitum, all now subsumed under "popular culture" and all produced and circulated within what Frankfurt School theorists Horkheimer and Adorno (2002: 120–167) famously called the "culture industry," although for this new cultural studies such popular culture is not intrinsically a hegemonic and negating domain as it mostly was for the Frankfurt School.

Williams initially distinguished such popular culture from what he calls the "traditional arts and forms of intellectual production," and it is quite clear that he is using the word "traditional" as in "Tradition and the Individual Talent," that is, the canonical (Eliot 1920). One may then take advantage of his usage to note a certain slippage by recalling that, in every-day usage, traditional arts can also be synonymous with folklore, although clearly Williams does not intend it this way. Had he lent it this other mean-ing as well, he would have filled a gap in his delineation of the field of cul-tural studies as media, popular culture, and canonical works.

Indeed, what of "traditional" arts of another kind? The history of folk-lore scholarship, including Paredes's work on the *corrido*, and jokes, tells us of such arts and other enactments and performances that have no clear origin point or circulation within either the canonical arts or the culture industry but rather appear to originate and circulate largely *within* the lived experience of peoples, especially peoples in subaltern positions, and exchanged freely among them predominantly in face-to-face interactions. Such behaviors we have habitually called "folklore," and its apprehension in English cultural studies is limited at best, as it will also be in Chicano/a studies.

For many intellectuals, especially on the left, the term "folklore" is politically vexed—hierarchical and colonialist—and perhaps that is the reason for its omission within cultural studies. Roger Abrahams (2005: 4–8), one of the leading folklorists of our time and another of my men-tors, recognizes this difficulty even as he fashions a compelling argument for continuing folklore studies.

Against static conceptions of "folklore"—rural, socially backward, self-enclosed, "authentic" past, formalized texts—Abrahams argues that the discipline has gone through profound changes commensurate with its object—folklore—and yet insists that we must still be attentive to what he calls traditional expressive practices residing and performed within com-munities, although these are always influenced by the rest of the world. Possibly to provide more acceptable alternatives to the term *folklore*, Abra-hams offers the somewhat synonymous "poetics of everyday life" and "vernacular culture" (8–17). Traditionally classified as discrete textualized genres such as ballad, tale, and proverb, such practices are better appre-hended within a more fluid and dynamic arrangement, or what he calls a "spectrum of genres": "conversational," "play," "fictive," and "static" (61). He then makes telling distinctions that bear directly on cultural studies, on its selected objects and its omissions, even as he also revoices the inter-actional, face-to-face performance context that is defining of folklore.

Other expressive genres with many traditional elements could also be usefully placed on this spectrum, but no one would want to designate them as folklore. The performance-audience continuum forms part of a larger spectrum in which all genres of expression, traditional or otherwise, could be placed.

A crucial distinction, which is to say,

> The difference between folklore and other expressive phenomenon lies in the range of relations possible in performance. Essentially, we distinguish between folklore and *popular culture* on the basis of dissemination methods; folklore exists only in face-to-face encounters that lead to oral transmission. This distinction is even sharper between folklore and high art or *belles lettres*.

Yet, he continues, it is important to recognize that,

> these genres do not differ greatly in expressive capacity, or even in the presence of traditional elements of composition. Setting folklore genres within the larger spectrum of aesthetic forms and rhetorical strategies reveals both its commonalities with other modes of expressive culture and its special defining features. (69)

Several points are worth highlighting here. First, folklore is to be seen in relation to other expressive forms, principally those of what Abrahams calls *belles lettres*, whose meaning is self-evident, and those of popular culture, the latter clearly understood in William's sense, that is, "journalism, fashion, and advertising." Second, none of these genres is inherently more or less expressive or artful, nor does Abrahams rule out interactions among these distinct domains. Yet, third, Abrahams does set folklore apart, but on the basis of "the range of relations possible in performance," which he then seems to specify with "face-to-face encounters that lead to oral transmission."

I would dare to add a fourth point that leads us centrally into the cultural Marxism that was so fundamental to cultural studies, an argument I made some years ago that is in fact partially indebted to Abrahams as well. For another attribute shared by *belles lettres* and "popular culture" is simply that for all of their often engaging and sometimes critical artfulness, they are also fundamentally market commodities with exchange value. Put perhaps too simply, all such artfulness is marketable even as some of it might even speak paradoxically against such marketability, and as market commodities, they are, in classical Marxist terms, products of alienated or estranged labor and cannot help but reproduce some such alienation in their consumers. By contrast, folklore, the poetics of every-day life—understood as democratically constructed and emergent, free-flowing performance either in language or in material craft or a combina-tion of both—largely escapes this alienating origin and consequence, and indeed by its very existence argues against such alienation (Limón 1983).

I am identifying an expressive domain something like what Michel de Certeau calls "the practice of everyday life," or, for him, "popular culture" but as crafted and shared by ordinary individuals and sometimes fashioned *against* the other mass media "popular culture." As do Abrahams and most contemporary folklorists, de Certeau (1984: 25) also criticizes traditional and now dated folklore scholarship that confined "the operational models of popular culture . . . to the past, the countryside, or to primitive peoples." He then continues an attack on what is clearly and surprisingly a very dated conception of folklore and ethnological studies, as if he is totally unfamil-iar with the new trends in folklore and cultural anthropology developing around him even though he was in residence in California during the writ-ing of his book. It is as if he is thinking of what in Chapter 3 I described as the historic-geographic method, or a very old-fashioned anthropology.[1]

> The authority of ethnological or folklore studies permits some of the material or linguistic objects of these practices to be collected, labeled according to place of origin and theme, put in display cases, offered for inspection and interpretation, and thus that authority conceals, as rural "treasures" serving to edify or satisfy the curiosity of city folks, the legiti-mization of an order supposed by its conservators to be immemorial and "natural." Or else they use the tools and products of a language of social operations to set off a display of technical gadgets and thus ar-range them, inert, on the margins of a system that itself remains intact. (de Certeau 1984: 26)

Such practices as he is interested in rather "exist in the strongholds of the contemporary economy" (25). Among and within such strongholds "are thus insinuated styles of social exchange, technical invention, and moral resistance, that is, an economy of the *gift* (generosities for which one expects a return), an esthetics of *tricks* (artists' operations) and an ethics of *tenacity* (countless ways of refusing to accord the established order the status of a law, a meaning, or a fatality)." He continues: "'Popular' culture is precisely that; it is not a corpus considered as foreign, fragmented in order to be displayed, studied, and 'quoted' by a system which does to objects what it does to living beings," but nor is it simply the products of the culture industry, although de Certeau's practices certainly can include democratically originated manipulations and transformations of such products (26). One needs to underscore the everyday-ness, the emergent artistry, the gifting rather than the cash exchange of such practices.

This emphasis on contestative everyday practices is not at all incompatible with that of Abrahams, who also believes that,

> objectifying the texts of expressive culture for the purpose of analysis without putting the pieces back together in situated performance is also unsatisfying, lacking in explanatory power and comparative reach.

"Vernacular cultural practices," he continues,

> can provide insight into the way others, and we ourselves, operate on a daily basis and amid the most profound disruptions of social life. Vernacular forms and practices should be approached through actual examples at a specific time and place, taking into account the audience's expectations and the conventions of performance. (2005: 38)

In comparison to de Certeau, Abrahams is far more conscious of the aesthetics and genres of such practices — of what de Certeau calls "artists' operations" — and their relationship to more traditional forms. An American pragmatist and social democrat, Abrahams also does not lend himself to de Certeau's predominant rhetoric of suspicion, to the latter's emphasis on *perruque*, which is to say expressive but antagonistic tactics of subversions and appropriations of the dominant order, such as a craftsman "borrowing a lathe" from his or her workplace "to make a piece of furniture" for his or her "living room" (1984: 25).

Abrahams put much greater emphasis on the ways in which such everyday expressive practices are also wagers of aesthetic achievement, friendliness, and goodwill among interlocutors performing in good faith (12–17). In this respect he is closer to Richard Sennett's recent ideas concerning craftsmanship, not as *perruque*, but as, whenever possible, doing work well and with pride in all social sectors, including within de Certeau's "strongholds of the contemporary economy" (Sennett 2008). Yet, in his review of Sennett's work, Julian Bell (2008) notes (and what is more likely so for folkloristic performances) that such moments of craftsmanship are perhaps better envisioned outside or at the margins of the workplace in zones mostly alternative to sites of paid labor.

Elsewhere, I have also suggested that folkloric verbal or material crafting in face-to-face encounters is a form of "gift giving" and metaphorically evokes the most fundamental Marxian concepts: use-value, nonalienated labor, and the denial of commodity fetishism. This is not a critical metaphorical "content" in folklore, but rather the folkloric performance/process as metaphor. In the very aesthetic act of performance may be found the inherent oppositional quality of all folklore (Limón 1983). What Abrahams (1981: 320) once claimed for Texas-style festivals, fairs, and display events may be true for all folkloric performances. All such performances may be displays of "the possibility of hanging on to the use and value of things . . . in the face of those who would turn all of life into acts of consumption." Indebted to Abrahams but also to new left-critical thinking, a younger generation of folklorists continues to develop a processual, rhetorical, and politically critical approach to the folk, folklore, and its adversaries (Gencarella 2009).

Abrahams offers us one now historical example—Texas-style festivals, fairs, and display events—of the sort of folkloric practices we are conceptually discussing here, and at this point the reader may wish for more. It is easy enough to gather and analyze examples of the mass media culture that so informs Birmingham and later American cultural studies such as Hebdige's exemplary work on alternative music and spectacular subcultures (1979). However, by their very emergent character, more everyday practices as we have been imagining may present more of a challenge for they may be concealed precisely in their everyday-ness and also because they do not always present themselves in traditional, formally defined "genres" such as the clearly marked Texas festivals that Abrahams cites. On occasion, however, and more in de Certeau's terms, they are brought out paradoxically by repression and their seeming challenge to the dominant order even when, in Abrahams's terms, they are the most friendly forms of goodwill.

It is this complicated kind of practice and this kind of world, for example, that Michael Bell (1983: 178–179) describes and interprets with such care within African-American society, the world of an urban, adult, African-American *middle class*—not peasants or proletarians. He examines this world as it is situated in a bar where the stylized conversation—not fixed genres—creates a "fictional world based in and re-creative of a conscious desire on the part of the patrons to have a place where they could be as black as they wanted to be." "A world," he continues, "in which they were able to identify what mattered to them . . . which allowed them to assert themselves that they were black in the face of the white world's desire that they be something more and the black world's fear that they had become something less."

In the preceding chapter, we have already seen examples of such everyday expressive poetics in Greater Mexico by way of Paredes's own studies, to which we can add at least contemporary examples from the current world of Greater Mexico by way of my own work on expressive culture in Mexican-American South Texas (1994). Lest one think that such practices are somehow only in Texas, where Paredes and I have done most of our work and only in the "past," as I write in Long Beach, California, the *Los Angeles Times* reports that ordinary and largely undocumented Latino day laborers have organized a "traveling theatre company," *Day Laborer Theatre Without Borders* (Bermudez 2010: A31–35). In the words of Juan José Magandi, its principal organizer and himself a day laborer, its central premise is, "you have culture, you have a story . . . you should share it with the world" (A31). These actors, mostly men, perform skits at various informal community locales dramatizing the trials and triumphs of day labor and immigration, and they perform these principally for other day laborers and mostly in Spanish, even as they constantly recruit and train other actors and even as they continue to support themselves principally through day labor. They have received some help from a nonprofit social activist theatre group and a Ford Foundation grant principally to fund this latter group, but it is quite clear that the day laborers came up with the idea, as well as the creativity and personnel. As the grant has dried up and the activist group has withdrawn its support, "the laborers are intent on finding ways to keep the company together on their own" (A35).

In an English context, Williams's and Birmingham's cultural studies seem to have difficulty recognizing such discrete folkloric activity, such a vernacular poetics, within the several signifying practices of modern social formations, especially working-class formations, an omission that largely continues to the present. In a relatively recent article in the *Journal of Folklore Research*, Barbara Henkes and Richard Johnson, the latter also closely associated with the Birmingham project, conducted a dialogue titled "Silences across Disciplines: Folklore Studies, Cultural Studies, and History" (2002). Johnson reports that when he raised the subject of folklore in Birmingham, "Faces turned blank when I mentioned the discipline." He continues: "Folklore Studies did not figure at all in the version of culture study developed at Birmingham" (128–129). Later he would discover that other geographical sites were studying folklore, but these were in continental Europe or Ireland, a point that will concern us later. He also discovers that Marxist historians such as E. P. Thompson, also associated with early cultural studies, were also employing folkloric sources in works such as the famous *The Making of the English Working Class* (1961) and that Thompson "was in sustained dialogue with folklorists. He wrote for *Folklore*, the journal of the English Folklore Society and was handsomely memorialized in its pages when he died. He was fascinated by custom and ritual and by popular practices like Rough Music" (130). But Johnson adds an important qualification, namely that this use of folklore was historical and not in the study of contemporary society.

Williams himself does somewhat allow folklore this historical and also literary space, although throughout he seems to subscribe to what Dundes (1969), another distinguished folklorist, called the "devolutionary premise" in thinking about folklore, namely the assumption that folklore is intrinsically of the past, defined by certain fixed genres, and characteristic of simple social formations only to die away with the advent of modernity and "progress."

For example, commenting on the role of newspapers in a working-class culture, Williams (1958: 309) says that "the historical counterpart of a modern popular newspaper, in its informing function, is not an earlier minority newspaper, but that complex of rumour and traveller's tales which then served the majority with news of a kind." But to speak of "then" and of the "historical" clearly suggests that for him these are of the past, now replaced by a modern newspaper. Moreover, Williams also acknowledges the persistence of dialect forms in English, noting that "certain selected sounds have been given a cardinal authority which derives from no known law of language, but simply from the fact that they are habitually made by persons who, for other reasons possess social and economic influence." While "particular uses of the common language have been taken and abused for the purposes of class distinction . . . the dialect which is normally equated with standard English has no necessary superiority over other dialects" (332). Yet he also tells us "modern communications make for the growth of uniformity," and discourses such as literature, but presumably also everyday speakers, "will be attracted to the dominant language mode" (323). But his rejection of the possibilities of expressive culture among the working class becomes even more explicit. Working-class culture, he says, cannot be based on "the small amount of 'proletarian writing' and art which exists." But then he conflates such proletarian artful forms with another, more properly folkloric:

The appearance of such work has been useful, not only in its more self-conscious forms, but also in such material as the post-Industrial ballads, which were worth collecting.

He continues: "We need to be aware of this work, but it is to be seen as a valuable dissident element rather than as a culture."
And then concludes,

The traditional popular culture of England was, if not annihilated, at least fragmented and weakened by the dislocations of the Industrial Revolution. What is left, with what in the new conditions has been made, is small in quantity and narrow in range. It exacts respect, but it is in no sense an alternative culture. (320)

How Williams knows all of this is unclear, as no evidence is provided for the "small" quantity of such forms, nor for their "narrow" range. But of equal concern is his conflation of written and plastic forms of what he calls "proletarian art" with what he calls "postindustrial ballads," as if the two had the same ontological and quantitative standing in working-class culture, with both having also the same level of dissidence. The recent work of Roger Renwick (2001) on such balladry in England argues against Williams's disavowal. Sparks quotes even the culturally conservative literary critic F. R. Leavis to this same effect as Leavis comments on the early-twentieth-century English folklorist Cecil Sharp, who

discovered that the traditions of song and dance . . . had persisted so vigorously because the whole context to which folk-song and folk-dance belong was there too. He discovered, in fact, a civilization or "way of life" (in our democratic parlance) that was truly an art of social living. (Sparks 1996: 15)

A later interview with Williams offers an overall and conceptual summary of his position on this question, but one that ends in a sort of irony that contributes to the dilemma of cultural studies as it also silences folklore. Williams is discussing one of his now quite famous ideas, "structures of feeling," which in this instance, initially at least, he seems to use as synonymous with culture as a whole, as he equates it with "the culture of a period," "the particular living result of all the elements in the general organization," "a very deep and wide possession, in all actual communities."

Under critical questioning from his interviewer, however, Williams then says,

> I now feel very strongly the need to define the limits of the term. There are cases where the structure of feeling which is tangible in a particular set of works is undoubtedly an articulation of an area of experience which lies beyond them. . . . What must be happening on these occasions is that an experience which is very wide suddenly finds a semantic figure which articulates it. (1979: 164)

The irony here is that Williams now seems to be returning to a "particular set of works," written and now canonical literary texts—"Shelley," "Byron," calling them "semantic figures," which, as he says, articulate the structure of feeling in a tangible manner, but as they do so, the structure of feeling—though tangible in these works—is "undoubtedly an articulation of an experience which lies beyond them." He claims that these were read and used by working people. Yet even though such a class read and used these texts:

> These works could only have been approximations or substitutes for their own structures of feeling, [that is the working class structures of feeling] . . . there are historical experiences which never do find their semantic figures at all. . . . Even though there is much more literary expression . . . there are still vast areas of silence. One cannot fill that silence with other people's structures of feeling. (1979: 165)

I couldn't agree more that written literary works, canonical or not, are only approximations or substitutes for working-class structures of feeling; that one cannot substitute them for other people's structures of feeling. Yet for Williams it as if in the absence of such literary works, there can only be "vast areas of silence," as once again Williams effectively silences this class. Didn't—and don't—working-class peoples and other subalterns have their own semantic figures to express their own structures of feeling without necessarily needing others—in written literary texts from above—and have we not habitually referred to such subaltern semantic figures as folklore, or now, the poetics of everyday life?

Folklore is placed in a similar historical and enclosed literary space in another of William's famous conceptual contributions: the knowable community. This concept refers to the social, face-to-face worlds and their boundaries represented in the English novel as Williams reads it. In his assessment of this idea in Williams's work, O'Connor (1989: 76) tells us that Jane Austen's knowable community, for example, is "composed of people in large houses who may be socially recognized and visited. The contrast with this apparently settled and poised community is the fictional world of Charles Dickens." In Dickens, as Williams himself then puts it,

> the popular tradition, which has been so much neglected, gives its life not only to continuations of itself—a crowded many-voiced anonymous world of jokes, stories, rumours, songs, shouts, banners, greetings, idioms, address. It gives its life also through its highly original use by this remarkable writer, to a very novel form of sustained imaginative creation—to a unique and necessary way of seeing and responding to what was then an unprecedented world; to the crowded, noisy miscellaneous world of the nineteenth-century city, and of the industrial-capitalist civilization of which the city and above all the metropolis, was the principal embodiment. (1970: 15)

Here we have Williams as close to folklore as he will ever get. Although he does not use the term, he is naming its genres, its democratic origins (that is, the crowd), but perhaps most importantly, the "continuations of itself," and its living presence within, not prior to, "the crowded, noisy, miscellaneous world" of "industrial-capitalist civilization." He tells us of its "imaginative creation," although the latter, he tells us, is "sustained" only in the writings of Dickens, as if this world has no creative life of its own and did not exist until Dickens constructed it. Moreover, he seems to imply, it does not sustain itself beyond the nineteenth century. But how do we know, I ask, that such "a crowded many-voiced anonymous world of jokes, stories, rumours, songs, shouts, banners, greetings, idioms, address" is not present in today's London, especially today's multicultural London, or immigrant Los Angeles?

Within English cultural history there is something both odd and yet paradoxically understandable about this disavowal of folklore. On the one hand, we are dealing with Williams's own England, where in 1846 William Thoms first coined the term *folk-lore*, "as a good Saxon compound to refer to what we in England designate as Popular Antiquities" (quoted in Stocking 1987: 55). On the other hand, it is the same country that in the later nineteenth and through some considerable part of the twentieth century cast folklore as remnants of the past in the face of modernity. Such a bracketing of folklore occurred, of course, as a result of the evolutionary thinking both in folklore and anthropology that was consistent with the industrial development of that country well under way in Thoms's time. We should also recall that in its invention through Thoms, folklore was immediately and deeply implicated in the advent of capitalist modernity. Thoms also offers an elaboration of his definition that is often overlooked when he is quoted. He adds: "the belief in Fairies is by no means extinct in England," and "where steam engines, cotton mills, mail coaches, and similar exorcists have not yet penetrated, numerous legends may be found" (Stocking 1987: 55–56). Such capitalist modernity was exemplified in the Crystal Palace (1851)—in the same short space of years as Thoms's coinage of folklore and the publication of Marx's *Economic and Philosophic Manuscripts of 1844*, the latter the beginning of the path that will take us to Raymond Williams and his own progressivist, devolutionary Marxist appraisal of folklore.

We see then a disavowal of folklore within the very birth of a Marxist cultural studies, a disavowal also perhaps influenced by the cultural Marxism of Antonio Gramsci, as noted in the last chapter. Gramsci is a clear influence on Williams in the latter's *Marxism and Literature*, especially on the question of the hegemonic, although in his articulation of the countervailing concept of the counterhegemonic, it is as if Williams momentarily opens up a space for folklore in his now very well known use of the "residual" and the "emergent" in culture. Although he continues to associate it with the past, there is now an important shift as such residual forms, though formed in the past, can continue to be effective in the present. It remains unclear, however, if Williams would have accepted folklore in such a space, and as we suggested above, new forms of folklore can also be part of the "emergent" (Williams 1977: 121–127). Later, in his *Marxism and Literature*, as he grapples with the idea of "form," Williams again veers between different forms of "tradition," seemingly between written literature and folklore, but cannot name the latter even as he seems to evoke it. "Forms," he says, "are thus the common property, to be sure with differences of degree, of writers and audiences or readers, before any communicative composition can occur." But we take notice of "writers," although other kinds of authors are not noted, and of the "differences of degree" in forms relative to their status as "common property," clearly implying that some forms are more private property and others more "common." This difference in their status as property, he continues, "is much easier to recognize in the case of stable traditional forms, where a specific relationship, of a collective or relatively general kind, is called upon and activated in the very processes of composition and performance."

But what exactly these "stable traditional forms" which occur in "a specific relationship, of a collective or relatively general kind" are he does not say, though such forms and presumably such specific collective relationships are "called upon and activated in the very processes of composition and performance" (1977: 188).

However, from another direction, folklore did make a more active, recognizable, though still momentary appearance within the early formation of cultural studies. Raymond Williams was, of course, not alone in the formation of cultural studies. Richard Hoggart also played an influential role both as the first director of the Birmingham University Centre for Contemporary Cultural Studies in 1964, but perhaps more so with his book *The Uses of Literacy*, which appeared in 1957, a year before *Culture and Society*. The book has two parts. In the first, Hoggart provides a kind of autobiographical ethnography of his own English working-class past, and in the second, he discusses what he clearly sees as the deleterious effects of mass communications on this older culture. The first chapter of Part 1 offers a general and economic sense of this working class, but it is in Chapter 2 that the folkloristic ethnography really begins with a large and engaging number of examples taken principally from everyday expressive speech. He analytically summarizes even as he notices the critical tension between such forms and capitalist modernity: "that tradition is now weakening, but if we are to understand the present situation of the working-classes we must not pronounce it dead when it still has remarkable life" (Hoggart 1992: 13).

Unlike Williams, Hoggart clearly admires and affirms this older urban folk culture, but, like Williams, he too is suggesting that such practices will not remain viable in the face of modernity. Yet unlike Williams, he is clearly angry about this erasure, although he expressed that with a note of lament at its passing before the onslaught of capitalist modernity.[2] Yet there is virtue in that he describes such a contemporary world at all and thereby goes where Williams would not or could not fully go, even though obviously Williams was very aware of his work. As Andrew Goodwin points out in his new introduction to *The Uses of Literacy* (1992), Hoggart's work is an effort "to move out from the study of literature as it is academically defined to work on many other aspects of contemporary culture, chiefly but not only in words." And he also reminds us "that the cultural studies project was originally centered on culture as lived experience, rather than culture as text or product," and recommends a rereading of *The Uses of Literacy* "for its focus on the relation between texts and something else, something more important than theory—how people live" (xvi–xvii).

Thus, the Birmingham group initiated cultural studies as a turn away from canonical literature as a selective tradition of the British ruling class and toward the everyday cultures of the English working class, or what Williams referred to as the lived experience of this class. While folklore was not the totality of such lived experience, I have suggested that it certainly should have been construed as a significant part of it, but it largely was not. Williams tells us of the silence, the absence of native semantic figures for this class. Put another way, I am referring to the discrepancy between this historical goal of cultural studies—the scholarly and politically committed apprehension of such democratic cultures—and what cultural studies ultimately came to identify as its objects of study, especially in the more current moment.

Within this discrepancy—this dilemma—I am interested in the place and role of those kinds of working-class behaviors that we might reasonably identify as folklore with the latter now understood as a flexible and wide-ranging category but keyed on the expressive resources generated largely within and shared by discernibly marginalized communities. For I am persuaded that English cultural studies paid insufficient attention to such behaviors within culture as lived experience, as a whole way of life. If the terms "expressive vernacular culture" or "the poetic of everyday life" can be used in somewhat substitution for folklore, then it is as if, for Williams, such democratic expression, especially artful expression, is not at all salient or important within the lived experience of the working class (Abrahams 2005). We see this broad sense and presence of such lived experience in Hoggart's *The Uses of Literacy*, even as he also signals the threat of capitalist modernity at mid-twentieth century.

Possibly because modernity did indeed wreak havoc on such lived experience or possibly because cultural studies lacked either vision or method for apprehending it, much if not all of subsequent cultural studies has now turned away from democratically based creativity and toward the texts of mass media, ethnic written literature, and public performances by cultural elites—few, if any, of these, with Hoggart's exception, attempting to identify and articulate the more creatively autonomous poetics of everyday life.[3] Perhaps the closest the Birmingham School came toward work on the poetics of everyday working-class life is in the volume *Resistance Through Rituals: Youth Subcultures in Post-War Britain* (1976), whose very subtitle conveys its limitation, namely its focus on youth and its very mass mediated expressive worlds, seen in cultural formations such as the "mods" and the "skinheads." According to Simon During (1993: 4), "as the old working-class communal life fragmented," cultural studies after Hoggart turned its attention "to culture as organized from afar—both by the state through its educational system . . . and by the 'culture industry'. . ."

My implicit contention throughout is that such a move in English cultural studies may have been (a) premature, resulting from a loss of confidence in the ability of the English subaltern to craft a relatively independent poetics of culture; (b) a methodological inability to apprehend such; or (c) possibly a particularly English encounter with modernity and postmodernity that did in fact wholly fragment English subaltern life and obliterate its autonomous creative resources.

Together with these general orientations, in the years since 1958, under the tutelage of Stuart Hall, the original Marxist theoretical framework for cultural studies was expanded to admit other and often vying theoretical perspectives: poststructuralism, postpsychoanalysis, feminism, race, and most recently transnationalism, globalization, and, of course, border studies (Morley and Chen 1996). One could go to many such examples flowing from post-Birmingham and from other geographical sites as well, such as Anthony Easthope's book *Literary into Cultural Studies* (1991), where the cultural studies part focuses on the popular films *Chinatown, James Bond,* and *Tarzan.* Finally, in 1989, and assessing the *future* of cultural studies, Raymond Williams was still thinking of the culture of everyday life in terms of mass media forms such as film, detective fiction, and soap operas (158–159). But along with all of these changes—or lack of them—by the 1980s cultural studies had also gone decisively American, and soon enough into Chicano/a studies, although Chicano/a studies also had to deal with the overlapping influence of Américo Paredes, a figure in many ways comparable to Raymond Williams . . . and not.[4]

. . . TO BROWNSVILLE

As noted, in 1958, the year of Williams's *Culture and Society,* and one year after Hoggart's *The Uses of Literacy,* Américo Paredes published *"With His Pistol in His Hand": A Border Ballad and Its Hero.* As it also happens, Paredes and Williams, the somewhat younger man, also shared the experience of World War II, albeit in very different circumstances: Paredes, as we saw earlier, largely in an army of occupation in Japan, while Williams saw considerable and up-close, ferocious combat as the commander of a tank destroyer during and after the Allied invasion of Normandy on June 6, 1944 (Williams 1979: 55–60). Both pursued a university education and academic careers after the war—Williams at Cambridge,

Paredes at the University of Texas at Austin. And, in addition to their academic work on culture, both also wrote fiction. But perhaps more to the point of folklore and everyday life is the manner of their upbringings and their reactions to them.

The comparison between these two men has not been lost on others. Both men shared what might be termed rural, regionalized, but also ethnicized and colonized backgrounds relative to the centers of power in the United Kingdom and the United States, respectively. We have already spoken of South Texas, and Williams was from a working-class family in Wales. Comparing Paredes to Williams, Ramón Saldívar (2006:36) tells us that in writing "about a similar border country tradition, Raymond Williams sought to preserve the history of the agency of the Welsh, Irish and Scottish folk within the history of imperial Britain."

Paredes certainly did with respect to Greater Mexico, but Williams's relationship to his native ground was far more vexed. His Wales was already a culture area that, as he says, "had been Anglicized in the 1840s," adding, "there was an intense and conscious pressure through the schools to eliminate the language, which included punishment for children who spoke Welsh." What he "did not perceive" in his adolescence, he continues, "is that the grammar schools were implanted in the towns of Wales for the purposes of Anglicization. They imposed a completely English orientation, which cut one off thoroughly from Welshness." Very much *unlike* Paredes, Williams concludes, "The result was a rejection of my Welshness which I did not work through until well into my thirties, when I began to read the history and understand it" (1979: 25).

This working through occurred in the "Welsh" novels he wrote, such as *Border Country* (1960), but does not get fully settled until much later with *The Fight for Manod* (1979) and the posthumous *People of the Black Mountains* (1989). As he says about his relationship to Welsh culture,

> a big change started to happen from the late sixties. . . . I began having contact with Welsh writers and intellectuals, all highly political in the best tradition of the culture, and I found this curious effect. Suddenly England, bourgeois England, wasn't my point of reference any more. . . . I want the Welsh people—still a radical and cultured people—to defeat, override or bypass bourgeois England. (Williams 1979: 295–296)

In his late "big change," his "curious effect," Williams sounds much less like Paredes and much more like some very bright, but highly acculturated, mobile, Mexican-American young person, perhaps the son or daughter of Paredes's middle-class joke tellers, a young person like Gúalinto/ George, who initially wholly adopts Anglo-American culture, but who, unlike Gúalinto/George, later returns to his "roots" out of late conviction and with the realization that his/her future is not in their present or future but rather in their past.

Américo Paredes had a very different formative experience, and it is to Ramón Saldívar's credit that he has Paredes vividly recollect this experience, one saturated with the Spanish language, Mexican popular culture, and native folklore (2006: 64–93). To be sure, as we saw with Guálinto/ George in Chapter 1, the forces of Texas-style Anglicization were certainly present, but in this war of position, in contrast to Williams, it must be said that Paredes won even as he also appropriated the cultural tools of the dominant Anglos. Unlike Williams, he left his border country with a firm base in Texas-Mexican folklore and culture, never lost it, and crafted a critical career based on it.

As we have already seen, Paredes's scholarly work is clearly an exercise in recovering the popular, principally but not only the folk balladry, the *corrido*, but also other forms of popular culture, as well as legend and proverb. Moreover, the popular in the present, the joke form, food forms, are seen not as residuals but as active elements of culture in the present, widely distributed as a democratic culture—a poetics of everyday life— among and originating with the Mexican people of South Texas. He is more like Richard Hoggart—but without the nostalgic lament. But as if that were not enough, WPH offers a surprising comparison that places him squarely in Williams's and Hoggart's and Thompson's own territory. Paredes (1958: 107, 243–244). compares the South Texas *corrido* and the Mexican people of that region to British Isles balladry and the Scottish and Irish people, and their resistance to English dominance, as if doing English cultural studies a favor from across the Atlantic.

Paredes, this Mexican American from South Texas, educated at a then-provincial university, had the vision to see the comparative linkages between the Mexican situation in Texas and that in England, a bit of an irony if one keeps in mind that British capital played a significant role in the nineteenth-century U.S. appropriation of South Texas (Montejano 1987: 62–63). We now have to inflect our pronunciation of "Anglo-American" with some emphasis on the *Anglo*. Though not a Marxist in the Birmingham sense, in Paredes's work we do find what Renato Rosaldo identifies as an embedded perspective that clearly relates culture to domination (Chabram-Dernersesian 2007: 116).[5]

Finally, unlike Williams, Paredes consistently acknowledged *his* border, cultural but also racial, and those of his people through his subtle understanding of what is now termed the postcolonial, and put these postcolonial analytical categories into full play in his writings. Thus, as a kind of organic intellectual, he was positioned to become an initial model for a new generation of Mexican-American college students who, like the later Raymond Williams, were fashioning a new critique of their own continuing sense of "Anglo" domination, the somewhat equivalent of Williams's new-found "Welsh writers and intellectuals, all highly political in the best tradition of the culture."[6] In this manner the Chicano movement of the 1960s found Paredes, although it must be said that he found it as well. In this mutual discovery, over time his work came to be defined as "foundational" for the initial emergence of Chicano/a studies, even though the relationship would not be sustained.

¡CHICANO!

The history of the Chicano movement has been often recounted in summary form and also explored in extended scholarly study such that I trust it will not be necessary to repeat it here, especially since I myself have already spoken on the subject in the preceding chapters.[7] What remains unexplored is the concomitant emergence and development of what has now come to be called Chicano/a cultural studies, the academic and arts component and legacy of the movement within colleges and universities in the United States.

As far as I know, there is really only one book-length treatment of this particular subject, Michael Soldatenko's *Chicano Studies: The Genesis of a Discipline* (2009), which, as the author acknowledges, tends "to overemphasize the role of the state" (190)—of California, that is. But even with this California emphasis, he does not overlook the work of the Texas-Mexican Américo Paredes in relation to Chicano/a studies, although his treatment is not wholly satisfactory. Soldatenko's most significant omission is simply but importantly Paredes's crucial role in the development of Chicano/a studies at the University of Texas at Austin after a period of intense advocacy in the late sixties in cooperation with the UT-Austin Mexican-American Youth Organization (MAYO). Paredes then became the founding director of the Center for Mexican American Studies (CMAS) in 1970 and remained an influential voice in CMAS affairs until his death in 1999.[8] More on this in Chapter 6.

Soldatenko does raise two significant issues germane to my argument concerning Paredes's relationship to CCS. First, he says that "the work of Paredes, like that of [sociologist Julian] Samora, was often distant to early Chicano activists. It did not resonate with their militancy and their form of cultural nationalism . . ." (118). He cites no evidence on this score, but it would seem very odd that such nationalist militants would *not* appreciate the figure of Gregorio Cortez, fighting off Texas Rangers "with his pistol in his hand." My personal recollections are quite different. Moreover, speaking of *WPH*, Paredes himself says: "It wasn't until the Chicano movement in California discovered the book in the 1970s that it really took off" (Saldívar 2007: 114).[9] And Soldatenko seems wholly unaware that the book's discovery was amplified when Paredes lectured several times in California beginning in the late sixties and into the seventies, and that during this period Paredes was also a visiting professor at UC-Berkeley, where he met and admired Octavio Romano.[10]

Moreover, though he discusses the seminal work of UCLA Chicano activist, historian, and cultural theorist Juan Gómez-Quiñones, Soldatenko seems not to know that the latter spent a 1972–73 postdoctoral year at UT-Austin's Center for Mexican American Studies under Paredes's mentorship. During this period, among other things, Gómez-Quiñones wrote his initially very influential essay "On Culture" (1977), where he says, "The best studies on culture of the Mexican people of the United States are those of Américo Paredes. . . . I draw on them" (291).

Soldatenko thus imagines an alleged and unsupported distancing that occurred between Paredes and the early Chicano/a activists, but this alleged distance disappeared, he says, by the late seventies as "Paredes and his work were reconsidered by the same activists, though now older and a new generation of scholars" (118). But the real reason that Paredes grew in importance, as the case of Gómez-Quiñones and my own experience illustrate, had less to do with age and far more to do with "a new generation of scholars," the marked and unprecedented entrance of Chicanos and, increasingly, Chicanas into programs of graduate study in which Paredes's work was one of the few available Mexican-American scholarly resources, including the very idea that he had successfully and brilliantly traversed such a course of study toward the PhD in a very brief period of time, making him a consummate role model.

However, Soldatenko is very helpful as he raises another issue even more germane to my argument, and it concerns the place of cultural anthropology in Chicano/a studies. He correctly notes that Paredes practiced participant-observation methods but that he did so in the context of a spreading distrust of cultural anthropology among young Chicano/a militants. This distrust had to do with the early Chicano/a critiques of such anthropology on Mexican Americans that, in the eyes of its critics, had resulted in a denigrating stereotyping of Mexican-American behavior (Romano 1968, 1970; Vaca 1970a, 1970b). He credits me with calling for a more subtle and engaged use of such methods in a future anthropology (119). However, others deserve even more credit, including Carlos Vélez-Ibáñez and Renato Rosaldo, as does Paredes himself, who also weighed in with such a critique from a folklorist's perspective and offered alternative ways to listen to people (1978a). Yet I believe such mistrust remained and continues among contemporary practitioners of cultural studies, especially when joined to a general critique of anthropology in the seventies and today as the so-called "handmaiden to colonialism" (Asad 1973).

As a result, although Paredes was initially widely read and admired both as a scholar and as a person, paradoxically, it cannot be said that over time he really exerted a practical, substantive and disciplinary influence on the later development of Chicano/a studies. Rather, or so I will argue, with the exception of a few figures such as Juan Gómez-Quiñones, Chicano/a studies actually veered away from Paredes's example, especially in terms of the cultural practices they chose to investigate. Put another way, over time, folklore as the expressive practices of everyday life, central to Paredes's work, as we saw in Chapter 3, seemed to lose its importance to Chicano/a studies, as did his fieldwork methodology. Put yet another way, the British cultural studies model flowing from the Birmingham Centre for Contemporary Cultural Studies, later refracted through an American prism, soon won out in its influence over Chicano/a cultural studies.[11]

CHICANO/A CULTURAL STUDIES

Even a cursory reading of what is written today in cultural studies demonstrates the pervasive British and American influence in all of its various generational manifestations, which have changed at the level of theory, particularly with the advent of feminist perspectives. What has remained largely constant, however—what has not changed appreciably— are the objects of cultural study and the methodology for their analytical apprehension. These still continue to be defined by their explicit connection to the mass media culture industry and to literary texts.

Let me begin by reviewing the work of a major figure in cultural studies in the present moment, José D. Saldívar, as he sets out the features and parameters of Chicano/a studies, even as he leads us back to the Birmingham School. Referencing Stuart Hall, Saldívar (1997: 10) notes that from its beginnings in the early sixties, the Birmingham School, as we have noted, sought to reorient the study of culture away from an elite sense of culture as canonical and largely artistic texts at a distance from the social and more toward an anthropological view. As we have already seen, cultural studies should take us to socially situated cultural practices as well as toward an understanding of such culture as intimately tied up with questions of domination, power, struggle, and resistance. According to Saldívar, a later and American version is exemplified by the groundbreaking volume *Cultural Studies* (Nelson, Treichler, and Grossberg 1992), where the editors also contend that "cultural studies is committed to the study of the entire range of a society's art, beliefs, institutions, and communicative practices" (4), not divorced, of course, from the aforementioned questions of power even as the specific studies in this volume tend to concentrate, once again, on mass media productions (Saldívar 1997: 11).

Saldívar (1997: 10–11) correctly takes note of the intellectual origins of such an expanded and critical view of culture for the Birmingham School and its American practitioners in the work of Raymond Williams. Moreover, he not only traces his own cultural studies practice back to Birmingham intellectually but also to Brownsville, Texas, because like Paredes, it is also his hometown. He explicitly acknowledges Paredes as a foremost practitioner of Chicano/a studies by way of *WPH*, although he says nothing about the rest of Paredes's folklore work. However, in keeping with Birmingham cultural studies, Saldívar spends most of his chapter on Paredes discussing his written fiction by way of *George Washington Gómez*, and indeed most of *Border Matters* is devoted to other Chicano/a literary texts. Later in his book he does make some attempt to move beyond literary texts, but in my estimation barely enters into the poetics of everyday life, turning instead to mass media performers such as Los Tigres del Norte, El Vez, Tish Hinojosa, Los Illegals, with only Los Tigres in some direct connection with the everyday life of ordinary working-class, and dare I say, adult Mexicans in the United States.[12]

His analyses of Tish Hinojosa and El Vez are the longest and particularly instructive. Hinojosa is a female "folk" singer, a distant approximation of Joan Baez though with nothing close to Baez's powerful voice, audience reach, politics, and popularity even today. A native of San Antonio now living in Austin, Hinojosa took some musical instruction from Américo Paredes in the singing of *corridos*, and in the performance that Saldívar reports, she indeed sings in the genre, including a *corrido* she composed *about* Américo Paredes called "Con Su Pluma en Su Mano" (With His Pen in His Hand), alluding, of course, to "El Corrido de Gregorio Cortez," which Saldívar misidentifies as "Con Su Pistola en La Mano" (188).

At this performance in San Francisco at the famous Fillmore, she sang along with other performers such as Don Walser and the Texas-Mexican accordionist Santiago Jimenez Jr. But it is Hinojosa's audience, as reported by Saldívar, that, for me, demonstrates the limits of the cultural studies approach that Saldívar is taking. His description opens with: "Shortly after dark on a foggy Friday night in San Francisco an excited crowd lines the sidewalk along Geary at Fillmore Street. The multiracial, transcultural crowd . . . have [*sic*] come here from all over the city for a performance by Tish Hinojosa, accompanied by the electric accordion Texas-Mexican riffs of Santiago Jimeñez, Jr., [*sic*] and the solitary yodeling of Don Walser" (186). Later, as Hinojosa sings an up-tempo traditional Mexican song, "the foot-stomping polka rhythms . . . and its shrieking accordion playing by Jimeñez [*sic*] lure many of us at the Fillmore into doing a hard *tacquachito* on the dance floor" (189).[13]

From a cultural studies perspective, such music is certainly an appropriate object of analysis, but who is this "us"—this audience—that so responds to Hinojosa and the music? I cannot know for sure since I was not there, but the "Bay Area," the "Fillmore," the many colleges and universities in the Bay Area, plus my own time in the Bay Area and at the Fillmore on other occasions, all tell me that it is *youth*, probably college-educated youth, probably ideologically committed youth, who in their youth and commitment respond with such marked fervor and excitement, and who in their Bay Area, highly educated, youthful sensibility dance a Texas-Mexican polka with a "foot-stomping" that would bewilder the distant South Texan, working-class Texas-Mexicans who created such music and dance as a potent part of their—not everyday, but probably weekly—vernacular poetics (Peña 1983; Limón 1994: 141–186).

A similar issue arises with respect to El Vez. As with Hinojosa, Saldívar offers an extended analysis of the mostly English-language performance texts of this Mexican-American Elvis impersonator who, in his act, riffs off ethnic Mexican, mostly humorous material as he offers a left-of-center social critique of the marginalized Mexican condition in the United States. But again, at least according to my direct observation of two performances in Austin, Texas, El Vez's audiences appear to consist largely of college-educated, already ideologically committed youths, and mostly non-Mexican-American youths at that. No doubt knowing that this is his key demographic, those who plan his bookings have slotted him mainly in large cities with large numbers of such young people, at least according to his upcoming online schedule.

Lest I be misunderstood, I am not objecting to the inclusion of youths as part of the cultural studies framework, but such youths, especially English-dominant, college-educated youths, are only a part of Mexican America. Both in the emphasis on this demographic and the focus on mass media staged performances like those at the Fillmore, Chicano/a studies continues in the Birmingham, and now also American, tradition.

Through her prodigious editorial work in this area, Angie Chabram-Dernersesian is also a major figure in cultural studies and furnishes a wide-ranging reference base for the current state of Chicano/a studies and Américo Paredes's place in it. In keeping with the Birmingham School, her *Chicana/o Cultural Studies Reader* (2007) is devoted chiefly to either con-ceptual/theoretical pieces with little ethnographic grounding or to essays that analyze literary and filmic texts, the latter mostly Chicano/a film pro-ductions with frankly little circulation in the wider non-university com-munity. Again, the emphasis is on young people as the consumers of these productions.

Most of these essays are splendid in their theoretical sophistication and in their fine-tuned analysis of their chosen, if predominantly un-grounded, texts. However, only the articles in Part 5 of the book really venture out into the world of everyday Mexican life in the United States, mostly by way of popular music although the musical productions chosen here have the virtue of a wider circulation beyond youths. These include Broyles-González's essay on Lydia Mendoza's *ranchera* music, as well as Deborah Vargas's on Selena. Most impressively for my taste and concerns is George Lipsitz, whose well-grounded review of Mexican music and dance (such as *banda* and *quebradita*, popular among working-class im-migrants at the time) actually has the word "work" in its title: "'Home Is Where the Hatred Is': Work, Music, and the Transnational Economy" (2006b).

Indeed, it is telling that in the entire volume only Lipsitz references Paredes at length, and with admiration, a Paredes who then makes only two other brief appearances in this entire volume (53–55). Velasco briefly acknowledges the importance of *WPH* (207). But editor Chabram-Dernersesian dismisses *WPH* as Chicano nationalism's "preferred revo-lutionary narrative" (166). As a whole, most of the studies in this volume do not live up to the benchmarks for cultural studies that Lipsitz (2006a) correctly sets forth in a second contribution to this volume.

Cultural Studies scholars bring anthropological and sociological perspectives to cultural practices and texts that have been previously analyzed largely on aesthetic grounds. They open up for sustained analysis the everyday life activities of popular culture consumers, youth subcultures, and ethnic minorities. More important they provide sophisticated and convincing arguments about the ways in which the commonplace and ordinary practices of everyday life often encode larger social and ideological meanings. (51)

While the texts and cultural practices analyzed in this volume are of considerable interest, I find little demonstrating distinctive "anthropological" or "sociological" perspectives, especially extended fieldwork, and precious little of "everyday life activities" or "the commonplace and ordinary practices of everyday life."

This volume is accompanied by another also edited by Chabram-Dernersesian called *The Chicana/o Cultural Studies Forum: Critical and Ethnographic Perspectives*. As with the other volume, and with considerable authorial repetition, of the thirty-eight participants in this volume, approximately thirty are in literary, communication, or film departments. The "cultural" that is discussed in this "cultural studies" forum turns out to be, again, a range of cultural artifacts, texts, and performances created mostly by yet other Chicana/o cultural elites, although as a conversational forum no extended case studies are offered, as with the other book.

Only three anthropologists appear (Ruth Behar, Renato Rosaldo, Carlos Vélez-Ibáñez) and one sociologist (Herman Gray), and it is telling that three of these voice a certain unease in their contributions to this conversation. In the small paragraph allotted to him, Vélez-Ibáñez reminds the forum that his own fine, truly interdisciplinary and partially field based *Border Visions* speaks of the "cultural *place* and *space* of the creativity and struggles of the *Mexican population* of the U.S." [emphasis added] (41). Rosaldo pleads that "there should be a prominent role . . . for anthropologists within cultural studies" (52) and suggests that "there are ways in which anthropologists can push cultural studies . . . it's important to talk to somebody who's actually viewing what you are studying . . . what I mean to say to people doing this kind of work is that they need to talk to people, and that they will learn something if they do" (120). Finally, Gray speaks of finding himself "frustrated by certain kinds of moves in cultural studies, including the textual move, which pushes me back toward sociology in an odd kind of way" (200), and by the manner in which "cultural studies got taken up in Spanish, Literature, Rhetoric and Communications Departments in particularly restrictive ways" (206).

Américo Paredes makes two appearances in this volume. Once again, it is George Lipsitz (2007: 196) who must remind this forum at length that "there is nothing that any cultural studies theorist of the 80s and 90s formulated about culture that was not already present in one form or another in Américo Paredes's '*With His Pistol in His Hand*' in 1958," even as he also says that Paredes's work "has all sorts of limits for today's readers." He lends emphasis to Paredes's "texts" and "the particular kind of work they do" but says nothing about the ethnographic fieldwork that Paredes did to acquire them. Yet here Lipsitz is clearly signaling the break between Paredes and the newer Chicano/a cultural studies. A second commentary on Paredes in this volume — Renato Rosaldo's — is also germane as it names one of the central reasons why Lipsitz thinks that Paredes's work "has all sorts of limits for today's readers." Rosaldo recounts his feminist critique of the patriarchal character of Paredes's construction of the "warrior-hero," such as Gregorio Cortez and of traditional South Texas-Mexican society as a communal culture, an influential critique that no doubt contributed to the schism between Paredes and the new Chicano/a studies, one in which in some real sense Rosaldo himself now supplants Paredes as a new originary and primal figure (18–19).[14]

If my assessment of these leading texts is correct, why are democratically grounded vernacular poetics and ethnographic fieldwork largely missing from today's Chicano/Chicana cultural studies as represented by these texts, and why has Paredes virtually disappeared?[15] One obvious but not entirely satisfactory explanation is that the cultural studies light that Paredes initially cast was really no light at all; that he never really mattered at all in California, not even in the beginning; and that he now matters much more by way of *George Washington Gómez*. And to the degree that he did ever so briefly, he was later swept aside by Rosaldo's feminist critique of the warrior-hero masculine syndrome in *WPH*. But, as we have also seen, Herman Gray alludes to another reason for this disavowal of Paredes's methodology, namely the way that Chicano/a studies was largely taken up by literary and communication departments in what he calls "particularly restrictive ways," by which I take him to mean no sociological or ethnographic methods.[16]

However, we must note that this departure from Paredes's example is quite regional in its character.

CALIFORNIA DREAMING

Beyond field methods and feminism, a robust sociology of knowledge also cannot escape noticing the fundamentally and predominantly Californian, indeed almost wholly *coastal* Californian, composition of Chicano/a cultural studies, if the lineup of contributors and topics in the Chabram-Dernersesian volumes is taken as evidence. After twenty-five years, that now also certainly includes the erstwhile Tejano José Saldívar. None of this work identifies itself as "Californian," and indeed, it implicitly casts itself in a national idiom of "Chicanos" and "Chicanas," yet it very evidently is predominantly Californian by any measure. One can only speculate that the insularity of Chicano/a studies and its interests may also have something to do with the very character of coastal California cultural life that Rickels (1991) has examined. He speaks of a coastal culture that lends so much emphasis to mass media, high technology, perfect weather, high mobility (in both senses), and beautiful, high-powered, if insulated, UC campuses, a culture enamored with itself that has undoubtedly shaped the sensibility of this mostly California native, and mostly young, Chicano/a studies cohort. That is, one wonders if the very cultural creation that is California with a concomitant though often overlooked insularity also played a role in the particular character of Chicano/a studies that we have seen. This insularity led to three intellectual disjunctions, two of which are regionally overlaid, that may have contributed to this particular formation and which return us to Paredes in a different modality.

Paredes himself told us that *WPH* was discovered in activist Chicano/a California as many such young men and women were moving into graduate programs with an emphasis on Chicano/a studies. Yet this was also at a time when there were precious few Chicano or Chicana professors with whom to study, even in California. However, the University of Texas at Austin had Américo Paredes, not to mention George Sánchez. The latter actually trained a large cohort of Chicanas and Chicanos from all over the country in the field of education. Yet, in the first disjunction, almost no one came from California, or for that matter from anywhere else, to study with Paredes. I have already noted Juan Gómez-Quiñones and his important postdoctoral work in history with Paredes, but as a result of that experience, he also wrote a seminal and path-breaking theoretical essay, "On Culture," which like Paredes's work is now largely ignored in Chicano/a studies in his own California (1977). Teresa McKenna, from the University of Southern California, and primarily a literary critic, also spent a postdoctoral year in Austin under Paredes's direction and carried that influence into her own study of the ballad form (1997: 1–30), but she is also not identified with Chicano/a studies.

Even with such eminent postdoctoral scholars, it remains oddly and perhaps sadly the case that from the 1960s until his retirement thirty years later, only two California Chicanos and two California Chicanas— Raymund Paredes (no relation), Manuel Peña, Olga Nájera-Ramirez, and Alicia González— came to do graduate work with Paredes and completed their PhD programs with him. Of these, only Peña and Nájera-Ramirez specifically studied anthropological folklore, completed the PhD, and returned to California to become, respectively, a full professor in Chicano/a studies at CSU-Fresno (now retired) and a full professor of anthropology at UC–Santa Cruz. More on both later.[17] But such a largely failed linkage only begs the question: why was there no great interest in ethnographic folklore among young Chicano/Chicana Californians, or at least not enough interest to warrant leaving costal California for a relatively brief period of time?

In fact, Californians did not even have to leave, for they had another alternative in matters of folklore. At the beginning of this chapter I mentioned the highly regarded UCLA program in folklore and mythology with Stanley Robe, also a distinguished Mexicanist folklorist, on its faculty. It fostered María Herrera-Sobek's early work on Mexican immigrant folklore and later her important feminist work on the *corrido* (1979, 1990, 1993); Elaine K. Miller and her *Mexican Folk Narrative from the Los Angeles Area* (1973); José R. Reyna's dissertation on Mexican-American prose folk narratives (1973); and the work of the late Michael Heisley on California Mexican labor and folklore.

Yet these were small in number and some are no longer with us. No others followed in their path at UCLA.[18] We should also recall the small monograph *Antología del saber popular* (Anthology of Popular Knowledge) (1971) and also the special issue of *Aztlán* (1982) on folklore specifically honoring Paredes and edited by Teresa McKenna, both published by the UCLA Chicano Studies Research Center. The late Guillermo Hernandez must always be acknowledged for promoting scholarship on the *corrido* by way of his collections, his very important annual conferences on the genre, and his writing (1999). One must also recall the special issue of *Aztlán* on the *corrido*, although none of the papers deal with California (Leal and Hernandez 1997). The very important ethnomusicological, field-based work of Professor Steven Loza (1993) at UCLA also cannot be overlooked. Finally, the aforementioned Juan Gómez-Quiñones, Paredes's postdoctoral student and a cultural theoretician, offers us a model, well-grounded, analytical, if essay-length, treatment of how Mexican immigrants practice a vernacular poetics in Southern California (2000). Yet, in this second disjunction, it must also be said that these numerically small, UCLA-centered efforts and these figures do not themselves appear to have had a decisive and continuing presence over time in what later came to be Chicano/a studies. Neither Gómez-Quiñones nor Loza are to be found in the Chabram-Dernersesian volumes, nor is Herrera-Sobek, the Luis Leal Distinguished Chair in Chicano Studies at UC-Santa Barbara.

This second disjunction has been amplified as it appears to be the case that Herrera-Sobek has joined her efforts to a distinctive feminist research path, one indeed grounded in ethnographically and democratically grounded folklore and popular culture — on the poetics of everyday life — of the kind and by scholars not predominantly represented in Chicano/a studies. This effort conclusively reaches beyond coastal California, particularly to Texas and New Mexico, an effort led by, among others, the aforementioned Olga Nájera-Ramirez but now also including the Tejana Norma E. Cantú of UT-San Antonio (Cantú and Nájera-Ramirez 2002). This is work of high magnitude that also has a close ethnographic affinity to that of the great folklorist Enrique Lamadrid and his colleagues centered at the University of New Mexico who are also habitually excluded from the California-centered Chicano cultural studies (Lamadrid et al. 2000). We should also note Charles Tatum of the University of Arizona and his book *Chicano Popular Culture* (2001). He is also wholly absent — referenced not even once — in the Chabram-Dernersesian volumes.

There is yet a third disconnection in Chicano/a studies which takes us generationally beyond Américo Paredes to the students that he trained within a social conflict model, but one now deeply influenced by Marxism from other sources. At his home institution of UT-Austin, this model intersected with other critical currents, both structural and cultural, beginning in the late 1960s and extending through the early eighties. Probably the earliest of these was the formation of a very active chapter of the Students for a Democratic Society, but it also soon involved a professoriate. This professoriate included Larry Caroline and later Douglas Kellner (philosophy), Harry Cleaver (economics), James Brow (anthropology), Gilberto Cárdenas (sociology), Gideon Sjoberg (sociology), and myself (anthropology), along with a very intense cohort of graduate students. Those of us working on everyday expressive culture within this theoretical climate, including Paredes, thus fashioned our own Texas- and Marxist-inflected version of Chicano/a cultural studies with folklore at its center. They include Manuel Peña and Richard Flores. I have already cited Manuel Peña, who is, of course, only too well known for his Marxist studies of

Mexican-American, democratically grounded, popular music, especially *conjunto*. Richard Flores has offered significant post-Marxist treatments of the Mexican-American Christmas folk drama, *la pastorela*, but also of the symbolic place of the deeply socially embedded Alamo in relationship to capitalist modernity in Texas (Flores 1995, 2002).

Others from or at UT-Austin continue to produce such work after Paredes. Domino Perez (2008) offers the most comprehensive and analytically advanced treatment of the legend of La Llorona to date. Deborah Paredez (2009) writes on the deceased Tejana singer Selena and the Mexican-origin community's expressive memorialization of her against the racist responses to that memorialization within the Anglo-dominant world, especially in Corpus Christi. John Moran González (2009) has explored the popular poetics of LULAC against the racist celebration of the Texas Centennial in 1936. Michael Trujillo's (2010) new work offers rich data and keen analytical insight into the everyday expressive responses by working-class Nuevomexicanos to the drug abuse violence that has befallen the so-called Land of Enchantment. Mexican-American lowriders, a subject much discussed in California cultural studies, continues to receive keen extended treatment from Ben Chappell, but now in Texas (2002, 2006, 2008). The politics and everyday poetics of Mexican immigration is the subject of Gilberto Rosas's evocative accounts of young Mexican immigrants (2006a, 2006b, 2007). Catholicism, still dominant among Mexican Americans, has received little attention from California cultural studies. Out of Texas, however, we now have the fine work of David P. Sandell (2009a, 2009b, 2010, forthcoming) on the often-overlooked category of folk religion among working-class Mexicans both in California and among former immigrants in the Republic of Mexico.

In the California-centric, yet supposedly universalist work that now constitutes the seemingly cutting edge of Chicano/a cultural studies, these Texas figures are rarely even cited or discussed, never mind included as contributors. While Chicano/a studies in California has largely veered away from Paredes, his influence continues for another generation of scholars in Texas and elsewhere.[19]

FINAL THOUGHTS

Américo Paredes was a momentary scholarly light illuminating at least the beginning of what has come to be called Chicano/a cultural studies, but a light that rather quickly gave way to a shadow: like a shadow, present,

sensed, perhaps even comforting, but no longer an enabling guide to trying to understand the full lived experience of the Mexican people of the
United States except in Texas and now also New Mexico.[20] I have suggested that in keeping with the legacy of Birmingham and largely for the
same reasons, Chicano/a cultural studies in its hegemonic California version has also reduced the domain of everyday lived expressive experience
to a focus on representative textualities from mass media, written literature, the plastic arts, and choreographed rather than unpredictable, democratic emergent performance.

Lest I be misunderstood, I am not opposed to such work in mass mediated popular culture, having done it myself (1973, 1998). Indeed, the analyses of such circumscribed textualties as are prevalent today in Chicano/a
studies are more than often executed with great analytical and theoretical
acumen and are instructive, indeed fascinating, and often do demonstrate,
if indirectly, the vital presence and resistance of the people of Greater
Mexico to their continuing, if now uneven, social marginalization. Such
mass mediated Mexican-American popular culture is important, but it is
not the whole or even the central story. As Storey (1996: 1) says, "although
cultural studies cannot (or should not) be reduced to the study of popular
culture, it is certainly the case that the study of popular culture is central
to the project of cultural studies." But if "the study of [mass mediated]
popular culture is central to the project of cultural studies," Storey is also
correct that cultural studies should not reduce its domain of study to such
"popular culture," and that is largely what the now hegemonic California-
centered Chicano/a studies has done.

Perhaps we can illustrate these distinctions with one final example
from the work of an important cultural studies practitioner closely affiliated with Chicano/a studies. Rosa Linda Fregoso is well-known for her
incisive analyses of film, especially the work of Chicano/a filmmakers,
mostly from California. In her most recent work (2003) she continues
to offer such treatments but with one significant change germane to my
interest and argument here. Her final chapter, "Ghosts of a Mexican Past,"
takes us beyond the images on the screen into a vivid ethnography of the
everyday Mexican-American world of her native Corpus Christi, Texas,
her family, and their relationship to the making and consumption of films.
I am quite certain that Américo Paredes would have lent particular admiration to this chapter in the work of our mutual Tejana *paisana*. Chicano/a
studies needs more of this.

In these pages I have argued for the expansion and amplification of
the cultural studies domain to recall and include what I have been calling

the expressive practices of everyday life, the contemporary folklore, if you will, especially of Greater Mexico, in the tradition of Américo Paredes. Such a reorientation, however, clearly requires a respectful entrance, if not immersion, into everyday life itself, and perhaps this methodological step may be the fundamental issue in cultural studies' current limitations.

In his own critique, John Fiske (1992) sees this issue as a methodological "distancing" that actually turns out to be profoundly and disturbingly theoretical. As he says, "the culture of everyday life is concrete, contextualized and lived" in contrast to the distancing that occurs between subject and the art object in the world of the canonical arts as part of the habitus of the arts. But a parallel distancing, he maintains, also occurs in current academic life, and he clearly means current cultural studies, where

> within this same habitus we may find the taste for congruent social and academic theories, a taste expressed in the disposition for macro-theories that transcend the mundanities of the everyday through distantiation, that move towards generalized, abstracted understandings rather than concrete specificities and that try to construct academic or political theories that are as distanced, detached, and self-contained as any idealized art object. This is, needless to say, the habitus in which most of us academics feel at home. But it is a habitus at odds with those through which the various formations of the people live their everyday lives. (155)

Such is also the difference, I would submit, between the practices and legacies of Raymond Williams and Américo Paredes in relation to cultural studies. Such abstracted theorization and distancing from the everyday seems to me to be characteristic of cultural studies in general and carried over into Chicano/a studies, the latter because it consistently failed to follow the methodological folkloristic practice of Paredes even as it has not attuned itself to new developments in folklore and ethnography. However, others, not academics, but rather ordinary citizens and expressive practitioners in everyday life, have responded to Paredes's influence in remarkable ways. In the next chapter I offer some sense of such spontaneous performances from everyday life.

FIVE

Tracking Culture

Contemporary cultural studies has largely overlooked the domain of folklore, or what in the preceding chapter I have also called "the poetics of everyday life." That the Birmingham School did so, and that its American practitioners have also, may be explained by the possibly now founded fear of the "culture industry" theorists: that the English and American cultural spheres have, indeed, come to be wholly dominated by such an industry. Such a dominance might also account for the attenuation of once flourishing folklore studies in the United States. Alternatively and paradoxically, cultural studies itself may have become enchanted with the culture industry and its products and much less interested in more traditional, face-to-face forms of everyday expressive culture, especially in methodological terms. I raise these as debatable possibilities without resolving the matter.

However, when it comes to the more culturally specific matter of Greater Mexico, the work of Américo Paredes, and contemporary Chicano/Chicana cultural studies, I have argued that the evasion of everyday vernacular expressive culture as a subject of inquiry and discipline has much less warrant. Earlier (to briefly illustrate my argument) I offered a brief example from this tradition taken from recent Mexican immigrant life: vernacular drama in Los Angeles. But consider also folk music in Texas, as well as in Mississippi, as Chávez (2010) has shown. He tells us of the autonomous, widespread, and dynamic presence of the folk musical form, the *huapango arribeño*, among Mexican immigrants from Querétaro and San Luis Potosí now mostly living in Texas, where such music flourishes in transnational, interactive, communal, dueling encounters called *topadas*. But it may well be counter-proposed that these are, after all, recent immigrants, perhaps from rural sectors of Mexico, and that later than sooner, these expressive performances—one "emergent," one "residual"—will also give way in the urban, mass media life of Los Angeles, but also in increasingly urban Texas or, in the case of *huapango*, incorporated into mass media musical culture as "the latest sound," perhaps beginning with participation in Austin's South by Southwest followed by bookings and so on. Perhaps, but there is no evidence of such attenuation, and more than enough at least anecdotal evidence of other kindred performances in other genres in immigrant life. We could speak of *tamaladas and posadas*, but consider the now ubiquitous *taquerías* and taco trucks in Los Angeles and other places—the food, yes—but perhaps more significantly as sites of expressive conversation akin to Michael Bell's Brown's Lounge.[1] But immigrants aside, the counter-argument might continue, what of third and later generation Mexican Americans—U.S. citizens? To the degree that they fashion their ethnicity through expressive forms, have they not become wholly the children of El Vez, George Lopez, Los Lobos, gang films, the occasional phrase in Spanish, occasional Mexican cuisine, lowrider shows and fashion, and Chicano art and literature? Perhaps, again, although I would say that the matter remains to be determined empirically before we reach such a conclusion, and I see little effort to do so, at least within the California cultural studies sphere that I have critiqued.

Yet even as I have foregrounded a poetics of everyday life, I also continue to insist that such a poetics, including that which will follow in this chapter, is not some hermetically sealed domain wholly impervious to the rest of the world, including mass media popular culture. On the contrary, even while we recognize and value the autonomous creativity of everyday performers, it is also often the case that they fashion their performances from the materials of commercial and popular cultural life even while their creativity is self-generated and democratically shared without a dominant cash nexus. As Narváez and Laba (1986: 1) note, "popular culture refers . . . to cultural events which are transmitted by technological media and communicated in mass societal contexts," whereas "folkloric performance is artistic performance which is transmitted and communicated by the sensory media of living, small group encounters." However, in today's world, it is often the case that, as Laba (1986: 17) also notes, "the social practice of folkloric communications is structured by the symbolic forms in popular culture and serves as a means by which individuals and groups ritualize, organize and make sense of those forms of their day-to-day experience." This folklore–popular culture continuum is not at all inconsistent with Abrahams's (2008) perspective, noted in Chapter 4, and will guide our understanding of the materials that follow. To Laba's continuum

I would only add that "the social practice of folkloric communications" can also be influenced, paradoxically enough, by scholarship: intellectual and journalistic commentary on such folkloric practices, the principal concern of this chapter.

Although I have noted California examples, I am far more familiar with Texas, and I now return to that cultural sphere—especially in its native, not immigrant, Mexican-American dimensions—to continue to make the case for a persistent vernacular poetics of everyday life today, an extension of the examples and argument I offered some years ago (Limón 1994). In doing so, however, I wish to once again recognize and honor the particular legacy that Américo Paredes left us, which, as I argue in Chapter 3, dealt substantially with the joke form and the ballad. I begin with a kind of update of our knowledge and analytical understanding of the joke form in the present day while hearkening back to Paredes's influential studies, which continue to influence today's joking. A second section of the chapter returns to Paredes's study of the ballad of Gregorio Cortez, but this time to trace its influence on various discourses over time, including the recent musical resurgence of this classical *corrido*.

ON JOKES AND THEIR MEXICAN-AMERICAN RELATIONS

As we turn first to the joke form, we also need to recognize the important work of another Mexican-American folklorist on this genre and other kinds of jokes that followed up on Paredes's own collections in the 1960s. José R. Reyna collected some two hundred, mostly Spanish-language jokes in the early 1970s and offered a relatively brief summary analysis of this material (1973, 1980). While the rest of his material is of some relevance to what follows later, it is immediately of considerable interest that by the early seventies he had collected only nine Stupid American jokes and could therefore, and I believe rightly, claim "that the trend is shifting away from this type of joke, for although I have recorded nine jokes of this type, most of these were solicited directly by me rather than occurring spontaneously" (Reyna 1980: 25).

He also explains this attenuation: "The fact that the anti-Anglo joke is not as hostile as it was in the past is indicative of a change in attitude towards the Anglo that may be explained by concomitant changes that have occurred in the socio-cultural context as it pertains to the relations between Anglos and Chicanos." He attributes this change to Mexican-American advances in civil rights. However, he might have added that this success in civil rights, especially in Texas, was premised on a concomitant educational and socioeconomic mobility for Mexican Americans by the 1970s, as noted by historian David Montejano (1987: 298–299). We saw its first instances in Paredes's joke narrators in Chapter 3.

The attenuation of the kinds of jokes Paredes collected does not mean that the Anglo-American has disappeared as a major conditioning element for new kinds of jokes. I would also argue that the "the Anglo-American in Mexican folklore" has continued in Texas into the late twentieth and early twenty-first centuries by a circuitous route, though still premised on a degree of social conflict. While such Anglo-American jokes have attenuated, Reyna continues to be correct for Mexican Americans even in our time, although "there is no doubt that they consider themselves an integral part of this country. . . . Chicanos are aware of the impossibility of gaining complete acceptance in the United States" (25).[2]

The paradox of social achievement and lingering doubt has made its way into new joking forms for this, our time. Let me offer three instances of such joking as it emerged in everyday life with neither any prompting on my part nor as a result of any programmatic fieldwork, followed by some comprehensive commentary. I also offer parenthetical translations from vernacular Spanish as needed.

EXAMPLE 1: BILLBOARD HUEVOS

I am driving up U.S. Highway 281 from the Lower Rio Grande Valley, one of the two highways that connect the Valley to the rest of Texas. There to my left is a large billboard, at first appearing like so many others along this busy road advertising the usual commodities and services: hamburgers, motels, gas stations, airlines, beers, cell phone services, and so on. But this particular billboard definitely catches my eye, so much that I leave the highway at the next off ramp, make the two requisite turnarounds and get on 281 so that I can see it again, this time at a much slower speed. There it is, in large, full-color lettering for all to see:

Martinez Egg Company
Our *huevos* are bigger.

I am totally by myself, but laughing so hard that I consider pulling off the road.

As Américo Paredes (1968: 110) reminded us in one of his joking studies, and as we saw in Chapter 3 with the *huevos rancheros* joke, for the people of Greater Mexico, *huevo* (egg) is "such a common synonym for 'testicle' that many prudish people avoid the word altogether substituting it with *blanquillo* which simply means something like 'small white thing.'" He might have added that it is more often than not women who prefer *blanquillo*, and that *huevo* takes on more sexual force in the plural *huevos*, suggesting two *huevos*, which the Martinez Egg Company is fully exploiting as a double entendre for the male testicles. Its public, face-to-face use is always a potential occasion for humor, usually among men, but to see it up on a billboard in this manner is hilarious.

EXAMPLE 2: THE A(NGLO) BOARDING PASS

I am in the local airport terminal in Corpus Christi, Texas, on the Gulf Coast between the Valley and Houston. Corpus is not a very large city, and all flights, including mine to Los Angeles on a Sunday in October 2009, go through either Dallas or Houston. I am flying on Southwest Airlines (SWA), which does not have assigned seating but not long ago initiated a way of boarding passengers that still seems to be solely theirs. When it is time to board the aircraft, passengers board in Groups A, B, and C, designated on one's boarding pass, with up to sixty passengers per group, and A goes first. It is to one's advantage to be in group A so as to minimize the chance of winding up with a middle seat or not having enough overhead space for carry-ons, and one maximizes the chance of having an A boarding pass by checking in before getting to the airport, which SWA allows one to do online no sooner that twenty-four hours before the flight. There are always those who don't care, or don't know, and have to print their passes at the airport, which very likely means a B or C boarding pass — as happened to me this time because I simply forgot to do it at the hotel where I was staying while visiting my brother.

As the SWA agent begins boarding the flight, he calls the A group, and passengers dutifully line up while the rest of us sit patiently waiting for our B or C boarding since SWA insists that the Bs and Cs "remain seated until you are called" to avoid confusion and congestion. Corpus Christi is about 50 percent Mexican-American, so it happens that six such — three heterosexual couples, who look to be in their forties — are also seated next to the gate where I am sitting, all of us waiting to board after the A group.

From their very audible conversation (they may have spent part of this Sunday morning at the small airport bar) it is clear they are on their way to Dallas, one air-hour away, to watch the Cowboys play in an NFL game, a destination also attested to by their full Cowboy regalia. As we all watch the A group lining up, one of the men, whose name turned out to be Balde (probably short for Baldemar), begins a barely audible mock complaint as to why *those* people get to board first. Either he does not really know the boarding rules or is pretending not to know them. Gesturing toward the A group with his head, he says to his wife, "¡Mira, hone, todos son white!" (Look, honey, they're all white!) The snickering begins within the group of six, and soon I and a few other Mexican Americans sitting around—also Bs and Cs—very quietly join in, slowly shaking our heads and twisting in our seats. In fact, as I sit there, surveying group A, Balde is quite correct about the group's racial composition. ¡Todos son white! In time-honored fashion, his wife tries to ssshh him but to no avail.

In time-honored fashion as well, he is then encouraged by one of his male buddies: "You're right, Balde!" he says, then code-switches, saying, "Así es in high school. They always got the As también!" (That's the way it is in high school. They always got the As also!) Not to be undone, the third guy in the group chimes in: "¡Te apuesto que 'A' is for 'Anglo'!" (I bet you that "A" is for "Anglo"!) More snickering, now louder, such that the people in the all-Anglo A line seem to notice, although I seriously doubt that they are aware of what exactly is transpiring. The agent calls for the A row to begin boarding, and as they begin to move slowly through the gate, Balde points toward each one of the first ten or so with his finger in consecutive order as they enter the ramp to the aircraft and says in a bare whisper: "¡Watchca! [Check it out!] white . . . white . . . white . . . white . . ." until his wife forces his finger down with her hand. The snickering gradually develops into barely covert laughter. But Balde is not done. When the Bs and Cs begin to board, he says: "¡Vámonos! ¡Ya se va la troca!" (Let's go! The truck is leaving!) Overhearing their conversation on the plane, I learn that the men are all highly skilled technicians at a local military base that overhauls and refits helicopters; one of the women is a teacher, and the others also seem to work outside the home, but I'm not sure. What is clear is that this is a special trip, and they have all arranged to be off work on Monday.

EXAMPLE 3: THE CENTIPEDE WHO PLAYED FREE SAFETY

Finally, and at greater length, the following was narrated by a Mexican-American insurance agent in 2005 during a *carne asada* (barbecue), again in Paredes's Lower Rio Grande Valley, where I was visiting friends and family.

Well, estos dos mexicanos anthropologists [these two Mexican anthropologists] were going to study a tribe in Africa, but they had engine trouble in their small plane and had to crash-land. So allí estaban (there they were); they didn't know where they were, or what to do; el tribe se había descontado [the tribe had split], they were just surviving you know, in their tent and eating whatever. Pretty soon they got bored, y no sabían que hacer [they didn't know what to do]. So one of them got an idea.

"Vamos a organizer los animals [Let's organize the animals] into football teams and play a game! We can be coaches!" So, lo hicieron [they did it]. Each bato (guy) would get a lion, or giraffe—you know the giraffes make great receivers! And pretty soon they each had eleven animales plus reserves, and the game started, and it was pretty even at first, but then the hippo linebacker on one team got a knee injury and had to go to the bench. But that meant that the water buffalo fullback for the other team started tearing them up, scoring touchdowns right up the middle just like Earl Campbell, sabes [you know]? Then all of a sudden the water buffalo gets the ball again but goes crashing down at the line of scrimmage, and he's really hurt, gritando [screaming], "Oh mothafuck!" and grabbing his knee, so the game stops and everybody goes out there, but everybody wants to know who brought him down, you know. But nobody on the defense takes credit—el tiger growls, "I didn't do it, Coach, I was double-teamed by two panthers!" Y tambíen [And also] el hyena says that he didn't make the tackle, but the hyena can't stop laughing, you know . . . and so he gets a penalty for unsportsmanlike conduct . . . until finally they hear this little voice coming from under the water buffalo. "I did it! ¡Sáquenme de aquí, cabrones!" [Get me out of here, bastards!] And so they rolled over the buffalo and sure enough, allí estaba un centipede bién agarrado del leg del water buffalo [there was a centipede with a really good grip on the leg of the water buffalo]. So they get him out y todo su team [and his whole team] is congratulating him and patting him on the back y todo [everything], hasta que el coach le pregunta [until the coach asks him], "Where did you come from, mi'jo [son]? I didn't know you were playing for us. We never saw you." "Simón [Sure enough], Coach," dice el centipede, "I was playing free safety and I came up to make the play!"

"Pos sí [Well, yeah]," dice el coach, "but este es el fourth quarter. Where were you before? How come we didn't see you playing before?"

Y el centipede dice, "¡Chingao, Coach, estaba en el locker room poniendo me los tennis!" [Fuck, Coach, I was in the locker room putting on my tennies!]

I have been indulging in Mexican-American humor practically all of my life, but this last joke may well represent the strangest, most creative, paradoxical instance of the form that I have ever heard, although I would suggest that it is of a piece with the other shorter and less complex instances that I have offered above and many more that I cannot record here.

Let's go back to the beginning—to the first of my texts—to try to offer some analytical insight into this material while putting it in relation to the jokes collected and analyzed by Américo Paredes that we examined in Chapter 3. Recall our claims about Paredes's material: the Stupid American and self-satirical jokes and his analyses. Rather than seeing them as expressions of simple repressed aggression or angst-ridden modernist ineffectuality, both kinds of jokes, I believe, fundamentally reveal the high degree of the Mexican-American narrators' and their audiences' social achievements. Such achievements, clearly evident in the description of Paredes's informants, were based on their correlated command of English and Spanish, but also their understanding of both American and Mexican culture and society, which allows them to critique Anglo-American culture but also the social failings of the Mexican state—all of this, we should also recall, in the historical period of the 1930s to 1960s. The narration of such joking material more fundamentally reveals the absurd joke that Anglos could continue their dominance over such Mexican Americans, for I will remind us again of Mary Douglas's (1968: 366) observation: "if there is no joke in the social structure, no other joke can appear."

If a totalistic Anglo dominance was already becoming something of a joke by the late sixties, this new material and its performance context seem to affirm that continuing "joke" but now carried into the realm of the absurd. Even when the "Anglo" is, for the most part, not textually present in these jokes, much as "he" was absent in Paredes's self-satirical material, "he" nevertheless deeply conditions this material.

The joke in the first example "works" because the play on *huevos* is funny, as we also saw in Chapter 3, but also because the success of the Martinez Egg Company is expressed in the expensive billboard itself as a materialized, succinct narrative competing with other, mostly "name brand" billboards, attesting to the very social existence of the people who travel U.S. 281 and enjoy this humor. To "read" this billboard written almost wholly in English, but with the Spanish word *huevos*, these readers would probably be reasonably successful Mexican Americans who speak fluent English but still retain sufficient Spanish and "Mexican" culture, and who now dominate the Lower Rio Grande Valley, as suggested in Chapter 1. That is to say, this joke will not work as well with Spanish-dominant speakers, such as Mexican immigrants, nor with the now few Valley Anglos who also travel this road unless the latter are highly acculturated *toward* Mexican culture, as can happen. It works most succinctly for reasonably successful Mexican Americans whose social *huevos* are, indeed, much bigger than they used to be.

Example 2 is, of course, not a narrative at all but much more like a comedy routine that one might see on a Mexican-American version of *Saturday Night Live*. Indeed, in his work done in the late 1960s, Reyna (1980: 21) astutely notes that at that time Mexican Americans did not "relate to the humorous entertainment of popular American entertainers," meaning specifically stand-up comics "whose delivery is usually very rapid . . . quite difficult to understand and appreciate for the average Chicano." However, times have changed for younger, socially and linguistically mobile Mexican Americans, who now routinely fly Southwest Airlines. Not only can they access American stand-up comedy, but Mexican-American comedians such as George Lopez are now part of the mass media scene. Moreover, there is also a native tradition of such comedic bantering and humorous routines that goes by various names such as *relajando* (cutting up), *haciendo* (doing), or *diciendo* (saying) *chingaderas* (fuckups) or *ocurrencias* (witty sayings or acts).

Balde and his wife and friends are somewhere in this total social and expressive universe as they head off to watch the Dallas Cowboys. The very trip itself clearly suggests the financial capacity to pay for regalia, NFL tickets, food and drink, lodging, and airplane fares, earned by their likely hard-earned mobility into well-paying technical jobs but also through likely commensurate employment for their wives. Our performer does explicitly name the Anglos—"white, white, white"—but he is not rendering them "stupid" so much as inert and passive relative to their own minicelebration at the airport based on and acknowledging their social success.

In this incongruity lies the humor, an incongruity accentuated by Balde but also his buddies "acting out," for other Mexican Americans, the part of regular working-class *batos* with slightly guttural intonations and the use of a vernacular "street" Spanish, as seen in the third example. But another part of the humor lies in their ability to recall and perform this incongruity between a likely working-class past and this now self-fashioned ability to fly to Dallas for a football game, hence Balde's announcement, "¡Vámonos! ¡Ya se va la troca!" (Let's go! The truck is leaving!), a humorous recollection of past times in Corpus Christi when trucks would come into the *barrio* very early in the mornings to pick up Mexican-American laborers to pick cotton in the surrounding fields. Thus while they symbolically and humorously recall this past, they do so as successful social actors in the present.

Such success, however, likely has been fashioned, again, against a still-felt adversity and Anglo dominance that does in fact continue in Corpus Christi, but in ways not as evident in other parts of South Texas, hence, perhaps, Balde's willingness to name and openly point to the Anglos as a racial category. That everyone in the A group is Anglo may not be such a coincidence after all, and perhaps speaks to the latter's greater computer cultural capital. Herein possibly there also lies another interesting social contradiction. One senses that Corpus Christi is not yet ready for the more subtle, self-confident, but still adversarial humor of Martinez's egg billboard in the Lower Rio Grande Valley. There are simply many more Anglos in Corpus, and in comparison to the Valley today, the city continues to have barely submerged tension based on a long history of racial conflict.[3] The controversy in the city around whether to display a statue of pop singer and Corpus Christi native Selena also attests to this tension (Paredez 2009). But I also hasten to apologize to the reader for this very tentative assessment of Example 3 because the fleeting, processual nature of the scene did not permit more interview data to lend more substance to these observations. Such is the nature of this verbal *perruque*, as I think de Certeau would agree.

Finally, what can we say about a centipede who plays free safety and tackles a water buffalo? The narration was occasioned by my efforts to collect such joke narratives as I have been discussing here, but its content was totally unexpected and prefaced by some good-natured teasing about the doing of anthropology and fieldwork—a process, I also discovered, not at all unknown to the Mexican-American insurance agent who narrated the joke. He had been an undergraduate student of Américo Paredes in a folklore class on Greater Mexico at UT-Austin in the late 1970s and had, in fact, done a bit of fieldwork himself for his term paper. He also remembered Paredes's articles on joking assigned as class reading. That is why, he told me later, he adapted the joke from one where the two human protagonists are Anglo anthropologists whose commercial aircraft goes down in Africa to this version now featuring two *mexicano* (Mexican-American) anthropologists.

What he did not seem to know is that I myself had reported this earlier joke based on fieldwork done in the 1970s (Limón 1989). The insurance agent did not appear to know of my 1989 publication, which is not at all surprising given that he had graduated from UT-Austin in the late seventies and returned to the Valley with a BA in business, and the article appeared in a professional journal of anthropology unlikely to circulate in the Valley, with only one caveat: the possibility that one of my anthropology colleagues at one of the local colleges had had their students read the article, opening the possibility that a scholarly publication on folklore produced even more folklore! The insurance agent, however, said he got it at another *carne asada*, and given that I collected it in the Valley at a *carne asada* in the first place, I had no reason to doubt him. In any case, it did not really matter. What is of interest here are the specific changes he made in his version.

Even though, like my 1970s informant, he likely intended his narration as a tease, knowing that I was an anthropologist, the very fact that he could now with some confidence insert Mexican Americans as professional anthropologists into his narrative continues to sustain my argument that Mexican-American social achievement, now in academic life, is explicitly foregrounded in the twenty-first century. Such an image is consistent with the very successful insurance agent's own professional life as well as those of his immediate audience at the *carne asada*: school administrators, lawyers, dentists, other professionals — and one anthropologist. And, as do real people in today's Valley, these fictive anthropologists/coaches communicate with some of their players in vernacular Spanish.

In the present instance, however, there may be even more at stake linguistically, for it is clear that the centipede is the *one* Spanish-speaking interlocutor for the anthropologist/coach. The only other jungle animals that speak are the tiger, who speaks in English ("I didn't do it, Coach,") and claims he was double-teamed by panthers, and the water buffalo, who, in pain, says, "Oh mothafucka!" after being tackled by the centipede. (The hyena also has an utterance as the narrator inserts a joke within a joke with the hyena getting an unsportsmanlike conduct penalty for laughing too much!) Therefore, is the centipede a Mexican American, with the tiger possibly standing in for the Anglo? Yet we must now broach the probability of a third racial actor here, namely African Americans, albeit in somewhat stereotypic fashion by way of "Mothafucka!," an expletive shared within working-class African-American culture as the ubiquitous *Chingar!* (Fuck!) is among working-class Mexican Americans (Abrahams 1964a; Limón 1998: 73–100).

At the further risk of stereotype, the jest may also be referring somewhat literally to the predominance of African Americans in real-world football, with relatively few Mexican Americans at either the college or professional level.[4] Mexican Americans are as fully engrossed with football as any other Americans. They closely identify with football, as Examples 2 and 3 clearly suggest.[5] They closely follow college football, especially as they personally come to be identified with colleges and universities either as alumni or through their children as students. And in the Lower Rio Grande Valley, at least, high school football is enormously popular, in large part because the teams are composed mostly of Mexican Americans (Huerta 2005). One has anecdotal evidence that the same is true in other parts of the Southwest where there are large concentrations of Mexican Americans.

This huge popularity does not translate into a substantial Mexican-American athletic presence in college and therefore in professional football. According to the *Los Angeles Times*, in pro football only, "[New York] Jets quarterback Mark Sánchez, [Dallas] Cowboys quarterback Tony Romo, [Chicago] Bears offensive lineman Roberto Garza and [Detroit] Lions guard Manny Ramirez" are Mexican American.[6] As if to accentuate this paucity, while Mark Sánchez was playing for the University of Southern California in the middle of heavily Mexican-American Los Angeles, he made it a point of pride to foreground his ethnicity. He had his dentist—also Mexican American—paint his football mouthguard in the green, white, and red colors of the Mexican flag, causing much controversy and race baiting.[7]

There are probably complex and controversial reasons for this marked ethnic discrepancy in football, ranging from body size to a strange kind of racism such that football recruiters perhaps feel no real need to look beyond predominantly African-American neighborhoods and schools and the occasional white one. But in a world where Mexican-American social achievement is everywhere evident, including in the very narrators of these jokes, such lack of representation in this most popular and visible of American entertainment may be particularly galling when Mexican Americans have so lent themselves to a sport in which they may watch but not play.

The centipede's triumph at the end may be a twofold statement on this question. Clearly identified as Mexican American by his speech style, much like the speakers in Examples 2 and 3, the *small* centipede, like Mexican Americans, is not in the game at first as he readies himself, laboriously tying the tennis shoes on his one hundred feet, as he explains in his punch line, whose very spoken exasperation may also speak to that of Mexican Americans. With the Anglo tiger out of the play, it is the little, now clearly Mexican-American creature who triumphs in the end in the wonderful absurdity of bringing down the water buffalo with a hard hit while presumably fighting off blockers as well. His struggle for recognition perhaps portends our future in this American sport, as rookie Mark Sánchez did in the 2010 season by leading his New York Jets almost to the Super Bowl.

The specific joke traditions that so attracted Américo Paredes in the 1960s may have disappeared, but new forms may have taken their place, with different characteristics perhaps reflecting a new sociocultural milieu. In comparison with what Paredes had to tell us about his informants, mine appear to have much more confidence in their achieved socioeconomic status but also in a more fully achieved bicultural stance and repertoire. By the latter I mean not only their control of various registers of Spanish and English but what seems to be their greater comfort level with the internal nuances of American culture—that is, the inner workings of American football—while others continue to demonstrate a similar ongoing comfort with such nuances in Mexican culture, as in the wordplay in Example 2. For its part, Example 3 also signals a kind of postmodern willingness to explore the surreal and the absurd. Yet I have also argued that the expressive critique of a still dominant Anglo-American presence continues implicitly in the very performances themselves by such performers who have achieved against the racial and class odds, and occasionally explicitly, as in Example 2. These and yet other expressive forms in today's culture continue to attest to an ongoing joking poetics of everyday life that I think Professor Paredes would have found intriguing although I never had a chance to discuss this new material with him. What I was able to bring to his attention before his passing, and which he did find intriguing, was the expressive return of Gregorio Cortez, another transformed continuation of vernacular culture in the present indebted to his work.

THE DISCURSIVE RIDE OF GREGORIO CORTEZ

My principal concern in this next section is to explore the musical reappearance of the ballad of Gregorio Cortez among the contemporary working class following a long hiatus of such performances. However, as a not-so-secondary matter, I also wish to trace how the ballad and its hero took another kind of ride—a historical, discursive ride—from their beginning in 1901 to their reappearance in musical form today. In Chapter 3 I spoke at length about the ballad of Gregorio Cortez as it was treated in the consummate scholarship of Américo Paredes. Yet Paredes's work is only one stopping place—albeit the most important one—in what I am now calling the ballad and its hero's discursive ride through a variety of appearances and representations in forums and discourses after its invention in the face-to-face poetics of everyday life of Greater Mexico in the earlier part of the twentieth century. I will further argue that each discursive reappearance signals a major sociocultural change for Mexican Americans.

Let us begin with the ballad's likely emergence. Paredes describes such a face-to-face setting in his also famous poetic dedication to "*With His Pistol in His Hand.*"

> To the memory of my father,
> who rode a raid or two with
> Catarino Garza;
> and to all those old men
> who sat around on summer nights,
> in the days when there was
> a chaparral, smoking their
> cornhusk cigarettes and talking
> in low gentle voices about
> violent things;
> while I listened.

But such men also sang in such settings.

According to Paredes himself, when sung in such settings, the ballad of Gregorio Cortez had a relatively attenuated history. He identifies only three historical periods when the ballad was more or less in full musical bloom. The first, of course, is the actual moment of the incident that generated the *corrido*'s beginning in 1901 with the gunfight, Cortez's ride to the border, and his subsequent capture and imprisonment, a time that Paredes calls a "period of high feeling," adding, "Tradition has it that men could get arrested or beaten, or lose their jobs if they sang *El Corrido de Gregorio Cortez*" (1958: 204).

The second period occurred between 1913 and 1920, when the Mexican Revolution "called forth heroic themes, and when friction along the

Lower Border was building up" toward the armed uprisings in 1915 and "Cortez was released from prison" (205). However, "from the 1920s on, the development of *El Corrido de Gregorio Cortez* is a gradually descending one," although it was in the 1920s when, as a child, Paredes heard his first *corridos*, including that of Cortez, as alluded to in his poetic dedication (205). That is, this *corrido* would not be literally heard again in any substantial and pervasive popular manner until a third period, paradoxically enough during World War II, when, says Paredes, "another recorded version of the *corrido* [probably a 1920 recording by a group called Los Trovadores Regionales] was played a great deal in cantinas on both sides of the river" as border Mexicans again felt the call to arms, albeit now as part of the U.S. military. "The feelings excited by the war . . . gave *El Corrido de Gregorio Cortez* one last period of vigor before it and the tradition that it represents gave way to a new music and a new age" (205–206).

Thus, it would seem that, according to its foremost scholar, "Gregorio Cortez" as a popular sung ballad was in nearly total abeyance after World War II, although no doubt occasional and relatively marginal performances could still be heard—an old record by Los Trovadores Regionales left on a cantina juke box, or the 1946 recording by the group Maya y Cantú, or a mariachi group in a restaurant playing a condensed version of the song on request.

Yet even though this heroic *corrido* largely gave way to other musics and a "new age," "Gregorio Cortez" found other discursive existences—scholarly, literary, and popularly—before returning musically once more in our own time. Indeed the first of these significantly precedes Paredes's own work. The first known discursive switch from face-to-face performance settings to other forms and forums occurred in unlikely hands and in an unlikely setting. In 1927, Jovita González, a emerging young female Mexican-American folklorist from South Texas, read her first professional academic paper before the Texas Folklore Society.[8] Its title was "The Folklore of the Texas-Mexican Vaquero."

By contemporary academic protocols, the TFS and other groups like it now seem quaintly peculiar, for they could provide an "appropriate" stage setting for papers upon request—early audiovisual aid, if you will. As I have noted elsewhere, newspaper accounts tell us that for Jovita González's presentation, "the stage was delightfully set to represent the great open places with cactus, prickly pear bushes and a campfire," and "about that fire were Mexican rifles, blankets, canteens, *morales* and saddles." But just before González delivered her paper, "three Mexican vaqueros sang songs of the trail in Spanish. Jose, dressed in his vaquero costume, was the hit of the evening," and we also learn that José sang one song particularly well, a song that the *Dallas Morning News* identified as "The Ballad of Gregaria Certes" [*sic*]. González then read her paper in a "delightful accent," according to the newspaper (Limón 1994: 64). Thus, in 1927, we have the odd conjunction of the masculinist *corrido* in a staged performance but before a mostly Anglo audience of folklore enthusiasts, save Jovita González and the singers. How many in that audience actually understood the combative lyrics, we cannot say.

As noted earlier, Paredes tell us that World War II occasioned a third historical period when Cortez was sung but principally in recordings. Since he did not leave Texas until 1944, perhaps this somewhat popular resurgence also occasioned Paredes himself to continue the discursive transformation of the ballad from song to scholarship. Although not yet a professionally trained folklorist, in 1942, as we noted in Chapter 2, he published his first scholarly article, "The Mexico-Texan Corrido" (1942), in which he discusses the thematics and style of the Cortez ballad, prefiguring what will come later in much more substantial form.

The 1950s saw this discursive transformation reach its apogee. Texas folklorist J. Frank Dobie published a newspaper article on Cortez in the *Austin American-Statesman* commemorating the fiftieth anniversary of the Cortez incident. Dobie renders what Cortez allegedly said when he was captured in what appears to pass as a poetic stanza. Cortez spoke little English, and Dobie was not present at the capture, so this rendering is wholly concocted out of Dobie's unfortunately racialized imagination: "I cannot walk no more. I find ole house nobody there. I fall on floor and I am asleep when I hear, 'Hands up!' Now I am here for feefty year for keel man I do not keel" (as quoted in Paredes 1958: 79–80). Dobie's 1952 article then gradually brings us to where I began, which is the publication of Paredes's *"With His Pistol in His Hand": A Border Ballad and Its Hero*, based on his 1956 doctoral dissertation but also preceded by his 1953 MA thesis on Texas-Mexican border balladry, in which "Gregorio Cortez" necessarily appears. Thus at a moment when the ballad as sung performance was presumably at its lowest ebb, Gregorio Cortez was riding high in the saddle as scholarly discourse.

Such a ride continued when, as we have seen, the Chicano movement adopted *"With His Pistol"* as a foundational text, although, as I suggested in Chapter 4, not much continuing scholarly work on heroic *corridos* in general or Cortez in particular resulted, save for four major instances (Peña 1982; Saldívar 1990: 26–45; Limón 1992; Flores 1994). However, the attention paid to the book by the Chicano movement did not translate into a musical resurgence of the *corrido* itself save for a few occasional performances at rallies. Paredes did record it once during a visit to California for such a rally, as well as at a private party at his home in Austin, Texas.

In 1983, however, as an indirect result of the Chicano movement, Cortez entered into yet another distinctive discursive realm: film. Moctesuma Esparza, a UCLA student who participated in the movement in California, produced *The Ballad of Gregorio Cortez*, directed by Robert Young and featuring Edward James Olmos as Cortez. The movie was based on the first part of *"With His Pistol"* and centered on Cortez's dramatic flight to the border after the gunfight in Karnes County. The film crew interviewed Paredes for the film, and, indeed, Paredes, playing his guitar, sang the ballad for the opening and closing soundtracks, accompanied by one of his graduate students, Pablo Poveda. Although the lyrics rolled on the screen as they sang, the filmmakers made a decision to mute their voices so that they can barely be heard. For this and other more significant reasons, Paredes disliked the film intensely. Indeed, in contradiction to its title, the film does not at all foreground the singing of the *corrido*.

As Paredes noted in a personal conversation, he had hoped for a scene something like a group of Mexican *vaqueros* around a campfire (as even the Texas Folklore Society was able to imagine), and they would be singing the ballad perhaps as the fugitive Cortez walks into their camp looking for food and rest. Seemingly influenced by the California Teatro Chicano of the 1960s, these California filmmakers instead inserted a *teatro* agitprop skit where the *corrido* is sung in a fast-paced, sing-song style and not in its traditional *lento* tempo. From Paredes's point of view, this erasure of the traditional song is then made worse by the manner in which the film's story is told, largely from an Anglo-American point of view, with few speaking roles for the Mexican characters. Paredes felt that the few lines given to Cortez, and the manner in which Olmos delivered the lines, rendered a man noted for his "coolness, dignity and courage" into "a scared little peon, a kind of Tex-Mex Charlie Chaplin" (Alonzo 2009: 119).

Juan J. Alonzo's fine work on Mexican-American film and literature also allows us to trace three other distinctive instances in which Cortez continued his discursive ride, but with only one gesturing toward musical performance. Like Esparza's *The Ballad of Gregorio Cortez*, Elmer Kelton's western novel *The Man Hunters* is also based on Paredes's book, although—unlike Esparza—he did not ask Paredes for permission to use his work. Yet, like Esparza, Kelton displaces Cortez as the central heroic figure of the story. Ironically, he substitutes a young Texas Ranger as the hero who comes to the assistance of Cortez to save him from an avenging local sheriff. Thus, "instead of exposing underlying notions of racial supremacy . . . Kelton flattens causes of conflict into differences among social equals, as if the novel's conflicts existed outside real racial/cultural hierarchies" — conflicts and hierarchies that are, of course, at the center of Paredes's story (Alonzo 2009: 130).

Alonzo also examines the contemporary film *Come and Take It Day* by Jimmy Mendiola to show how the story of Gregorio Cortez is transformed and adapted to critically inform a new postmodern and hybrid Mexican-American urban youth identity at the end of the twentieth century (143–153). Mendiola's film continues the critical ideological thrust of the original ballad and legend — reversed by Esparza and Kelton — and the Mexican-American and Texas poet Evangelina Vigil also offers such a critical perspective, but does so attendant to musicality as Alonzo continues to assist us. In a wonderful poem called "with a polka in his hand," dedicated to Américo Paredes, the Mexican-American speaker critically surveys the commodified Anglo-tourist aspects of the famous downtown market, historically the center of Mexican-American life in that very Mexican city.

She is aware of the irony of her own participation in that touristic culture by way of having a drink in a trendy, Anglo-dominant bar until she sees a poor, old Mexican-American man walking outside, "in his left hand / a transistor radio / yes, a transistor radio/ blaring out accordion."

> I utter to myself out loud
> "He's carrying a polka in his hand!"
> and the anglo client seated next to me
> glances over uncomprehendingly
> and I think of Gregorio Cortez
> and Américo Paredes
> y en que la defensa cultural es permitida
> [and that the defense of one's culture is
> justified]
> and that calls for a drink and another toast.[9]

For Alonzo,

> . . . the old man and the radio stand at opposite ends of a long temporal shift that has seemingly overtaken Mexican American culture in San Antonio. Yet paradoxically, the old man proves the endurance of Mexican culture by its near absence hinted at in the picturesque quality of

his surroundings . . . The old man carries not a weapon, like the famous Gregorio Cortez, but a radio that transmits culture . . . as Mexican radio is even heard in a ritzy downtown bar. (162)

Alonzo correctly concludes that the music is indeed Mexican, or Mexican American, because the key line in the original ballad, "Con su pistola en la mano" (With his pistol in his hand), directly informs the poem's key, playful yet critical line, "He's carrying a polka in his hand!," as once again the Texas-Mexican polka returns as a signifier of deep-rooted, native, working-class musical culture, as we saw in Chapters 1 and 4, and which we now revisit at length in relationship to the ballad of Gregorio Cortez.

In Chapters 3 and 4, I discussed the ballad of Gregorio Cortez in detail, but for the purpose of what follows, I want to rehearse some of this material while adding a few words on Paredes's collection and reproduction of the original folkloric texts so that we can better judge the song's reappearance in our own time as the most recent moment in Cortez's ride. Paredes (1958: 179–180) identifies nine variants of the song that he was able to collect, labeling these alphabetically from A to I. He also offers a printed broadside from Mexico City but clearly thinks this not to be a sung version. For Paredes these variants, "collected from different stages of oral tradition, are none of them in any way complete," implying that there was a "complete" and very early version possibly composed even as the actual events were transpiring in 1901.

"My search," he says, "for the earliest variant of the Border *Corrido de Gregorio Cortez* . . . has been up to the present time entirely fruitless" (179). That is, he was not able to find any actual versions that render the Cortez story in sufficient detail and with sustained narrative fullness and flow, on the assumption "that the original ballad was intended to inform and that it was therefore more detailed and factual than its later variants" (180). Therefore he offers a Variant X, a "reconstruction" that he put together within these rules and procedures.

I did not begin by attempting to set a limit on the number of stanzas for Variant X. I took as my general outline the story of Cortez and chose from the variants available to me those quatrains that tell the story most fully and most accurately. This, I believe, corresponds with the Border singer's own views about the ideal *corrido*, one that tells all the story. I ended up with a ballad of twenty-eight quatrains. Full-length *corridos*

have between twenty or thirty quatrains, though some go as high as forty
. . . the original Border *corrido* [of Cortez] may have been about thirty
quatrains long. (180)

It is also important to know that "X is made up entirely of quatrains
from Variant A to I, with the exception of a few variations within lines,
coming from versions *with which I have been familiar for thirty-five years or
so*" (180) (emphasis added). That is, at the time of this writing circa 1956–
1957, Paredes was also remembering the song as he may have heard it since
circa 1921, when he would have been six years old and the events of 1901
were still fresh in the minds of older border people. Let us recall his poetic
epigraph dedication to his father in *"With His Pistol in His Hand"* and
his recollection of old men talking around the campfire of violent things
"while I listened." If so, then he may have heard a close approximation to
Variant X, and this memory may have also played a part in his reconstruction. Therefore, in what follows, I will lend some comparative emphasis to
Variant X, but with some attention to the others as well.

SINGING IT BACK TO THE PEOPLE

After riding through newspapers, novels, scholarship, films, and poetry,
the venerable folk *corrido* of Gregorio Cortez acquired a new musical life
in our time as it substantially intersected with the another traditional and
popular musical form, the *conjunto*-polka-Tejano musical universe and its
largely working-class audience. To be sure, such an intersection had occurred before when the *conjunto* groups Los Trovadores Regionales and El
Grupo Maya recorded the *corrido* in the 1920s and '40s, respectively. But
the revival that began in the 1980s was very different in two broad, important respects. First, it had the huge advantage of a much larger and tech-
nologically sophisticated market circuit of recordings, radio, television,
dance venues, and even web sites. Second, it transformed the otherwise
lento tempo of the original ballad into a faster paced polka rhythm also intended for dancing. There are two such instances.[10]

The first rendition is by Ruben Ramos and the Texas Revolution, a
Tejano band and not a small conjunto group (1992). Tejano musical aggre-
gations are somewhat modeled on the classical American "big band" with
a lead vocalist and assorted wind instruments backed up by electric guitars,
keyboards, and percussion. Like the smaller *conjunto* groups they also play
an assortment of genres—*boleros, cumbias,* some rock—but the domi-

nant genre is polka. Moreover, in comparison with the *conjunto* bands, they tend to be much more popular with a much wider range of Mexican Americans in terms of class, region, and age (Peña 1999).

In 1992 Ramos and his group produced a lengthy variant of "Gregorio Cortez" which they both recorded and played many times at dances both in commercial venues and on ritual occasions such as weddings and *quinceañeras*. This is the song in four-line stanzas in my translation. The original Spanish version is footnoted.[11]

EL CORRIDO DE GREGORIO CORTEZ

I am going to sing you the story
In which Gregorio Cortez,
In nineteen hundred and one,
Killed a sheriff of the law.
During an investigation,
About a stolen horse,
He killed the sheriff,
In defense of his brother.
The sheriff fired first,
Exploiting the situation,
Leaving Romaldo wounded,
Without any compassion.
When Gregorio saw his brother
Falling to the ground,
He unholstered his pistol
And took the sheriff's life.
The badly wounded Romaldo,
Was taken to the prison,
In the Karnes City jail.
He died of his wounds.
They followed him with hound dogs,
Trying to capture him.
They offered a reward
To whoever found him.
They found him in Ottine,
At Martín's house,
In order to escape,
He killed another sheriff.
By the Guadalupe River,
He rode toward the border.

He was tired when he got to Cotulla,
Where everyone saw him.
To get the reward,
The thousand dollars they offered,
Jesús González, "El Teco,"
Turned him in to the police.
They took him to San Antonio,
They gave him a life sentence.
The sentence was revoked,
After eight years he was freed.
Here ends this corrido,
That I have sung of this man.
Very decisive and valiant,
Such was Gregorio Cortez.

The second example, called "Los Hermanos Cortez" (The Brothers Cortez) (2001), is from the *conjunto* group Ruben Naranjo y Los Gamblers, composed principally of a lead accordion with percussion and one or two guitars, electric and not, and with vocalizations. The original Spanish version is footnoted.[12] This is my English translation in six-line stanzas.

THE BROTHERS CORTEZ

In nineteen hundred and one
On horseback they searched for him.
The sheriff was very sure,
As he questioned Cortez,
Since he didn't speak English
Another man translated.
It was a good response
That Rumaldo gave them.
The tragedy came because of the mare
That Rumaldo had traded
For his bridled horse
Known in that region.
In that instant the sheriff
Began to fire.
With bad luck Gregorio
Saw his brother in agony.
He killed the sheriff
In self-defense.

To capture Cortez,
They offered one thousand dollars.
Rangers with their hound dogs
Came all the way from Laredo
To the town of Gonzalez,
And they could not kill him.
At Rendado Lake,
They wanted him to die of thirst.
The Rangers got careless
With that wildcat.
He went to the water with the cattle,
And even drank their coffee.
Fifty years without clemency,
He was sent to prison.
With his valor and intelligence,
They made him a trusty.
He served twelve years,
And they gave him his freedom.

A close analysis of a confluence of textual and contextual characteristics of these songs and their performances offers interesting insights into the sung reappearance of Gregorio Cortez at the end of the twentieth century, nearly one hundred years after the gunfight that spawned ballad and legend. How do they compare with the variants that Paredes collected and other subsequent productions, and what, if anything, does such a comparison reveal? Following Paredes's variants A–I, I will label these two contemporary versions as J (Ramos) and K (Naranjo), respectively, which is to say they are not repetitions or variations of any of Paredes's versions, especially X, but rather distinctive compositions in their own right. That is, they are not true variants of oral tradition, but separate treatments of the same material. For convenience, I will say "J-K" when referring to both together.

While the general narrative of J-K corresponds loosely to that of the others—the setting, the gunfight, the ride, the capture—they stand apart from the others in their attention to known and verified historical detail. Thus, in a way, they tend toward Paredes's X and his informed sense that the ideal *corrido* be faithful to the details of the story, although they end up doing so in a paradoxical manner, as I will show. I offer several such textual instances.

Only the Mexico City broadside—not very well known in the United States—names the year 1901 as the one in which the precipitating incident occurred, as do both J and K, and only J-K offer any details whatsoever about the misunderstood horse/mare trade that generated the gunfight. The actual gunfight itself receives more detailed treatment in J-K than in any other variants, and like some musical legal brief, clearly lays out the basis for a plea of self-defense. None of the other Paredes variants tell us that Cortez's brother, Romaldo, died of his wounds in the Karnes City jail, as does J. Only J notes that during his flight Cortez was found near the village of Ottine at the home of his friend Martín Robledo. Only K reports the true detail that Cortez masked his approach to drinking water with a herd of cattle, although it adds that he also drank the Rangers' coffee, a detail not reported in the historical record. No other version, including J, reports these two details. None of the other variants name the village of Cotulla, Texas, as a place where the tired Cortez stopped presumably to rest, nor do they say that he was taken to San Antonio after his capture, as does J. J also specifically reports that he killed only two men, both sheriffs, a fact reported only by Paredes's Variant D. A and X also report two specific sheriffs, but they each add "several men" to those killed by Cortez. No other versions except J report that Cortez was turned in by a man named Jesus González (nicknamed "El Teco"). Finally, only J and K accurately report that Cortez was sentenced to life imprisonment and had his sentence commuted, although they differ in the length of time he served; J says eight and K says twelve, but, like a parole board, K is clearly counting the total time served in various jails from the time of his arrest, while K is counting only the time he served after he was finally sentenced to the state prison in Huntsville.

We must, of course, allow and even welcome embellishments and changes of the known historical record in mythic poetic song, but in J and K I am tracking such historical fealty to the actual known events in the interest of establishing the compositional impetus and sources for these two songs. And, of course, my basic source for such a known historical record is "*With His Pistol in His Hand,*" particularly Chapter 3, called "The Man," based on Paredes's careful research in archival data and the legal record of the Cortez case. My question is simply how did the composers of these songs, particularly the much longer and more detailed J, know these historical details so as to incorporate them in their compositions? That is, how is it that they go beyond Paredes's X and respond with great detail to the requirements of the ideal *corrido*?

Ruben Naranjo died before I could talk to him, and his family simply doesn't know how he came by the song, but Ruben Ramos identified Salomé Gutiérrez as J's composer. Gutiérrez is a freelance composer, the author of more than a thousand popular songs, a record producer, and a very well known figure in Mexican-American musical culture in Texas. In a phone interview he told me that he composed J on October 20, 1987, according to his records. Before turning to his response to my general question, we can consider three possible answers.

For a living composer like this one, steeped in his time and place, the seemingly most likely scenario is that he had heard previous versions of the song and then composed his own. Certainly he was aware of these other songs; indeed, he told me that he was present at the 1949 recording of Jesús Maya and Timoteo Cantú. Yet he disowns these prior renditions, claiming his to be quite original, a claim certainly justified by the historical detail in his version largely not found in any other variants, including Paredes's. That is, he could not have learned such detail from songs that did not have them in the first place. A second possibility, not entirely divorced from the first, is knowing and remembering a kind of vernacular nonmusical history about the Cortez matter, and such is the stronger claim that Gutiérrez makes for his composition: that he drew from his knowledge of the affair gathered principally, he said, from his father, Florencio, born in 1885, a native of San Antonio and therefore a teenager in 1901 and potentially quite aware of the matter as it unfolded and as it was covered by San Antonio newspapers in English and Spanish. Moreover, after his capture Cortez was brought to San Antonio. But to this paternal endowment, as a source of information, Gutiérrez also added what he called "*el vivir*," which is to say, his own lifetime in San Antonio. Why the song was not written until 1987 he could not exactly say except that the idea came to him then.

There is, of course, a third way to learn all of the details in the song and that is simply to have read "*With His Pistol in His Hand*," where each of the aforementioned factual details is carefully reported and supported. I asked him if had read the book, and he said he knew of Paredes but had not read it, if only because his reading of English was not that good. I then asked him if perhaps he knew of the Spanish translation of the book published by the National Institute of Anthropology and History in Mexico (Paredes 1985), and he said he did not. Yet in her own discussion of Gregorio Cortez, Harvard professor Doris Sommer (1999: 304–305) quotes James Nicolopulos as follows: Salomé Gutiérrez "felt compelled to write down his own version [of the eight-year imprisonment] because he felt that the transcriptions and translations that he had seen in the pamphlet to Folkloric 9004 and Paredes's books did not tell the whole story or told it accurately," even though he adds no detail that is not in "*With His*

Pistol in His Hand." Respectfully, I could get no further with Gutiérrez, as he simply repeated his version of how he came to compose his song.[13]

Finally, one or perhaps two of these details might also have been gleaned from the film *The Ballad of Gregorio Cortez*, such as the length of the sentence or Cortez using a herd of cattle to mask his approach to drinking water, but for the most part the film does not dwell on historical details such as these. Of some considerable interest, however, is K's report that Cortez drank the Rangers' "coffee." No other variants, including J, report such, nor does Paredes in his historical account, and such a detail is rather odd though poetically and politically intriguing.

One has to imagine a great deal of poetic license to envision Cortez with such bravura as to walk up to a Texas Ranger campsite, probably in some sort of disguise, to drink a cup of coffee with his deadly adversaries. That is a *corrido* hero of a wholly different magnitude! What I think happened is that K's composer obtained but changed this wonderful little detail from the Robert Young film, which does have a scene in which the very tired Cortez shares a cup of coffee with a stranger, though not a Ranger. In what seems an effort to enlist the sympathy of an Anglo audience, Young and his team created a wholly fictional scene in which Cortez comes upon a very kind and chatty Anglo cowboy, probably a fence rider. The cowboy invites Cortez to have a cup and something to eat, having no idea who Cortez is. Perhaps he thinks him to be a fellow, though Mexican, cowboy out riding fence as well, a not unusual occurrence. Young took poetic license with the historical record but also the balladry, and K's composer likely took poetic license with Young's film.

Elizabeth Fine (1984) has written a welcome intervention on the rendering of a live folkloric performance into useful evocative scholarly print. But here we have the exact opposite trajectory where folklike composers of *corridos* have transformed scholarly print back into performance. After making his way from musical face-to-face performance and into scholarly writing, fiction, poetry, and film, we now have the novel and paradoxical reemergence of Cortez as sung performance probably as a direct result of new composers having read *"With His Pistol in His Hand"* and/or seeing the film that it inspired.

Recalling Paredes's three periods when the song was in musical ascendancy, we can now argue for a fourth in the present moment. Through this improbable route, Gregorio Cortez is riding again in sung performance at the turn of the twenty-first century, but doing so for predominantly working-class Mexican-American and/or Mexican immigrant audiences. The audiences for Naranjo and Ramos are indeed Mexican-American working class, which these days may also include some second-generation immigrant Mexicans. Ramos tells me that the song is often requested at the dances he plays for such audiences, although Naranjo passed away before I could put the question to him.

Why and in what ways, might we ask, does the ballad in these specific renditions speak to them? Why, after his ride through various and largely elite, nonmusical discourses, has Cortez returned to the people, especially in the kind of nearly face-to-face transaction that is a Mexican-American working-class dance, and why now, rather than, let us say, in a rendition by Little Joe y La Familia in their famous Chicano movement–related album *Para la Gente* of the 1970s. I was able to do fieldwork on Texas-Mexican polka music and dancing in the seventies (1994). At my age, and with compelling family obligations in the early years of the twenty-first century, when the song was at its apogee, it was difficult, indeed impossible, to conduct systematic fieldwork, especially because fieldwork in such a late night dance scene is already difficult. Thus I offer only these textually keyed but ethnographically ungrounded speculations, and more as questions.

I wonder if the Paredes-informed addition of historical detail in J and K—especially the references to place-names such as Karnes City, Ottine, and San Antonio—might now make the song more intimately familiar to its contemporary audiences in our far more mobile time? Do the new lines about Cortez's right to self-defense, his subsequent legal history, and Romaldo's death in prison resonate with working-class Mexican Americans at a time when the policing and incarceration of Mexican-origin persons is controversial and disproportionately high, and has drawn much critical publicity (Olguín 2010)? The Mexican-origin community has been under a severe attack led by the Republican Party and its Fox News and right-wing radio, but also academics such as Samuel Huntington. Yet, at the same time, this community is also mounting a counter-offensive through its political leaders, its intelligentsia, and mass demonstrations, but also the arts, including music, most evident in the resurgence of Tejano music, a resurgence co-led by Ruben Ramos (Limón 2011). Is the new, resurgent "Gregorio Cortez" musically articulating this new defiant stance in detail? Have these composers and musicians then also hit upon the perfect way to bring this musical stance to the people by rendering it in the massively popular Tejano polka form, which also musically energizes the message?

On the other hand, one cannot help but recall certain key instances of reported speech in Variant X and some of the others. In these instances, either Cortez speaks in defiance of the Texas Rangers, or they do, saying how fearful and yet admiring they are of Cortez for his bravery. Such instances are wholly absent in J and K. I can only surmise that while attentive to historical and sociological detail, these new composers are also mindful of the energetic requirements of polka dancing but also playing time for radio and recording, and chose to leave out such instances that do not add to the historical detail and would lengthen the song.

Gregorio Cortez rides again, and this recent musical resurgence, but also his other appearances over time, would be impossible without the pivotal book "*With His Pistol in His Hand.*" I have also suggested that the joke forms that Paredes studied continue to be transformed in the service of such a struggle in the present day, a struggle now more mature and sophisticated. Through his meticulous, well-researched folklore scholarship on both genres now acting on the present, Américo Paredes—no longer with us—may have joined the fight once more, a fight in our time in another tempo.

SIX

Valor Civil

W e have come to know Américo Paredes as a creative writer; a journalist, largely in Asia; an academic folklorist; a progenitor of cultural studies with its dual beginnings in the interesting year of 1958; and, through his writing, as a paradoxical influence on the creation of more and contemporary expressive practices of everyday life. With some inevitable overlap, these identities occurred in a rough chronological order over a multifaceted and immensely productive career spanning a good portion of the twentieth century—a career centered on writing in various forms. In this final substantive chapter, I want to bring together these themes and identities, but in relation to yet another that might be associated with Paredes, that of public intellectual.

Most would agree that Paredes produced a corpus of work committed to social change largely on behalf of the people of Greater Mexico. Such a commitment might then lead some to think him to be what has been called "a public intellectual," meaning one involved in praxis. By the latter term we mean something like drawing from one's intellectual and artistic commitments and practices to engage in more direct action for social and institutional change, even as that action also acts back upon such commitments and practices. For public intellectuals, direct action may also, and usually does, involve writing and other forms of discourse, but a critical discourse now addressed to a general public on behalf of social change.

One of the foremost exponents—and examples—of this particular intellectual stance, the late Edward Said, describes it in this manner:

> . . . the intellectual, in my sense of the word, is neither a pacifier nor a consensus builder, but someone whose whole being is staked on a criti-

cal sense, a sense of being unwilling to accept easy formulas, or ready-made clichés, or the smooth, ever-so-accommodating confirmations of what the powerful or conventional have to say, and what they do. Not just passively, but actively willing to say so in public. (1994: 23)

Raymond Williams is another example of such an intellectual. Earlier I noted his ambivalent return to his Welsh ethnic culture in contrast to Paredes's forthright defense of Greater Mexico. But to note this particular ambivalence may be a small criticism — if at all — a criticism that shrinks when one considers Williams's direct involvement in English public life from the stance of a Marxist, which took him into adult education, journalism, and the Campaign for Nuclear Disarmament, among other such activities (Williams 1979).

Drawing on Greater Mexican culture, Américo Paredes also offered his own close version of Edward Said's formulation with the concept of *valor civil*, with *civil* meaning much as it does in English, or better yet, *civic*. A more interesting semantic load occurs with the word *valor*, which again can certainly and easily translate as "valor" in English, synonymous with "bravery," but in Spanish also carries the meaning of "value" or "virtue." *Valor civil*, said Paredes (1977: 125), "is courage that requires no weapon but the will itself; it is the courage of the unarmed and peaceful citizen who will not flinch before threats of violence. *Valor civil* is the ability to stand steadfast for what you think is right, come what may."

In his formulation Paredes was defining the work and person of George I. Sánchez, the great activist, historian, and long-time professor of education at the University of Texas at Austin, Paredes's friend and colleague. Beyond their professional proximity at UT-Austin, Paredes has been compared to Sánchez as this kind of public intellectual (Saldívar 2006: 227–240). In this chapter I want to explore this and other comparisons to define the manner and degree of Paredes's own identity in this regard, anchoring this exploration to the identities and time periods we have already noted. And since most of his career was devoted to Greater Mexico, my comparative inquiry will take up other intellectuals from this transnational sphere, beginning with Sánchez but not ending there as we also return to a rough chronological arrangement corresponding to epochal moments in the history of Greater Mexico and Paredes's own life.

For Paredes and Greater Mexico the first and originary moments would have been the Mexican Revolution of 1910 and the South Texas uprisings of 1915. Except in writerly retrospection, Paredes, not yet or barely born, had nothing literally to do with these momentous events surrounding his birth, which we have discussed at various points in this writing, although obviously they did much to shape his sensibility as he grew up in their immediate aftermath. But three more historical moments followed for Greater Mexico, where opportunities for a public intellectual life based on his beliefs presented themselves for a now mature Paredes.

1936–1944

The first historical moment occurred between Paredes's coming of age at twenty-one in 1936 and his departure for Asia in 1944, a period of great activity for the older Sánchez as well as for several other comparable intellectual activists. For the world and the United States, this, of course, was the time of the continuing Great Depression, Franklin D. Roosevelt's New Deal, and World War II, each of great consequence for Greater Mexico. However, for Mexican Americans, as for African Americans, we must always add a continuing pattern of intense racial discrimination, often institutionalized, in direct relationship to an expanding Mexican-origin population after the Mexican Revolution.

Saldívar (2006) correctly identifies Sánchez as a leading figure in the Mexican-American struggle against such oppressions as have others (García 1991: 252–272; Blanton 2006). Most of this oppositional career was centered on the educational exclusion of Mexican Americans and took the form not only of his many writings, both in professional journals and in the public media, but also in his role as an expert witness and counselor in the several legal cases carried by Mexican-American attorneys against such exclusion. But he also wrote on matters of culture and history in his 1940 *Forgotten People*. Blanton (2006), the best scholar on Sánchez, has called him a "New Deal 'service intellectual'" who utilized academic research in an attempt to progressively transform society" (574), working through governmental agencies but also as president of the League of United Latin American Citizens, which was briefly noted in Chapter 1.

In this same assessment, Saldívar (2006) also compares Paredes to a very different activist of that time, the Texas Communist Party labor organizer Emma Tenayuca, also noted in Chapter 1. Very active in organizing militant Mexican-American labor strikes in San Antonio, she also wrote on matters of ideology and political practice with her husband, Homer Brooks (1939). All are also placed in critical relationship to Roosevelt's New Deal ideology, rhetoric, and practice, and the painter Norman Rockwell's rendering of Roosevelt's "Four Freedoms."

While praising both Sánchez and Tenayuca and Brooks for their very different forms of engagement, Saldívar finds them still curiously wanting, even as he reserves a special place for Paredes, at that time a young poet still living in Brownsville, Texas. This is his claim:

> Despite the profound discontinuities among the varieties of ideologies represented by Roosevelt's and Rockwell's liberal New Deal Four Freedoms, George I. Sánchez's *Forgotten People*, and Emma Tenayuca and Homer Brooks' "The Mexican Question in the United States," each shares with the others a deliberate construction of consciousness, reflecting a particular cast of modernity and modernization that seems to speak for the age. Liberal and Popular Front politics alike participate in similar ideological justifications of modernity and modernization. (241)

As "Mexican-American intellectuals," Sánchez and Tenayuca

> deployed the liberal rhetoric of American national unity to justify its reformation—but not to imagine the framework of a new modern *mexicano* consciousness. In stark historical contrast, Paredes, as a young native intellectual seeking to invent a site of decolonized consciousness, offered a difference. (241)

For Saldívar that difference is articulated in Paredes's poetry, especially a critical poem called "The Four Freedoms," although others expressed similar ideas. These are the opening stanzas of the poem, originally written in Spanish circa 1941:

> Language, Culture, Blood:
> my song is yours,
> you are rock of the seas
> the hearth wall of the home;
> this "Four Freedoms" nation
> can offer us nothing.
> Justice . . . does it even exist?
> Might is justice,
> amusing words: Justice and Liberty.
> We have but our Race,
> We have but our Tongue;
> may we always preserve them

and maintain them alive
for an eternity.
(Paredes 1991: 95)

"With his poetic reprise of Roosevelt's Four Freedoms," says Saldívar, Paredes's "artistic work represents an important shift in consciousness and prefigures an era of renewed cultural integrity in the imaginary ground between two worlds in the borderlands of culture" (241). This primal cultural sentiment for language, culture, and blood is the basis for "a new modern *mexicano* consciousness," a "decolonized consciousness" that by comparative implication leaves intellectuals Sánchez and Tenayuca presumably as colonized, as not quite *mexicano/a* enough. Moreover, such a posture "prefigures an era of renewed cultural integrity," so that one can only conclude that it will be given a full figuration later. As with George Washington Gómez, one can think only of the "Aztlán" movement of the 1960s, where such exact sentiments abounded, as we seem to have another version of "the future in the present." Such a posture and identification, however, are not without risk and perhaps should be treated with more critical circumspection. As Saldívar (2006) himself notes of this same time period,

By 1937, evidence of the nightmares that uncritical cultural nationalism and celebrations of racial purity could lead to was plentiful with the ascendancy of fascism and Nazism in Europe. Race and nationalism, blood and soil, were the very principles of National Socialism thought, and they were echoed in eerily frightening ways by American Jim Crow racism. (218–219)

There is yet another and more practical issue in configuring Paredes against these two other Mexican-American activist intellectuals. These individuals were acting in the public realm, often against great adversity. By practical comparison, this and most of Paredes's poems were largely unpublished, read publicly only, if at all, to a small group of friends. That is, while the poem does seem to speak a new consciousness, it remained onc largely unheard in the public realm. Published or not, this primal sentiment is evident and certainly can be the basis for identifying the youthful Paredes with a new way of thinking, as Saldívar clearly wants to do. However, there is no evidence that Paredes made any attempt to put his sentiments into some sort of organized practical form, a precursor to the

Chicano movement, if you will. They remained largely poetic and private. Such nationalist sentiments would have been closely tied to the *sediciosos* insurrection of 1915 in South Texas, one year before the Easter Rising in Ireland and W. B. Yeats's full emergence as a public poet of Irish nationalism. Here, however, we have no Yeats.

Paredes did appear to share a great deal of Tenayuca's leftist thinking, which he suggested might lead to practical action in this direction: "my own politics were really quite radical," he said. "I've often thought that if there had been a Communist Party cell in south Texas at the time, I would have joined it" (quoted in Saldívar 2007: 91). In point of fact there was an active cell in South Texas, with Emma Tenayuca in San Antonio less than three hundred miles from Brownsville. Tenayuca and the Communist Party had played critical roles in organizing strikes in the pecan-shelling and cigar-making industries in 1936–1937 that turned violent and were widely publicized throughout Texas and the nation. In 1939, fearing for her life, Tenayuca left San Antonio and the state of Texas for California.

If, for whatever reasons, these regional involvements in the public realm were not viable options, there was yet another one for a young poet "whose politics were really quite radical," whose first language for conversation and poetry was Spanish, and who was decidedly opposed to the Catholic Church. From 1936 to 1939, in Spain, Francisco Franco and his right-wing followers, in collusion with the Catholic Church in Rome, initiated their vicious civil war against the new leftist and secular Republic. Franco sought to restore a pure, conservative, Catholic, and monarchial state and received direct support from Nazi Germany and Fascist Italy, and tacit support from most Western powers. Leftist, progressive volunteers from around the world, including many writers, journeyed to Spain to fight for the Republic. These included the distinguished Mexican writer Octavio Paz, who would later become Paredes's intellectual nemesis. For American volunteers the famous Lincoln Brigade was the primary organizational conduit to Spain (Beevor 2001).

For leftist progressives around the world, it was *the* cause of their time, and, not surprisingly, Paredes was clearly aware of the issue and records it and his anticlerical sentiments in *George Washington Gómez*. He satirically and even sarcastically recounts the Mexican-American Catholic churches' custom of having "kermesses" to raise money from the Mexican-American poor for the parish. Today these are called *jamaicas*, or bazaars, with booths, games, food, and music. In a mock religious tone, Paredes imagines a priest at mass preaching to his flock: "Don't sit there and tell me you have no money for the Church, who is your Mother, who is the guardian of your soul. Don't forget the kermesse. . . . Blessed are they who are generous in the cause of God," followed by: "Now we shall say a short prayer for the deliverance of our brothers, who are suffering the loss of their liberties and their beloved king. Let us pray that the Lord in his righteous anger shall give their just due to that anti-Christ Zamora and to Azaña, his partner in sin" (211). (Niceto Alcalá Zamora initially headed the Spanish Republic, followed by Manuel Azaña Díaz, who was president throughout most of the conflict.)[1]

At age twenty-one, had Paredes left for Spain, lived to tell the tale, and brought its more culturally specific lessons back to Greater Mexico, one can only imagine what his reputation as a progressive, true transnational would now be.[2] Short of such an active, fighting transnationalism, a young intellectual, especially a young journalist, might also have taken part in the domestic counterpart of the battle for Spain as both sides worked actively in the United States to garner support for their respective causes. Again, I know of no evidence that Paredes participated in efforts to rally support for the Spanish Republic in Mexican-American Catholic Texas, but I would be pleased to see such.

By comparison, another famous folklorist of the U.S.-Mexico border-lands, Aurelio M. Espinosa, did think a great deal about the Spanish Civil War and acted on that thinking, activity not at all separable from his work in folklore. In his own and later career as a folklorist, Paredes clearly came to know Espinosa's work, although they probably never met. As Paredes was returning to the United States from Asia in 1950, Espinosa was in the twilight of his long career. He died in 1958, just as Paredes's own career was being launched with the publication of *"With His Pistol in His Hand."*

We can turn to Paredes himself to define Espinosa as folklorist, a career dating from the early 1900s to the eve of his death and based largely at Stanford University. From the southern Colorado/northern New Mexico culture region, Espinosa studied at the University of New Mexico and later taught there after earning a PhD in Spanish from the University of Chicago. He later moved to Stanford, where he continued to develop as the foremost example of what Paredes called the "Hispanophile" perspective toward the Spanish-language folklore of the U.S.-Mexico borderlands.

Such folklore came not so much from what came to be Mexico, but rather from Spain transmitted to the borderlands almost directly during the Spanish colonization of these regions, particularly New Mexico with its very early Spanish settlement. By these chronological and spatial measures, the thus "Spanish" folklore of New Mexico and adjacent areas is thought to be superior to that later associated with Mexico "since the latter is mixed with indigenous elements which have diluted its grace and elegance" (Paredes 1993a: 4). Paredes strongly disagreed with this view, stressing instead the mestizo and Mexican regional identity of most such folklore. While Espinosa did make some "admirable discoveries of remnants of Spanish folklore in the southwestern United States . . . he was rarely concerned with the purely Mexican elements, which were decidedly in the majority—or if he did collect them, very seldom did he recognize them as Mexican" (4). Paredes's view of Espinosa has come to be shared among scholars of the U.S.-Mexico borderlands, and he has been reduced almost to a historical curiosity.

What we did not know about Espinosa until very recently is the way his deeply emotional identification with Spain, where he had done fieldwork, but also his devout Catholicism led him into the domestic struggle over the Spanish Civil War. Working from a newly found Espinosa archive, Renata Limón, a young historian, has discovered that this famous folklorist of his time also wrote tracts fiercely attacking the leftist, secular Spanish Republic and its American sympathizers. These appeared in Catholic Church publications and other forums and were also delivered as speeches to civic organizations. He particularly targeted the Catholic, Spanish-speaking communities in the United States, especially in California. Using his academic position as chair of the Department of Spanish at Stanford University, he corresponded with and encouraged right-wing, Catholic faculty colleagues in Spanish universities. He also brought some of them to Stanford for visiting appointments, during which they also participated in fomenting public support for Franco. Conversely, and again, using his Stanford prestige, he tried to subvert efforts by other U.S. academics to bring anti-Franco Spanish faculty to teach in American universities, including the distinguished Ramón Menéndez Pidal (R. Limón 2010). The latter were in dire danger as Franco came closer to his final victory.

"Just as Espinosa voiced direct political support for Franco in his writing," concludes Limón (2010: 31), "his folklore studies, based on an exaltation of sixteenth-century Spain, in effect contributed to the ideological project of Franco's State as it implicitly argued for the primacy of a pure Spanish and Catholic culture."

Another New Mexican literary intellectual, Fray Angélico Chávez (1910–1996), was far more cogenerational with Paredes than Espinosa. Indeed, as Meléndez (2010) has pointed out, his career parallels that of Paredes in many ways, although with different ideological emphases, such as Chávez's obvious affiliation with and devotion to the Catholic Church.

Like Paredes on South Texas he was a prolific writer in different genres on matters New Mexican and also served in the U.S. Army in World War II in the Pacific.[3] But before that, in 1936–1939, Chávez wrote poetry, fiction, and tracts but also took an active public advocacy role in the United States on behalf of the Franco forces and against what he saw as a communist Republic (McCracken 2009).

As far as I know, Paredes had nothing to say about these two intellectuals from New Mexico in regard to the Spanish Civil War. In 1936–1939, Paredes, of course, did not have the older Espinosa's academic power and prestige, but he was comparable to the much younger Chávez. It is still surprising to me that he appeared to have taken no significant public stance on this subject when everything in his developing profile would seem to point in this direction—a road not taken.

Paredes also had to deal with two other prominent folklorists of Greater Mexico, these much closer to Paredes in time and space, and active in the public arena. If Paredes characterized (and dismissed) Espinosa as an "Hispanophile," Jovita González and J. Frank Dobie, who worked among Mexicans in Texas from the 1920s through the 1950s, were labeled (and also dismissed) as "regionalists," which for Paredes meant another very specific but wrong-headed way of capturing and interpreting folklore. Many of their materials, he tells us, "have been vitiated by a limited knowledge of the language and by either a too romantic vision of the folk or an attitude of arrogant condescension. Their supposed informants talk like Castilian grandees or else stereotyped Mexicans in a third-rate film"; moreover, such regionalists, "have been romantics through and through. The romantic point of view deals not with living things but with idealizations of them, in a world where there are no contemporary problems." Such folklorists "look for local color, for the rare, the archaic, the bizarre" (Paredes 1993a: 17).

For Paredes, J. Frank Dobie was the most prominent such regionalist, and we shall soon turn to him. However, as Paredes's graduate student in folklore studies for several years, I became quite aware that he had the same critical sentiments toward González, who, in fact, had studied with Dobie at UT-Austin in the 1920s. Curiously, he never specifically named her in print the way he did several times for Dobie, nor did he ever spend any extended time with her or correspond with her that I knew about, although they may have met briefly at the annual meetings of the Texas Folklore Society.[4]

While González's work might be loosely characterized as "romantic regionalist," I, and others such as María Cotera, have tried to free her from the critical onus that Paredes principally placed upon her, or at least to argue that she represents a more complex case (Limón 1994; Cotera 2008). For one thing, this life-long teacher of Spanish and native of South Texas could hardly be accused of having "a limited knowledge of the [Spanish] language." Cotera has advanced the most elaborated case for rethinking the work of Jovita González, arguing, among other things, that just below the surface of her presumed idealizations is a consistent critique of Anglo-dominant society in Texas and its subordination of Mexicans. In a not dissimilar manner, one can also trace a firm feminist critique in her work. For Cotera, the manner of González's fieldwork and her subjective writing overcame a rigid subject-object binary, anticipating contemporary and welcome experimental practices in ethnography. Finally, Cotera values González's public performances of Mexican folklore, primarily for Anglo-American audiences, arguing that they constituted a needed cultural intervention in such a dominant world.

In Chapter 1 we also came to know Paredes as a social critic in fiction, and Cotera (2008) argues a parallel case for González and her coauthorship of an important novel, *Caballero*, written at exactly the same time that Paredes was writing *George Washington Gómez*. Like Paredes, she and her coauthor were not able to publish it in their own time. At one point González considered applying for graduate study in Spanish at Stanford, probably to work with Aurelio M. Espinosa, given her interest in folklore, but she did not follow through. She was a devout Catholic, although it is impossible to say how she would have come out on the issue of the Spanish Civil War.

González did go beyond folklore and literature to participate in the public sphere in another compelling manner. Adding this public dimension to Cotera's work on Jovita González, John Moran González (2009) has carefully traced this public career, especially around the critical year of 1936, when Texas was organizing the statewide celebration of its centennial, commemorating the one hundred years since the founding of the Texas Republic in 1836. Mexican-American leaders feared that the celebration would be wholly a celebration of Anglo-Texan triumphalism and hegemony, denigrating or wholly excluding the Spanish and Mexican people living there since before there was a state or a republic. To combat this triumphalism, they organized within the League of United Latin American Citizens (LULAC) (noted in Chapter 1), which had been formed in Corpus Christi, Texas, in 1929.

González was very active in LULAC, especially in this bicentennial moment. In addition to participating and speaking at LULAC meetings, she wrote articles for the group's newsletter and other public outlets intended for lay audiences in Texas, especially as 1936 approached. Some of these articles were based on her master's thesis at UT-Austin, where she demonstrated a vital and progressive Mexican presence but also spoke to the racialist domination of Anglo Texans in the nineteenth century and later. But, as noted earlier, she also spoke publicly and gave musical and other performances at centennial events with the same intent. According to John González (2009), she also had another intention for her public work and that was to contest male dominance within LULAC itself. One particular such publication, "Catholic Heroines of Texas," published in a Catholic newsletter, uses Catholicism as a cultural synonym for Mexicans and shows the vital presence of ethnic Mexican women, including in defense of Texas liberty at that most central icon of Texas triumphalism, the Alamo. Thus, she "turned to the strong historical identification of ethnic Mexicans with the Roman Catholic faith to insert the agency of Spanish and Mexican peoples into Centennial discourses that otherwise dismissed their accomplishments as feeble and inconsequential to the history of Texas."

In 1936, at age twenty-one, Américo Paredes took no part in this particular public struggle, no doubt because in large part he viewed LULAC with some disdain. He felt that "at that time the LULACs were extremely assimilationist. They counseled their members not to speak Spanish at all to their children, to bring them up as American citizens and nothing else" (quoted in Saldívar 2006: 125). Retrospectively, it now seems clear that Paredes was very mistaken, although his assessment has proved to be very influential in how most younger Mexican-American scholars have come to see LULAC.[5]

Clearly González's own work within LULAC is hardly assimilationist, and even though critical of the organization in some respects, the radical Emma Tenayuca and her coauthor, Homer Brooks (1939), noted that LULAC was a more complex and evolving organization than its critics then and today wish to recognize: "An amendment to its constitution recognizes Mexico as the cultural motherland. In several cities . . . LULAC has entered into cooperative relationship with other Mexican groups, including labor organizations" (266). Finally, and never to be forgotten, the founder of LULAC, the lawyer, diplomat, and public intellectual Alonso Perales of Alice and San Antonio, Texas, authored a major polemic (in Spanish) called *En defensa de mi raza* (In Defense of My People).[6]

Johnson (2005) has offered an informed and nuanced examination of LULAC. Buttressed by original primary research, he closely identifies this organization with a long-term tendency that he aptly calls "Tejano progressivism." LULAC flourished and continues to do so within the Mexican-American community, having become "the oldest surviving and most prominent civil rights organization for Mexican-Americans" (192). Among other things, he notes that LULAC mounted major social and legal struggles against segregation, particularly in the schools, some involving great personal risk.

LULAC members did indeed struggle mightily to learn English, recognizing that it was the only language for an effective politics and civic culture in the United States (as Paredes himself obviously recognized). But if they insisted on speaking English during their meetings, it was to set an example for the rest of Mexican America, and not to imply that this population should not also continue to speak Spanish, as all of these members did in their less public lives (Johnson 2005: 185–194). And if language shapes culture, we can easily imagine its members with a decisively Mexican comportment in other aspects of their cultural selves in the 1920s and 1930s. Contrary to charges of being mindless assimilationists, there is this LULAC statement:

> Our efforts to be rightfully recognized as citizens of this country do not imply that we wish to become scattered nor much less abominate our Latin heritage . . . but rather on the contrary, we will always feel for it the most tender love and the most respectful veneration. (quoted in Johnson 2005: 192)

John Moran González also offers us new and fundamental archival research and nuanced readings of a wealth of hitherto unknown LULAC *literary* materials (including a hilarious knock-knock joke) to clearly demonstrate another and much more likely LULAC. Calling LULAC members "Lulackers," González concludes that "despite scholarly assessments to the contrary, Lulackers advocated neither an uncritical assessment of Anglo-American values at school nor the abandonment of ethnic Mexican customs at home."

Most LULAC members never relinquished their loyalty to their Mexican culture even as they fashioned a bilingual and bicultural creative and proactive existence in defense of their community, contesting nativist Anglo-Texan symbolic actions such as the Texas Centennial. And "far from advocating the disappearance of Mexican Americans into a whitewashed mainstream, LULAC proposed the institutionalization of Mexican American studies some three decades before the Chicano movement managed to implement the concept albeit in a radically reconceptualized form" (González 2009: 241).

J. Frank Dobie was a major figure in the formulation and implementation of the Texas Centennial, with all of its Anglo-Texan triumphalism, and thus was Jovita González's opponent at least in this particular instance, although there were others. Yet he had also been her mentor and champion in her promotion of Mexican folklore and culture, and this contradiction in Dobie marked this man who became a significant figure in Paredes's life as well.

Older than Paredes, Dobie was considered the major folklorist and scholar of Texas culture, including its Mexicans, prior to Paredes, although González certainly competed as she grew in stature. Given his iconic status in Texas, and indeed the world, as well as his pronounced presence in Paredes's own work, Paredes's relationship to the famous Texas folklorist and icon also deserves some extended commentary in a comprehensive evaluation of each man's full significance to the other. I have written on Dobie before (Limón 1994: 43–59), but my present task is greatly assisted by the recent appearance of a welcome and well-done biography (Davis 2009). Much of what follows biographically is indebted to Davis's fine work.

Born and raised in a ranching family in upper South Texas on land that had once belonged to Mexicans, Dobie graduated from Southwestern University in 1910 with a major in English. Like Paredes later, he also tried his hand at journalism, but eventually took up college teaching as an instructor in English, most significantly at UT-Austin, which would remain his intellectual home. The University of Texas required an advanced degree if he was to advance to a professorship, so in 1913 he moved to New York to earn a master's in English from Columbia University with a total emphasis on canonical literature, particularly English Romanticism.

Master's degree in hand, Dobie returned to UT-Austin for the fall semester of 1914, just as the "guns of August" went off in Europe. An adventurous young man with stories of the Mexican and Indian wars in Texas in his head, Dobie enlisted after the United States entered the bloody fray in 1917, but he did not see combat, arriving in France in late October 1918, on the eve of the Armistice. However, this young man with a largely regional formation up to that point fell in love with France, as Paredes would with Japan, and chose to remain in the army through May 1919 so that he could visit the famous French sites of culture and take classes at the Sorbonne.

After France, Dobie returned to his post at UT-Austin. Throughout this early phase of his career, he remained profoundly depressed and dissatisfied, finding the life of a professor of composition and canonical literature unrewarding and even a threat to his masculinity. Severely depressed, in 1920 he left the university to return to ranching, managing an uncle's ranch back in the Nueces River area. Since his undergraduate days, Dobie had always been interested in the folklore and vernacular culture of Texas and the Southwest, and during this brief, déjà vu stint as a rancher, and with his literary sensibility, he discovered the rich Mexican folklore from the *vaqueros* who worked on the ranch.

Immediately Dobie sensed that he had found his life's calling, for not only did this folklore flow from his home region, but he felt it was material that could or should be introduced into the curriculum of university literary departments. To this end he was supported by the example of John Lomax, a fellow Texan who had been a student at UT-Austin in the 1890s and had gone on to a PhD at Harvard and a career collecting Texas and other regional folklore while teaching at Texas A&M University. Dobie could never persuade himself, or be persuaded, to get a PhD, the lack of which would have impeded his academic progress under conventional circumstances. Dobie, however, was not conventional.

He gave up ranching to return to UT-Austin and to launch his new program of research and teaching in Texas regional folk culture. While he never lost his interest in Mexican folklore, he never developed fluency in Spanish, and this obstacle seemed to be the principal factor in his turn away from such to the culture of Texas cowboys and others of his own ancestry. But there was perhaps also a subconscious sense that Mexican folklore belonged to a racialized "Other" that had been and continued to be oppressed by his own people, and that his parents' very land was part and parcel of that subjugation. He then turned to a more generalized region that might be described as "southwestern Texas."

Beginning with a book called *A Vaquero of the Brush Country: The Life and Times of John D. Young,* based on the reminiscences of Young, a working Anglo cowboy, Dobie wrote and published a series of books of collected and archival Anglo-Texan and southwestern folklore and vernacular culture which he typically rewrote in a more literary style. Appearing from the 1930s into the post–World War II period, these books were enormously popular. Together with his teaching of the very popular English course "Life and Literature of the Southwest" at UT-Austin and numerous speaking engagements across the country, Dobie soon came to be called

"Mr. Texas" and considered the foremost exponent of Texas regionalism.[7] It was at this point that his career first intersected with that of Paredes.

Let us recall that in the late thirties and early forties, Paredes was completing *George Washington Gómez*, whose final sections are also set in that time period. In one of those later scenes, Guálinto/George is about to graduate from high school and make his way to UT-Austin. For graduation, his school decides to invite a prominent commencement speaker named "K. Hank Harvey," a professor at a place referred to as "the University," and described as an expert on Texas history and culture, including its Mexicans. In the commencement address, Harvey extols the virtues of Anglo Texas while making racist and condescending remarks about Mexicans in Texas to a predominantly Mexican-American audience, who politely listen since most of them don't understand his English.

With thinly veiled sarcasm, the narrator describes the commencement speaker: "Harvey's fame grew too big even for vast Texas, and soon he was a national and then an international figure" who "filled a very urgent need; men like him were badly in demand in Texas." The narrative continues in an editorial vein.

> They were needed to point out the local color, and in the process make the general public see that starving Mexicans were not an ugly pitiful sight but something very picturesque and quaint, something tourists from the north would pay money to come and see. By this same process bloody murders became charming adventure stories, and men one would have considered uncouth and ignorant became true originals. (271–272)

Harvey's speech embitters Guálinto/George even more toward Anglo Texas. However, as we saw, the bitterness will not last, and the protagonist takes a decisive turn at its end. Guálinto/George will eventually become a seemingly fully assimilated American subject, now fully "George," especially after attending Dobie's UT-Austin.

Paredes tells us that, in fact, he modeled Harvey after Dobie, who did come to Brownsville in the 1930s to give a speech which Paredes heard, although it was not a commencement address. "Dobie was constantly in the news at that time," said Paredes. "His books were being touted for the truth of their representations of Texas folklife" (quoted in Saldívar 2006: 117–118). The young Paredes was not at all impressed, but his relationship with Dobie would continue later.

1944–1967

As noted in Chapter 2, after his Asian interlude Paredes returned to the United States in 1950, specifically to Dobie's UT-Austin, to resume a college career. But by 1950 it was no longer Dobie's school and platform, for much had happened since the young Paredes had last seen him at that speech in Brownsville, principally occasioned by Dobie's political turn to the left. Perhaps consistent with his condescending and sometimes racist attitudes toward Mexicans but also African Americans, Dobie's general politics in the 1930s had been decisively right-wing conservative, especially when it came to the election of Franklin Roosevelt and the coming of the New Deal, construing his opposition to Roosevelt and his policies in regionalist terms. For him Texas was the last depository of personal freedom, symbolized by the open range of the nineteenth century, and he thus called for opposition to an expanding activist federal government. Matching Paredes's enmity for Roosevelt, but from the right, he said: "I have no use for Roosevelt and no use for his plans" (quoted in Davis 2009: 99).

But slowly things began to change in the early 1940s as a much greater threat to Dobie's vision of Texas began to emerge. For Dobie the threat revolved around the seemingly unlikely conjunction of Great Britain, oil, and UT-Austin, all in relation to an increasingly conservative right-wing and white Texas political and business establishment which continues to the present day. In keeping with his love for the English literary classics, Dobie was an ardent supporter of Britain in its battle against Nazi air and submarine attacks. Before December 7, 1941, this same Texas establishment, in league with isolationists, also opposed Roosevelt's attempt to help Great Britain while maintaining U.S. neutrality, and some openly sympathized with what they saw as an industrially and militarily dynamic and Aryan Nazi Germany. This same establishment also abhorred Roosevelt and the federal government's increasing regulation of big business, especially oil, but also Eleanor Roosevelt's "call for equal rights for African Americans," and the president's "support for an antilynching bill" (Davis 2009: 144). Increasingly Dobie threw in his lot with Roosevelt, even as he also began to advocate for racial integration, particularly of the university. The latter became even more of a focal point of resistance when this establishment, operating through the university's politically appointed Board of Regents, openly tried to suppress or fire professors who were, in their eyes, engaged in "subversive activities," including the use of certain books in their classes, such as John Dos Passos's *U.S.A.* Indeed Dobie was also attacked for advocating the teaching of Russian.

Eventually Homer Rainey, the university's progressive president, was fired when he defended academic freedom and openly opposed the regents. The campus erupted in protest, and students boycotted classes. According to Davis,

> More than any other factor, these attacks on academic freedom caused Dobie to reassess his deeply held, almost instinctive political beliefs. He realized that the greatest threat to individual freedom was no longer the government—it was right-wing business interests. With this insight, fifty-three year old Dobie became a political liberal.

He wrote to a friend,

> Here in the University we have a fight for academic freedom on, against a board made up almost entirely of millionaires and corporation lawyers, Roosevelt- and new-style fascists. I am expected to take the lead on the side of the liberals, and I am expecting to be called on the carpet for taking part in politics. (Davis 2009: 152–153)

And henceforth Dobie did indeed take a liberal-left stance on most issues, at some considerable distance from his former conservative, anti-Roosevelt views of the 1930s—views that he associated with his sense of Texas as a region. He supported, for example, labor's right to strike even in wartime. It cost him dearly in popularity as "Mr. Texas" within some conservative circles, and his new views strained his friendship with intellectual figures such as the famous regional folklorist John Lomax, an archconservative, who accused him of "stirring up class feeling." Lomax went on: "You're disgracing yourself," he told Dobie, "and you're disgracing Texas. You'll ruin your reputation writing trash like this" (quoted in Davis 2009: 157).

In 1943 Cambridge University invited Dobie to spend a year there teaching American history and culture. With his ardent Anglophilia, Dobie readily accepted, seeing it also as a way to help the British cause given that so many English faculty had enlisted in the war effort. Dobie loved the experience so much that he extended his leave of absence another year on an unpaid basis, which he was able to do because he was making a good living from the sales of his very popular books and other investments. In 1947 he applied for yet another extension of his unpaid leave so that he could finish another book project. The new UT-Austin president was an arch segregationist who had requested the FBI to investigate subversive activities on campus. Dobie had publicly referred to him as "a flunky of the Laval pattern." Dobie's request went through administrative channels and was approved at each level but was ultimately denied by the president. Dobie was told to report for teaching duties in the fall of 1947; he refused and was fired.

The firing not only added to his liberalism and his popularity with ordinary Texans, but across the world as well, and Dobie continued to write about his beloved Texas in new books such as *The Voice of the Coyote*. For good political measure, he did not support Harry Truman in the 1948 presidential election. But did he support Dewey? No. True to his now decidedly leftist perspective, he backed the third-party, leftist candidacy of Henry Wallace. He would continue to fight from the left through the fifties and early sixties opposing the House Un-American Activities Committee (HUAC) and supporting the Supreme Court decision on *Brown vs. Board of Education of Topeka*. His opposition to HUAC drew the personal attention of J. Edgar Hoover, who ordered the FBI to investigate Dobie for "subversion." In his final few years, Dobie led a counter-attack on a right-wing group called "Texans for America," which among other causes demanded that school textbooks at all levels delete references to authors disloyal to America, including "Albert Einstein, William Faulkner, Ernest Hemingway, Willa Cather, Langston Hughes, Carl Sandburg, and several others," including . . . J. Frank Dobie (Davis 2009: 228).

In 1944 Paredes left Texas for Asia, where he remained until 1950, even as Dobie was fighting his own war against Texas reactionaries. Life is often a series of difficult choices, but for Paredes, remaining in Asia for an additional four years after his discharge—when most veterans might choose to go home—does not appear to have been an agonizing decision. No doubt there were any number of compelling reasons not to stay—more on this, a bit later—but stay he did. There, as we have seen, he produced a distinctive body of largely journalistic work chiefly focused on Japan and China. It was during this period that he fully defined himself as a professional journalist to the point that he considered it as an alternative career when he returned to the United States in 1950.

His decision to remain in Asia after the war did have other consequences for Paredes as a public voice in the affairs of Greater Mexico, namely that he missed a singular opportunity to take part in the Mexican-American civil rights movement from 1945 until well into the 1960s, a movement that continued the reformist politics of before the war but that now added returning Mexican-American veterans. By choosing to remain for five years in Asia, he effectively removed himself from joining what we must now see as a watershed, politically active generation of Mexican-

American World War II veterans, for whom his journalistic skills would have been of great service (Rivas-Rodríguez and Zamora 2009).

Albert Armendariz Sr. was one such World War II veteran. In a recent story in the *El Paso Times*, Diana Washington Valdez reports that he was "honored recently by the Texas Civil Rights Project" for his activism on behalf of Mexican-American civil rights. Armendariz, then eighty-seven, a judge and former president of the League of United Latin American Citizens, "recounted the kind of racism he experienced in the 1950s when he and other LULAC members went to Pecos, Texas, to look into complaints about discrimination. 'In Pecos, the schools, the churches and the dog pounds were segregated,' he said. 'When we got there—this was around 1955—we saw one of the (public) schools had a sign with big letters on it that said "Mexican school." We were there on a Sunday and went to church only to be told that we were in the wrong Catholic Church because it was for whites only. We also learned they had separate dog pounds for dogs that were found in white, black and Mexican-American neighborhoods.'"

"The group found a sympathetic federal judge," Valdez tells us, "but they fled after being warned that a mob was on its way to get them. In another case involving discrimination at a former El Paso Catholic orphanage, Armendariz and others threatened to sue the bishop and Catholic diocese over the fact that the orphanage existed exclusively for Anglos. Then Bishop Sidney Metzger promised things would change" (*El Paso Times*, June 28, 2007).

Efforts such as this one also included activist groups such as the Political Association of Spanish-Speaking Organizations (PASSO) which were coming on the scene. Upon returning in 1950, Paredes dedicated himself to his family, graduate school, and the beginning of his professional academic career, and there is no record that he took up an activist role in the 1950s as he pursued these other vital concerns.

In the afternoon of September 18, 1964, J. Frank Dobie died at his home in Austin near the university. That morning he had received the first advance copy of his latest book, *Cow People*, on a variety of Texas and southwestern characters. Though he had expressed some doubts about Texas, in the end he returned to it. "It was a handsome book," Davis (2009: 233) tells us, ". . . and the portraits he assembled contained some of the strongest, most disciplined writing he had ever achieved. He no longer romanticized the old-timers; instead he saw them for what they were— fellow humans who were tough and admirable in some ways, limited in others."

When Dobie died, Américo Paredes was already an associate professor of English in Dobie's old department. The very university that had fired Dobie had hired one of its first Mexican Americans—and certainly the first in the English department. At this moment the careers of the two men overlapped in a more personal manner.

Dobie, of course, never saw Paredes's scathing, satirical portrait of himself by way of "K. Hank Harvey." The manuscript of the novel *George Washington Gómez* was not retrieved and published until 1990. Paredes had also mildly criticized Dobie's views toward Mexicans in *"With His Pistol in His Hand"* and in other of his writings, and these Dobie did see. Nevertheless, Dobie admired and promoted the book when it appeared (Davis 2009: 210–211). In an exquisite irony, given Dobie's ranching origins,

> Dobie's reading of Paredes also influenced his view of the King Ranch. Paredes made him aware, at last, of the extent of Mexicano enmity toward Anglo landowners. Dobie now understood that the King Ranch and the Texas Rangers who worked on its behalf were accused of illegally dispossessing Mexicano land grant families. (214)

The King Ranch was and still is often credited with inventing cattle ranching itself, but Dobie observed that "millions of Spanish-Mexican cattle had been raised in south Texas before King owned an acre or a cow" (quoted in Davis 2009: 214).

During Paredes's early career at UT-Austin, Dobie and his wife were still living very close to campus, even after he was dismissed in 1947. Of this overlapping time, Paredes had this to say in an interview with Ramón Saldívar in the 1990s:

> I was pretty harsh on Dobie in the novel because I didn't know him when I was writing the novel. Later, when I came to the University of Texas, I finally did meet him. I found him to be a very lovable old . . . fraud. I was invited to his house several times, and I think we even visited him at his Paisano Ranch. But as I said, he was a lovable old fraud [laughter] as far as Mexican materials were concerned. (Saldívar 2006: 117)

"When I did get to know him," continued Paredes, "we would talk about a number of things, but never about Mexicans" (119).[8]

There is no record that Paredes ever returned the courtesy by inviting the Dobies to his home, and he developed a kind of ambivalence toward

Dobie somewhere between "lovable" and "fraud." To judge from Dobie's invitations, "several times," it appears that he was trying to get to know Paredes much better and to learn from him, as Davis suggests.

In 1964, shortly before Dobie's passing, Paredes declined a request from the esteemed Ronnie Dugger to contribute an essay for a special issue of the *Texas Observer* on Dobie, saying, "I would be best qualified to write on Dobie as a folklorist, but disagree with so much of what he has done (while respecting him as a pioneer in the field) that anything I would write would be either hypocritical praise or would strike a jarring note."[9] Dugger replied with the following, clearly suggesting Dobie's awareness of Paredes's criticisms:

> I do not see why it would be inappropriate for you to disagree with Dobie's work as a folklorist; to subject it to the objections you have about it. Dobie has said to me several times about this issue that he vastly prefers intelligence to charity. I wish you would reconsider and go ahead and write on Dobie as a folklorist—a serious piece.[10]

Paredes did not take up the invitation—unfortunately—for it deprived us of a serious public engagement between these two eminent Texas folklorists over what O'Sullivan (1845) and later Tenayuca and Brooks (1939) had called "the Mexican Question" in Texas.

As if perhaps regretting his decision, in the year following Dobie's death Paredes did publish a review of two of Dobie's edited books on Texas folklore, where he, in effect but too briefly, responds to Dugger's request for a "serious piece" on Dobie as folklorist. Again unfortunately, this very brief review appeared in a professional journal of folklore, one not read by the general public. In it Paredes contrasts a professional and methodologically rigorous approach to folklore (implicitly his as well, as we saw in Chapter 3 on balladry) to Dobie's approach, which endorses W. B. Yeats's criticism that scientific folklorists "tabulate" their materials "like grocer's bills." For Dobie, "folk-lore, as it is given forth by the Texas Folk-lore Society, should express the life of the folk; it should reveal the social background; it should suggest raciness, color in character" (Paredes 1965: 163). But for Paredes, in the hands of non-natives, as we have seen, such a literary approach also too often led to condescending racist stereotyping of Mexican Americans, and he held Dobie culpable in this regard, although he does not go this far in this particular review. Yet he also closes the review by quoting John Lomax's 1944 assessment, which Paredes calls still "pertinent," suggesting that he would seem to agree.

No Texas library—pretty soon it will be no library in the world—can be called a complete library without a set of the Dobie folklore books. All of the contents may not be accurately called folklore but there is a world of priceless stories about the basic beliefs, manners, customs, and legends of the people of Texas and her neighboring states. (1965: 164)

In the same exchange with Dugger, Paredes also says, "I value Dobie most highly as a person and believe that his lasting importance will be as a bridge between the beliefs and attitudes of the backwoods and those of a new and liberal generation. That is to say, his influence on others is his greatest contribution."[11] In another letter to a colleague, Paredes notes Dobie's passing with the words: "It is a great personal loss for all of us."[12] And in what might be Paredes's ultimate tribute, he sang a *corrido* about Dobie at the next Texas Folklore Society meeting (Davis 2009: 212).

Such expressions suggest but do not specify that Paredes was perhaps lending appreciation to Dobie's stalwart politics in defense of racial equality and academic freedom, which were legendary on the UT-Austin campus and in liberal circles in Texas during Paredes's early career. Undercutting such a seeming appreciation of Dobie, Paredes's use of the phrase "old fraud," uttered later in his life in his interview with Saldívar (2006), seems uncharacteristically unkind. Uncorrected, it will significantly contribute to what Steve Davis sees as the marked tendency of younger Mexican-American scholars to see Dobie solely, and in my view, narrowly, "as a perpetrator of racist histories" (236).

1967–1999

Paredes's general nonparticipation in the public life of his time changed to a significant degree with the onset of the Chicano student movement beginning in 1967. We have already noted the movement's reception of *"With His Pistol in His Hand,"* but Paredes also began working with students demanding a research center dedicated to the study of Mexican-American life, anticipated by LULAC, although we did not know it then. As his teaching assistant and graduate student, I functioned as a kind of go-between for the mostly undergraduate students and Paredes. In 1970 the administration of UT-Austin established the Center for Mexican American Studies (CMAS) with Paredes as its founding director. As someone who was present and active every step of the way, I can testify that Professor Paredes worked actively with the movement: attending meetings, advocating to the administration, helping to draft position papers, traveling to coordinate with similar efforts throughout the Southwest, and, of course, serving as the center's first director. In 1972 he resigned from the position in the belief that the central administration had betrayed him. However, over time he did return to serve as interim director twice and to chair search committees for hiring new directors. Until his final days, he lent his support to CMAS, which published a volume of his collected essays in 1993 and a small volume of eulogies upon his death in 1999.

It is also certainly worth noting that during this same period the Chicano movement also brought Paredes into a different kind of public engagement in defense of the Mexican people of the United States. His adversary came from an unlikely quarter: not from Anglo-America, but from Mexico by way of that country's most esteemed public intellectual, Octavio Paz—he who had participated in the Spanish Civil War in 1936 when Paredes had not. As noted in Chapter 3, in 1951 Paz had published his arguably most famous work, *El laberinto de la soledad,* translated into English as *The Labyrinth of Solitude* in 1961, shortly after the publication of *"With His Pistol in His Hand."*

The first chapter of Paz's book, "The Pachuco and Other Extremes," is based on his experiences in Los Angeles, where he was able to observe *pachucos,* Mexican-American "street" adolescents characterized by their distinctive dress (the zoot suit), speech style, gestures, dance styles, and perhaps occasional illegal activities. For Paz they represented an extreme form of Mexican identity, one he characterized as antisocial and performative; the *pachuco,* he wrote, is an "impassive sinister clown whose purpose is to cause terror instead of laughter" (Paz 1985: 16). Given the relative absence of work on Mexican Americans in the early 1960s, the essay became an important text for the Chicano movement, although in two distinct ways. For some, Paz's characterizations were actually consistent with their own adoption of the *pachuco* as a kind of folk hero in rebellion against Anglo-American culture, even as he was also a victim of Anglo racism.[13] For others, including Américo Paredes, Paz's characterization was offensive and itself racist. In October 1969, Paz lectured at UT-Austin, and Paredes was present. In part, the lecture dealt with Mexican culture and its relationship to the 1968 massacre by Mexican troops of protesting students at Tlatelolco. For Paz a deep-rooted Mexican cultural propensity to violence had something to do with the massacre, a linkage that deeply offended Paredes (López-Morín 2006: 120–121).

I also attended the lecture, but I cannot recall with certainty that Paredes engaged Paz from the audience. Such an encounter, had it occurred, I think would have been memorable to me as a young graduate student just beginning my work with Paredes. I do recall that we talked that evening, and I clearly recall his anger. I also recall that he told me he had been invited to an after-lecture party for Paz. I have always wondered what might have happened there other than what he reported to me when I asked him a few days later. The always understated Paredes simply said, "We talked a bit."[14]

1999–2012

We may conclude that in comparison to his fellow intellectuals from 1936 to his passing, Paredes's politically critical work remained confined largely to his writing; that is, he largely eschewed any public, active political participation. He showed much admiration for but did not actively pursue participation with Emma Tenayuca and leftist labor. In another political direction, I believe he misread LULAC in 1936 and thus missed an opportunity to join George Sánchez, but especially Jovita González, in the public fray concerning the momentous Texas Centennial. After 1944 he spent some very critical years in Asia doing other important work, but missed out on the great Mexican American civil rights struggle led by former World War II veterans, where his talents would have been most welcome and efficacious. When he returned to the United States in 1950, to be sure, for largely familial and professional reasons and later illness, such participation was not a real option during his graduate student and early professorial days. He did reach out to a larger public through a few writings in the *Texas Observer*, but not in the way that Dobie did as the latter publicly fought the forces of Texas reaction. From their correspondence, it is quite clear that Ronnie Dugger wanted Paredes to be even more involved in the *Texas Observer*. That Paredes was not able to do so with his very accessible writing remains a most unfortunate missed opportunity. He might have helped forge a link between Anglo-liberal Texas and an emerging Mexican-American Texas, one largely still missing through the present day, and that, in part, has permitted the nearly complete ascendancy of the reactionary and racist forces that Dobie fought.

Yet in 1967 Paredes did become very involved with the Chicano movement and the creation and institutionalization of Mexican-American studies, his most extended public involvement as an intellectual. To the present day, UT-Austin's CMAS has been a very influential force in the field and may certainly be seen as Américo Paredes's most important public, institutional achievement. That is why I am mystified that he seemingly chose to say not a word to Saldívar about this active moment in his life, nor did Saldívar choose to add this activity to his monumental biography, although Paredes's other biographers have.[15]

Family obligations, political differences, misreadings of history, and other factors, including simple lack of interest in the public realm, may all serve as some explanation for why Paredes and some other modern intellectuals may choose to stay within the ambit of their work, scholarly and creative. With Paredes, at least, while some of these may obtain, I do wonder about a more fundamental reason that had everything to do with his early formation and the onset of modernity. For while I personally believe it to be vitally necessary, all such participation does indeed commit one in some form or fashion to the project of modernity. From his work and many extended conversations with him over thirty years, including long drives and flights together to attend Chicano movement gatherings, I think Paredes was never fully able to make such a commitment. Although he obviously lived within modernity, I have always felt that he did so as a kind of modernist with a disdain for his modern present, what I have elsewhere called a modernist sense of tragedy, or in Unamuno's words, *el sentimiento trágico de la vida*. Speaking of his earliest days in Brownsville and evincing already the modernist-in-exile within, Paredes said, "to a great extent I was a loner: I was not a joiner" (Saldívar 2006: 125).

Paredes's early poetry does show an anchoring point with a premodern and pure border Mexican past of blood, language, and culture articulated by the old men while he listened as a child. Against this background, his later short stories set in South Texas largely show us a corrupted modern world. The painful example of George in *George Washington Gómez* further demonstrates the dangers of modernity and shows us not so much the assimilated subject, but rather the incipient modernist manqué, as I suggested in Chapter 1. Even Paredes's marriage to the very nonbourgeois South Texas singer Chelo Silva might be construed as part of this modernist posture, as might his extended excursion in exotic Asia, the classical Western modernist-in-exile away from native soil, though this time not to Paris, Vienna, Zurich, nor indigenous Mexico. The military and modernism provided the opportunity, and he took it. Even though Japan was experiencing its own new version of modernity after the war, perhaps it and China still offered—not a comparative model for his future work—but rather a temporary respite of cultural difference before he reentered the now even more fraught world of Texas modernity to engage it on the terms he knew best from his prewar past.

Paredes has correctly insisted that *George Washington Gómez* is "*not my autobiography*" (Saldívar 2006: 120). Yet I also sense an over-insistence here, for indeed Paredes followed Guálinto to Dobie's University of Texas, although obviously with very different outcomes, even as he narratively left behind the wholly admirable Feliciano, a man really much more like the Paredes I came to know, even within an academic setting. Obviously Feliciano could never have lived in such a setting, but for Américo Paredes, such an academic existence offered the best compromise, as it did for Dobie, between the fundamental falsity of a new Texas modernity, as they saw it, and the past. The same university that Paredes held responsible for Guálinto's assimilation now provided a site from which he forged a brilliant career based on his ancestral culture. Good universities can do that, even though they too can be set upon by the more nefarious forces of modernity, as indeed is happening to higher education in Texas at this writing. In the so-called real world that is Texas public political culture today, there is something to be said for ivory towers.

For Paredes, nothing really was the same after 1915 and, after Asia, for his central work within an academic setting he again chose the past, before 1915, by returning to Gregorio Cortez in 1901, because "that was Gregorio Cortez, and that was the way men were in this country along the river. That was the way they were before these modern times came, and God went away." John Moran González has taken note of an interesting, seemingly minor character in *George Washington Gómez*, as noted in Chapter 1 in our discussion of Elodia, the fiery restaurant owner and activist married to another of George's old school chums. Her husband was the then young boy who had led the *corrido* singing after Guálinto and his group were refused admission to the graduation party at the restaurant in Harlanburg. While she ran the restaurant and did her electoral politics, González says, her husband was relegated to entertaining the customers singing "old *corridos*," a musical genre thus now "fallen from its heroic heights" (40). The husband's name was Antonio Prieto, initials: AP.

Within a modern world gone fundamentally corrupt, why become a public intellectual who must eventually always involve her- or himself in modernity? Occasionally we may have need of someone who will recover the past to show us the fundamental error of our modern and now postmodern ways.

Despedida

A corrido such as that of Gregorio Cortez often ends with a verse of farewell—in Spanish, a *despedida*—sometimes implied and sometimes with the literal word enunciated. I have not written a *corrido* here, but as I take leave with some closing thoughts, *despedida* is poetically better than "Conclusion" and consistent with the unfailingly courteous Américo Paredes and Greater Mexico. Indeed, I have not written a *corrido*, if by the latter we mean something like the heroic epic that so occupied Paredes and that he defined thematically as having "one theme, border conflict; toward one concept of the hero, the man fighting for his rights with his pistol in his hand" (1958: 149). I think that such has been the tendency in defining Paredes himself, a tendency, as Renato Rosaldo (1989:151) has said (perhaps overstated), to venerate rather than debate, most notably in the three extant intellectual biographies to date—in short, to think of him as a hero akin to those of the *corridos*. Indeed, I myself have suggested that there may be some truth to this, but only some (Limón 1992).

Jesse Alemán (1998) has argued that after Paredes, many of us who have written on the heroic *corrido* have tended to emphasize its heroic monological thematics and then extended such a thematics to contemporary Chicano literature. He proposes instead a diaglossic approach to both kinds of expression. I think him to be less right about the *corrido*, but certainly quite correct about contemporary Chicano literature. However, his proposal is useful for me in that I have tried to approach the work of Paredes with such a diaglossic perspective by noting the different voices and views that emerge from or can be brought to his texts—voices and views that he may not even have intended—rather than simply to see in it the monolithic work of the cultural hero in resistance, an evaluation that

I began in 1992. Ralph Rodríguez (2009) has also weighed in on the on-going discussion of Paredes's work; he asks if it is not time to move beyond monolithic heroic constructions of Mexican-American oppositional forms or figures such as Paredes toward a closer consideration of "the nuances, complexities, and subtleties of contemporary culture and life" (181).

To this end in the present work, I have offered treatments of different aspects of Paredes's work, but also that of his critics, beginning with his capacious and increasingly central writing, the novel *George Washington Gómez*. There I tried to correct what seems to me to be an overempha-sis on the figure of George in the novel. While understandable—he is, after all, the central character—such an emphasis has largely ignored his uncle, Feliciano, a "middle-class" representation of what, after Jonathan Lear (2008), I called "radical hope." Feliciano's formation in the first third of the twentieth century is consistent with what historian Robert D. John-ston (2003) has identified as that period's tradition of American "middle-class radicalism." In such a middle-class persona—more often than not disparaged by the novel's critics—I believe Paredes crafted a figure of deep Mexican values, familial responsibility, and entrepreneurship and a flex-ible, skeptical politics that for me represents the best model for Mexican-American social achievement. It is a model, I think, far more resonant with what most Mexican Americans and most Mexican immigrants believe and practice than the "critical" imaginings of elite academics, including my-self in prior moments. Whether he intended it or not, Paredes's Feliciano strikes me as the real future in the present.

The question of Paredes and Asia in Chapter 2 may loom largest for some, though not necessarily for me. Yet, clearly, when matters of massive, racist, and bloody imperialism are directly at issue, one's attention will focus. Here it would seem that Paredes thought such imperialism to be characteristic of the Allies, particularly the United States, against the Japa-nese in the Second World War, and it certainly also seems to be Ramón Saldívar's position as he interprets Paredes's Asia writings. Moreover, such imperialism, they argue, was akin to that which the United States had prac-ticed on Greater Mexico. I wholly reject that understanding of these trans-national relationships. In their conflicted relationship with the United States, the people of Greater Mexico were never guilty of first aggression as were the Japanese. But far more importantly, Japanese aggression of the most massively vicious sort was first initiated against China, particu-larly its women, an aggression and a people who are virtually ignored in the Paredes/Saldívar assessment of the war and their later enchantment with postwar Japan. Such planned, racist, sexist aggression in Asia was simply unmatched by the random atrocities committed by American soldiers in the U.S.-Mexican War, Allied troops in the war with Japan, and even unmatched by the planned Japanese atrocities against Allied prisoners, as pervasive and horrible as the latter were. This debate about Asia and Paredes also occasioned an exchange concerning pan-Asianism—or not—but the "not" seems to me so evident as to not say much more. This morning, before this writing, I read that India is buying sophisticated Russian weaponry in anticipation of Chinese military movement in the Indian Ocean.

Far more debatable is Saldívar's assessment concerning the influence of Asia on Paredes's postwar writings. He thinks it immense; I think it negligible, nearly absent, but surprisingly so. That is, one would think that Paredes would have said much more about Asia after 1950 given his journalistic six years there, but he simply does not. I may ultimately be wrong on this matter, and I am waiting to see evidence to the contrary—evidence of the sort one can clearly see in the writings of W. E. B. DuBois. My sense is that Paredes had said what he wanted to say about Asia in his journalism, and that's it. It largely came to a halt as other concerns took over. Once back in the United States, he needed to be far more focused on making his second marriage work, attending to a young son from his first marriage who was living in Corpus Christi, raising a new family, working for a living, and completing his education. The latter included a doctoral dissertation executed relatively quickly because he chose a prewar subject that he already knew very well, the balladry of Gregorio Cortez. He then very quickly turned it into the famous book, if only for tenure job security in the very department where he had received his PhD, and where not everyone had been receptive to his professorial hiring after only one year's absence. In this context, Asia became a memory, although never entirely forgotten, of course, as any veteran of the Second World War would likely say, although many might like to forget.

Having explored issues in a transnational framework myself, I am in great admiration of the idea when it can be demonstrated with specific data (Limón 1998). However, academic concepts and theories like the "transnational" or "border" can sometimes become so attractive and even seductive that they override all evidence to the contrary. In this case Saldívar's well-known affiliation to deconstructionist theory is married to a transnationalism now in vogue to produce the provocative, if wrong-headed, reading that "With His Pistol in His Hand" and the rest of Paredes's work has an Asian genesis and presumably an Asian form, theme, and structure. I beg to differ. In expeditiously professionalizing his career, given his obligations, Paredes took full advantage of what he already knew, as evidenced by his prewar scholarly publication on *corridos* and Gregorio Cortez, material he had already collected. Overlooked by Saldívar, that 1942 article is the evidentiary linchpin of my counterargument that, after Asia, for all manner of good reasons, Paredes returned socially, emotionally, and intellectually to Greater Mexico, principally Texas. He then stayed there, with little evidence of a continuing sustained interest in Asia, important as that work was—past tense—as Saldívar has indeed demonstrated. From that fertile Austin, South Texas ground, he critically engaged the world around the problems of modernity, race, and colonization, practicing an anticipatory version of what is now called "critical regionalism" (Limón 2008).

Border balladry such as that of Gregorio Cortez is about heroes typically in conflict with a racist and oppressive Anglo America, a theme that also appears in many of Paredes's other writing before and after Asia. But in Asia, or so I have argued, it is as if Paredes at least momentarily subverted this dominant concern to explore the internal workings of the Anglo subject to show, in the case of "The Gift," the possibility of a kind of stoic Anglo heroism—indeed, against Japanese oppression—even as the leading Mexican figure deserves only contempt. Only somewhat by contrast, in "When It Snowed in Kitibamba," Captain Meniscus cannot consciously recognize and bring to the fore his stigmatized Mexican identity, but even more so when it is compounded by his closeted homosexuality. The result is a kind of hero, but of the tragic variety.

As we have already noted more than once, heroism of the border balladry kind was Paredes's dominant thematic concern, but that did not mean that he lost sight of the need to professionally research and record not just the politically compelling thematics but also the formal poetics, the musicality, and the historical genealogy of such balladry. In the first part of Chapter 3, I charted his landmark professional emergence as a ballad scholar in relationship to the profession of world ballad scholarship and found the latter wanting before Paredes. On the other hand, I found his work on the joke form wanting, not in its fine field research, nor even in its analysis as far as he took it, but in his perhaps too disciplined refusal to historicize and thereby see the full social implications of his material, perhaps as he might not wish to have seen it. For compared to the heroic ballad, these are, after all, jokes. This joke form scholarship of the 1960s, we must never forget, was also at a time of continuing and now enhanced great familial and professional responsibilities, but also serious illness, so perhaps this is far as he could go. Yet his joke scholarship and his work on the ballad still mark him as a thoroughly accomplished figure whom I have no hesitation in naming the foremost folklorist of our time, and I have studied with the best. Meticulously and rigorously crafting a professional identity is also part of the war of position for those of us in difference to the dominant society, for only through such a politicized professionalization do we make our necessary mark on the academy, or any other profession or craft, for our own sake and that of our constituencies. Feliciano understood that, and so did and do many of our parents. The Mexican *gritos* at the Frank Erwin Center on graduation night at UT-Austin still reverberate in my mind.

Yet for all of his distinguished work on the folklore of Greater Mexico, in Chapter 4 I strongly argued that after an initial period of intense recognition, the later-emergent scholarly area of Chicano/Chicana cultural studies, chiefly sited in coastal California, chose to disavow the work of Paredes and continues to do so today. To some considerable degree, this disavowal has much to do with a confluence of factors, chief among them the continuing post-Birmingham dominance of mass media popular culture, perhaps stemming from California culture itself, but also the attenuation of folklore programs in that state. Unfortunately, the feminist attack led by Renato Rosaldo on Paredes and the image of the warrior hero no doubt also played a critical role in this disavowal.

However, in effect, we may now have two wings of Chicano/a cultural studies, the second one flowing out of Paredes's Texas, with representation in New Mexico as well. Such work is far more ethnographically grounded in the poetics of everyday life and adheres more closely to the critical traditions of Birmingham Marxism. For the moment I see minimal overlap between the two, although Texas has been far more receptive to the admission and training of graduate students from California who may return to that state to influence matters there, as indeed some already have, if higher education in California traverses its current severe economic crisis.

In Chapter 5 I suggested that the poetics of everyday Mexican-American life continue, and critically so, in the present moment, in part paradoxically influenced by Paredes's work. Such an influence continues in new joking forms, but most notably in the sung Tejano revival of the ballad of Gregorio Cortez. One suspects that Professor Paredes perhaps might not be entirely happy with people polka dancing to the tune, but perhaps a collective and participatory heroism is better suited for our time.

Finally, I have taken the measure of Paredes as what has been called a "public intellectual" and found him less than what one might have expected in comparison to some of his far more socially active contemporaries. There were probably very understandable and material reasons for this relative absence from the public life of Greater Mexico, most having to do with other pressing obligations. Yet I also suspect a deep-rooted antipathy toward modern life as a more fundamental motivation.

This study of Américo Paredes's work has thus tried to address specific and, I hope, novel issues within that corpus, issues both contained within the work and/or raised by other of its commentators. But I have also not wholly addressed other issues in Paredes—or not at all. For example, Ramón Saldívar and others have examined his prewar short fiction set in the Lower Rio Grande Valley and read it as a formal and ideological part of a whole with his total work, as part of an idiom of resistance. I quarrel with such an understanding, and these critical results might well have been placed here as part of the diaglossic contradictions that appear in Paredes's writings. However, I have reserved such a treatment for another place where it may be better understood in comparison and contrast to certain Anglo-American writers of Texas in a book in progress called *Neither Friends, Nor Strangers: Anglos and Mexicans in the Literary Making of Texas*. I also have said almost nothing about Paredes's postwar novel *The Shadow*, mostly because Juan Alonzo (2002) has said anything I could have said and said it better, although I think Saldívar misconstrues Alonzo's work in his own reading of the novel.

We remember and honor Américo Paredes for his creative writing and his scholarship, both of which substantially illuminate the world of Greater Mexico in a manner not known before his time and not superceded since. Yet as with any distinguished scholar and writer who has addressed complex human issues, this work must continually be evaluated and reviewed through distinct perspectives and expectations, and with sometimes very different interpretive outcomes. In the foregoing I have critically reviewed aspects of his fiction and scholarship with one such set of perspectives, expectations, and interpretations set in critical conjunction with those of others. One hopes there will be more. What is undoubtedly the case for the short and long term is that for anyone interested in an enhanced understanding of an amplified twentieth-century American fiction, folkloristics, and cultural studies, a meeting with Américo Paredes is mandatory. Though he is no longer with us, his work still speaks to us, and we will continue to listen carefully, if not always agree.

Notes

1. Although other such primary figures would include Julian Samora (sociology), Ernesto Galarza (public policy), George I. Sánchez (education), and the New Mexican/Coloradoan folklorists, Aurelio M. Espinosa, Juan B. Rael, and Arthur J. Campa.

2. María Herrera-Sobek (2000) offers a very useful article-length review of most of Paredes's work, although she necessarily could not devote extended attention to its individual aspects.

3. Appearing as it did in 1994, Bruce-Novoa's criticism could not have taken account of my own 1994 (76–94) critical commentary on Paredes.

4. See, for example, Alonzo 1998; DeLeon 1983, 1997; Montejano 1987; Tijerina 1994; and Zamora 1995, 2009.

5. Paredes also wrote a series of short stories with a south Texas setting during his earlier, prewar period in Brownsville. I treat these in a chapter of a book in progress, *Neither Friends, Nor Strangers: Mexicans and Anglos in the Literary Making of Texas.*

6. We must, however, also take account of a relatively new, recent resurgence of immigration from Mexico into the United States, substantially and largely since the 1970s, mostly in undocumented status and in unskilled occupations, producing two distinct groupings in the United States. As one later-generation Texas Mexican American, or Tejano, social commentator put it in less than generous terms:

> . . . the rift between the recently arrived Mexican immigrant and the old time *Tejano* community has widened and deepened. Aside from being Americans of Mexican descent, we have little in common. We speak, read and think in English while they do not. Other than the desire to fulfill the American dream we are far apart socially, politically and economically. . . . The majority of the new immigrants are the dishwashers, construction workers, gardeners, day laborers, etc. The *Tejanos* are the Senators, Congressmen, Doctors, Lawyers, Professors,

PhDs, Realtors and Authors that also participate in the political process. (Arellano 2007)

7. Following the general practice in the academy, Mexican-American studies consists of three broad disciplinary areas: the social sciences and education, historical studies, and cultural studies, the latter including literary criticism, anthropology, arts criticism, and folklore/popular culture analyses. Cultural studies and history often overlap, but rarely with the social sciences. See Soldatenko 2009.

8. It will not escape the discerning reader that I have switched ethnic nomenclature here, from "Mexican American" to "Chicano." In the 1960s we see the ideologically motivated self-conscious adoption of "Chicano" and later "Chicana" not only by members of the Chicano movement, but also by those—often the same—fomenting the establishment and development of academic programs focusing on the Mexican-origin peoples of the United States. Recognizing the prevalence of the term for naming these specific practices, especially in California, I now use it here and wherever appropriate for naming such practice. Elsewhere, I discuss the origins of the term *Chicano*, the ideological uses to which it was put, and the limitations and contradictions of those uses (Limón 1981).

CHAPTER 1

1. Here, of course, I allude to the foundational text for "resistance" readings, Barbara Harlow's *Resistance Literature* (1987).

2. Paredes greatly admired Emma Tenayuca and was clearly aware of her activities in San Antonio, Texas. He told me, and later Ramón Saldívar, that, in his words to Saldívar (2006: 91), "my own politics were really quite radical. I've often thought that if there had been a Communist Party cell in south Texas at the time, I would have joined it."

3. To be sure, some important Mexican-American Democratic Party elected officials into our own time did have an initial formation within the college-based Chicano movement, but not all, and those who did had to adjust their politics to the liberal "center." A case can also be made for a Mexican-American left-liberal political tradition *independent* of the Chicano movement and sometimes at odds with it, as exemplified by Congressmen Henry B. González and Edward R. Roybal of Texas and California, respectively.

4. Paredes is presented with a problem in his construction of Feliciano. On the one hand, he can make a stronger case for Feliciano's outstanding personality if he keeps him single and totally and unselfishly devoted to María and her children. On the other, he crafts him as such a good man—and an attractive one—that is hard to imagine that he would *not* be sought after as an eminently marriageable bachelor, one who "longed for a wife and family of his own" (263). Paredes, at that time a very young novelist, "solved" the problem by having the sometimes neurotic María insist that she

will not share a household with another woman, and threaten to move out with her children if Feliciano marries. While it is not stated, we are implicitly asked to recognize that he cannot support two households, so in his devotion to his family and Guálinto, he accedes to his sister's demands (263–264).

5. I was a student in such a school in the mid-1950s in Corpus Christi, Texas.

6. An 1864 Manet painting in the Chicago Art Institute depicts a small steamboat leaving the port of Boulogne. Centered in the painting, the small craft is moving from left to right at a shallow upward diagonal, as if chugging out of the picture, but doing so with an optimistic upwardness while leaving a clear wake through a host of seemingly more stationary sailing ships. Actually smaller than its pictorial companions, the little steamer's engine gives off a brownish smoke of sufficient thickness to block the sun's rays and cast a dark shadow on an otherwise lovely blue sea. Though the sailing vessels are themselves commercial craft, their very sails, their languidness in the blue sea, more than suggest a version of the seafaring pastoral to which we are all more than susceptible. Yet, to judge from the painting's title and the singular and centered steamboat, it is as if Manet was intent on subverting such pastoralism and, if not celebrating, at least insisting that we focus on the little steamer and its energetic presence and purpose. Though we might lend our invested pastoral sympathies and nostalgias to the sailing craft, Manet invites us into an admiration of the modern little steamer as well.

7. And we are reminded, for example, of the recent proliferation of internationally competitive chess clubs among Mexican-American youths in today's Lower Rio Grande Valley.

8. Here two caveats may be immediately noted and ultimately set aside. One of these is the legal and moral question of Feliciano's participation in the informal economy of smuggling. In the novel such smuggling principally involves transporting goods into Mexico while avoiding the enforced payment of bribes and duties that would go to an increasingly corrupt Mexican state after the failed revolution (79–81). And, as Paredes notes elsewhere, "smuggling and the trading of contraband of all sorts as a way of life already had a deep tradition in the borderlands, long before the American Civil War" (quoted in R. Saldívar [66]). It is certainly not to be equated with the hyperviolent drug smuggling of today. There is also Feliciano's occasional moderate to heavy drinking, occasioned chiefly by his gnawing concern that Guálinto is changing (and for the worse) before his very eyes. As González notes, he also drinks when one of Guálinto's unmarried sisters becomes pregnant by her Anglo lover, and the boy's father arranges another marriage for him. Feliciano realizes that he cannot redeem his family's honor "with his pistol in his hand," as he might have done in another time, "before the changed conditions of border modernity prevent[ed] . . . full masculinist expression" (34). Instead he becomes, in Paredes's words, "as pathetic as a drunken old man can look" (237). But what González might have added is that under the changed conditions he now lives in, Feliciano fully realizes that armed retribution will likely mean his own death, either at the hands of professional gunmen hired by the boy's father or by the state, and he is counseled to this effect by his attorney (239). With this realization, and

knowing he is the family's principal means of support, Feliciano puts the long-term interests of his family first. Surrounded by such crisis, the narrator tells us that "Feliciano had been drinking lately, something he had rarely done before" (269).

CHAPTER 2

1. He did return briefly to Brownsville in February 1948 because his mother was quite ill. His father had died while Paredes was in Asia. Paredes, Personal Correspondence, letter to his fiancée, February 20, 1948. Paredes Papers, Box 1, Folder 1.

2. For a summary account of Japanese settlement in Texas, see http://www.tshaonline.org/handbook/online/articles/JJ/pjj1.html.

3. Paredes, Red Cross Reports. Paredes Papers, Box 11, Folder 8.

4. Paredes, Red Cross Reports, February 2, 1947. Paredes Papers, Box 11, Folder 9.

5. Paredes, Personal Correspondence, March 3, 1947. Paredes Papers, Box 11, Folder 9.

6. Paredes, Red Cross Reports, April 1947. Paredes Papers, Box 11, Folder 8.

7. Paredes, Personal Correspondence, October 28, 1946. Paredes Papers, Box 11, Folder 3.

8. Paredes, Personal Correspondence, October 28, 1946. Paredes Papers, Box 11, Folder 3.

9. Paredes, Personal Correspondence, December 20, 1946. Paredes Papers, Box 11, Folder 3.

10. Paredes, Red Cross Reports, January 19, 1947. Paredes Papers, Box 11, Folder 8.

11. Paredes, Red Cross Reports, February (?), 1947. Paredes Papers, Box 11, Folder 8.

12. Paredes, Red Cross Reports, February 7, 1947. Paredes Papers, Box 11, Folder 8.

13. Paredes, Red Cross Reports, January (?), 1947. Paredes Papers, Box 11, Folder 8.

14. Paredes, Red Cross Reports, December (?), 1946. Paredes Papers, Box 11, Folder 8.

15. Paredes, Red Cross Reports, November 15, 1946. Paredes Papers, Box 11, Folder 8.

16. A bit later in the war, in 1942, the Japanese Imperial Second Army Division that had centrally participated in the Rape of Nanking was posted to Guadalcanal in the South Pacific. There they would find no innocent civilians . . . no Chinese women . . . just U.S. Marines, including many Mexican Americans from Greater Mexico.

17. See http://www.neta.com/%7E1stbooks/bataan1.htm.

18. See http://www.tshaonline.org/handbook/online/articles/JJ/pjj1.html. John M. González also reminds us that in 1935 a group of German Nazi naval officers visiting San Antonio extended a stiff-armed "Heil Hitler" salute to the memory of the dead Texans at the Alamo.

19. However, in his first usage in 1958, Paredes actually restricts the term *geo-*

graphically to refer only to "the area now comprising the Republic of Mexico with the exception of the border regions" (129–130). Only much later does he expand the term in the transnational sense taken up by Saldívar to now mean "all of the area inhabited by people of Mexican culture—not only within the present limits of the Republic of Mexico but in the United States as well—in a cultural rather than a political sense" (Paredes 1976: xiv). One suspects that this expanded 1976 definition had everything to do with the beginning of a new and ongoing growth in Mexican immigration to all parts of the United States in the early seventies, rather than, by then, some very distant Asian influence.

20. There is, by the way, a second, more extended, and more interesting instance (Paredes 1977).

21. The content of the 1969 publication is self-evident from the title; however, the one from 1963 is not. In it Paredes compares the North American cowboy to the Argentinian gaucho.

22. Paredes, Personal Correspondence, Letter to Amelia Paredes, September 16, 1967. Paredes Papers, Box 1, Folder 10.

23. In Paredes's novel *George Washington Gómez*, the central character—the fictional young Guálinto, or George—leaves Jonesville (Brownsville) on the lower border of Texas in the 1930s to attend and graduate from the University of Texas at Austin with the support of his middle-class uncle. With two years of junior college completed, even with the Depression, it is not at all difficult to imagine Américo Paredes directly following his fictional character to UT-Austin at some point, perhaps in the 1940s, had the war not made that move circuitous. He was gainfully employed after junior college, saving money would have been possible, and he surely had the support of his family. Such a move toward higher education, especially at UT-Austin, would not have been that unusual for a young Mexican American from the South Texas border even at that time, especially for those as ambitious, hard-working, and precocious as Paredes. Before Paredes, these include scholars, writers, and public intellectuals such as Manuel García, who was the first Mexican-American UT-Austin graduate (classics) in 1894, eleven years after the university's founding, but also J. T. Canales, Carlos Castañeda, Elena Zamora, Jovita Gonzalez, Hector P. García, Virgilio Roel, Ed Idar, two Gus Garcías, Rolando Hinojosa, and more recently, John M. González and Oscar Casares, as well as an entire family named Saldívar. Had he done so directly and not gone to Asia, I have no doubt whatsoever that Américo Paredes would have still become the scholar of Greater Mexico that we know today, whether at UT-Austin or elsewhere. And yet in a letter to his wife written while he was a visiting professor at UC-Berkeley, Paredes does express some doubt on this point in discussing his career trajectory, saying, "I don't think I would have got a PhD and have taught at UT if I had stayed in Brownsville during World War II. Academically there is a parallel between Brownsville and UT." It is not clear if he is saying that he would not have got a PhD at UT-Austin specifically or not at all. The odd and seemingly disparaging "parallel" that Paredes sees between UT-Austin and Brownsville seems to suggest that he thought he might have

done better academically than UT at that time, perhaps UC-Berkeley, from where he is writing. However, my gut feeling is that if he stayed in Brownsville, he would have eventually made his way to UT-Austin if only because of the strong interest in folklore in the English department. Paredes, Personal Correspondence, September 16, 1967. Paredes Papers, Box 1, Folder 10.

24. Finally, after talking to several of Paredes's colleagues and students during his postwar career, none of us can recall that he ever substantially referenced Asia in his conversations and rarely in his teaching. He and I talked a great deal about his Asian period, but I cannot recall a single instance where he connected it to his work on Mexican Americans or Latin America.

25. A stronger "transnational" argument might even be made for Paredes's South Texas, Mexican-American contemporary, the distinguished writer Rolando Hinojosa, whose fiction and poetry to this day explicitly and substantially address his combat experience in the Korean War and his time in Japan.

26. Following the *corrido* tradition, Anglos can also be cowardly. The one interesting exception is Judge Norris in GWG, although as a longtime resident of predominantly Mexican-American Jonesville, the judge is very "Mexicanized" and said to speak a "clear Spanish" (33).

27. In the early days of the war the Japanese sank the heavy cruiser USS *Houston* in the Java Sea, with many of its men taken prisoner and subjected to the most atrocious treatment. Commander Arthur L. Maher, "the *Houston*'s senior surviving officer, faced questioning from as many as a dozen Japanese at a time. 'They were anxious to find out almost anything they could regarding our Navy, the operations of the ships, the officers in command, the number of men on board, the modern installations, radar, and so forth'" (Hornfischer 2006: 245).

28. For a comprehensive and state-of-the-art study of this most famous of Greater Mexican folk legends, see Perez 2008.

29. I am very grateful to Professor Pamela Thoma of Washington State University for first calling my attention to the peach boy story at the 2008 annual meeting of the American Literature Association.

30. But Paredes also faced a problem in creating this character, which, as Sandra Soto (2010) shows us, he also faced in his short story "Over the Waves Is Out." The problem is how does he, in his historical moment, represent gayness, especially closeted gayness? In "Over the Waves Is Out," as Soto has noted, Paredes uses music as the subtle idiom of sexual difference. But in this story Paredes tries to do so by turning to signifiers that may be questioned as stereotypic, such as the contempt for women, the feminine handwriting, the slight and slender body type, and so on. And so we get to the killing secret in the 1940s through these now too stereotypical bodily signifiers in the hands of a still very young and heterosexual male writer from South Texas.

31. There were many Mexican-American and Latino officers in World War II. Probably the highest ranking of these, Lt. General Pedro Del Valle, a graduate of the Naval Academy, commanded the 1st Marine Division at the battle of Okinawa.

32. While in Asia, Paredes befriended several Anglo Americans in the military and elsewhere, something not easy for a Mexican American to do in South Texas, frankly even today. It is difficult to say, but perhaps these new, extended relationships encouraged these new explorations in his fictions.

CHAPTER 3

1. Underscoring my point about the pungency of these debates, Coffin (1964: 201) opened his talk with these words: "Even with the guns of John Greenway primed at my very flank . . ."

2. Taylor 1931: vii–viii.

3. I have asked Roger Abrahams about Paredes's involvement with this panel. Nearly half a century later, it is understandable that he cannot clearly recall what that involvement might have been. In the early 1990s, when I first started writing this chapter, I asked Paredes about this matter, and he simply replied, rather matter-of-factly, "I was not invited." Perhaps because I was a bit stunned by his answer, it did not occur to me to ask if he attended the meetings in general and this session in particular. However, a copy of the program is among his papers in the Mexican-American Library Project Archives at the Nettie Lee Benson Latin American Collection at UT-Austin. It is also worth noting that, like Paredes, most of the organizers and panelists were at the junior stage of their careers. It is also worth noting that Professor Paredes was in poor health and aging considerably when I asked him this question. It is possible that he was recollecting another incident involving the Texas Folklore Society, with which he had a tense relationship. However, in a footnote in his article, Richmond takes brief note of "*With His Pistol*" as one of two recent analyses in which ballads "have given impetus to literary or historical studies," the other being Christophersen's (1952).

4. Abrahams (1964b: 200) recognized this absence of music and added a fifth paper (Foss 1964) to the published version of the panel presentations.

5. Paredes was thoroughly familiar with these various theoretical perspectives and others. In a recent review of contemporary scholarship on the ballad, Roger de V. Renwick, a faculty member at UT-Austin since the mid-1970s, opens his review with the following observation:

In the mid-seventies a question that occasionally appeared on the PhD comprehensive examinations for folklore majors in my university's program asked the examinee to discuss how the work of six or seven folksong scholars—one list I remember began with Herder, ended with Albert B. Lord, and included Child, Gummere, and Alan Lomax—could stand as representative of folklore scholarship in general over the past two centuries or so. I admired the question enormously and wish I'd thought of it myself, even wished I'd had it on my own comps in 1972 as a doctoral student at Penn. (1992:74)

I myself had the privilege of responding to this question on my folklore PhD comps at Texas. I have verified that the daunting question that so impressed Renwick, and which I will never forget, was constructed and offered by Américo Paredes.

6. Other reviews (Simeone 1960; Ferris 1970) tend to focus on Part 1.

7. However, a decided exception to this disavowal is McDowell's (1981) close analysis of the full poetics of the ballad of Gregorio Cortez, which is to say, both Parts 1 and 2.

8. And, indeed, more mature Mexican-American studies scholarship on "With His Pistol" has continued to focus on Part 1 (Peña 1982; Rosaldo 1989; R. Saldívar 1990; Limón 1992; Flores 1992; Bruce-Novoa 1994; J. D. Saldívar 1997).

9. And yet, I would also argue that Chapter 2 of "With His Pistol" offers something like a performance analysis of *corrido* singing.

10. Within the then still professionalizing discipline of folklore, Texas was also closely identified with J. Frank Dobie, the Texas Folklore Society, and the amateur, free-form literary treatments of folklore noted above.

11. Recurrent serious illness during the last third of Paredes's life did not help. Together with his wife, Amelia, he also had to care for a daughter born with severe birth defects.

12. Bronner's footnote is only in reference to Paredes's coediting of and preface for *Toward New Perspectives in Folklore* (1972), a task that fell to him because he was the editor of the *Journal of American Folklore*, where this volume first appeared as a special issue. Zumwalt (1969) has one reference in her bibliography to Paredes.

13. The reference is to Jacobs 1959: 124.

14. The collection *Folklore and Culture on the Texas-Mexican Border* (1993), put together by Paredes's colleagues, represents a late effort to produce just such a book although its focus on the Lower Border and its inclusion of *corrido* material worked to the exclusion of other of his essays noted here.

15. The third category seems to refer to those new legalized Mexican immigrants that came to the United States with the agricultural *bracero* program and then stayed on with their families. In 1966 Paredes could obviously not foresee the massive new waves of Mexican immigrants that would begin entering the country after 1970 to the present day, complicating his tripart division.

16. As Oring (1992: 17–19) notes, folklorist Roger D. Abrahams was also associated with jokes as forms of Freudian aggression by way of his work on "elephant" jokes told by whites ostensibly about African-Americans. However, Abrahams initiated his career with a Freudian-keyed analysis of joking material collected from African Americans (1964a). In 1963 he joined the nascent folklore program at UT-Austin and became a close colleague of Paredes. It remains unclear what flows of influence there may have been, if any.

17. For utmost effect, her punch line should always be uttered in a heavily English-accented Spanish.

18. I do not know why eggs prepared in this manner came to be associated with ranching. The word *huevos* is so laden with testicular significance as to almost over-

power its literal meaning; thus, in polite Mexican-American company (meaning females present) the word *blanquillo* (small white thing) is often used instead. Historically there are two broad kinds of Mexican restaurants, those that serve a kind of cuisine sometimes called "Tex-Mex" and cater largely to an Anglo public, and smaller "Mom and Pop" neighborhood places (such as Joe's Bakery in Austin, Texas) that serve a very different kind of Mexican-American "home cooking." However, a third and fourth kind have also recently emerged: the restaurant specializing in Mexican *haute cuisine* ostensibly from the "interior" of Mexico and not the border, and *taquerías* that cater largely to new Mexican immigrants, although the latter have been well-known in Los Angeles for some time.

19. Although one must allow for some cultural overlap among these various groups relative to factors such as time and place of immigrant arrival and intermarriage, as with my own parents, he a post-Revolution Mexican immigrant, she a descendant of one of the old Spanish-Mexican families. They met in Laredo, Texas, a very different place to meet and live than, let us say, Houston.

20. López-Morín has commented very briefly on these jokes, largely repeating what Paredes (2006: 105–106) himself said about them.

21. See also Limón 1983b. In a footnote, Saldívar (2007: 444) also aligns Paredes with the Italian Marxist folklorist Luigi Lombardi-Satriani. This is, in fact, a more acceptable pairing, but it fails to note that Lombardi-Satriani (1974: 104–105) was trying to correct the "problematic questions" evoked by Gramsci's observation on folklore. I introduced Lombardi-Satriani's work to Paredes in the mid-seventies and used it in an early publication (1977).

CHAPTER 4

1. Such work has been reviewed in recent retrospectives even as they also discuss contemporary cultural anthropological practice which shares much with contemporary work in folklore (Ortner 2006; Rabinow and Marcus 2008; Westbrook 2008; Faubion and Marcus 2009).

2. It is telling that as an epigraph for this chapter Hoggart uses a line from T. S. Eliot's *The Wasteland* and its sense of religious loss: "What are the roots that clutch . . . ?"

3. Probably the best-known among these are Hall and Jefferson 1976; Willis 1977; Hebdige 1979; Hall et al. 1980.

4. Both in its theoretical framework and in its data field, the harlequin romance, Janice Radway's *Reading the Romance: Women, Patriarchy and Popular Literature* (1984) is one decisive marker of the appearance of cultural studies in the United States. Radway has gone on to become a major figure in American cultural studies.

5. Let us also recall Paredes's youthful interest in joining the Communist Party (Saldívar 2007: 91).

6. I say "a kind of organic intellectual" because, for reasons that will be more

fully explored in Chapter 6, Paredes and his work could not fully be described in these terms: "The organic intellectuals of the working class are defined on the one hand by their role in production and in the organization of work and on the other by their directive political role . . ." (Hoare and Smith 1971: 4).

7. See Gómez-Quiñones 1978; Muñoz 1989; and García 1997. Yet, more such serious work remains to be done on the complexities of the Chicano movement, which in contemporary Chicano/a scholarship is too often reduced to a facile repeatable phrase, "Chicano male nationalism," and thus made a straw*man* and an easy point of departure for such scholarship.

8. Why Texas chose "Mexican-American" for most of its major centers versus "Chicano/Chicana" is an interesting issue worthy of serious comparative analysis.

9. For the record, it is also worth noting that Soldatenko is also mistaken about Julian Samora who, at the University of Notre Dame in the late sixties and seventies, attracted and trained several young, militant, and critical sociologists including Gilberto Cárdenas, Miguel Carranza, Alberto Mata, and Jorge Bustamante.

10. At the time, as his research and administrative assistant, I accompanied Paredes on some of these visits. However, Soldatenko is right in that the ever culturally conservative Paredes did draw an unfortunate impression of California Chicano activists as urbanized, highly acculturated, ghetto-type ultra-nationalists (Paredes 1976: 118).

11. The famous 1990 University of Illinois cultural studies conference was one likely relay point between Birmingham and Chicano/Chicana cultural studies.

12. Los Illegals are a Chicano punk rock band in Los Angeles. Los Tigres are arguably the best-known conjunto-style group in Greater Mexico.

13. *Tacquachito* is a dipping, shuffling polka dance style supposedly in imitation of the movement of a *tacquache* (possum). Why Saldívar thinks it to be "hard" mystifies me. Sometimes considered sexually suggestive, it is sometimes associated with the Mexican-American "lower" class. I also wonder how Saldívar hears the accordion as "shrieking" when, for a polka, it is typically played with a very staccato, yet flowing tempo and tone. I am reminded of Saldívar and the famous polka dance scene in *George Washington Gómez* discussed in Chapter 1, where the culturally conflicted Guálinto/George also hears the accordion tone as "shrieking" (Paredes 1990: 242). But in San Francisco, at the Fillmore, with artists and intellectuals, I suppose anything is possible.

14. In this earlier critique Rosaldo (1989: 150–155) argues that Ernesto Galarza and Sandra Cisneros are much more progressive than Paredes in these gender terms. In his commentary in this forum, Rosaldo claims that Paredes stopped talking to him as a result (19). However, Paredes did have a kind of last word. In one of his conversations with Ramón Saldívar, he says Rosaldo "was way off the mark" because the latter did not appreciate that Galarza was writing autobiography and Cisneros fiction, while Paredes was writing a critical historical ethnography in the 1950s, and it was important to lend emphasis to such heroic patriarchy and communalism when Mexicans were

thought to be cowardly, treacherous, and dysfunctional. Obviously, said a clearly exasperated Paredes, there could also be dissension and low, unheroic behavior in such a society. He simply chose not to emphasize it (Saldívar 2006: 69–71).

15. Yet one must note some exceptions, though they tend to be *historical* cultural studies, such as Anthony Macías's (2008) on Mexican-American popular music and dance in Los Angeles, and Catherine Ramirez's (2009) on pachuca culture in California, both archivally well grounded. Much more contemporaneous is Curtiz Marez's (1996) effort to articulate a working-class "Chicano" style. To the degree that he bases his effort on the late Freddy Fender, a popular Texas-Mexican singer, he is closer to my argument, although he too tends to veer in the direction of a coastal, youth-centered California with figures like El Vez and toward a definition of such practices, such as "Chicano aesthetic objects," as "elaborate, extravagant, excessive" (122). Raul Homero Villa's (2000) work on the culture of East Los Angeles and San Jose, California, makes extensive use of sociology and cultural geography although it too lends great emphasis to literature and the plastic arts rather than the poetics of everyday life. However, a volume on Latino Los Angeles that Villa coedited offers some important, if all too brief, contributions to such a poetics, particularly the essays by Camilo José Vergara on *paleteros*; James Rojas on the use of space; and Margaret Crawford's "Mi Casa es su Casa" (LeClerc, Villa, and Dear 1999). Debra Blake (2008) also focuses on written literature and the plastic arts as her primary expressive materials, but, as if responding to Renato Rosaldo, she collects oral data from ordinary women with respect to these expressive productions. Ramón Saldívar has also offered some brief commentary on contemporary *corridos* by Los Tigres del Norte in relation to the poetry of Américo Paredes (1999). Much better yet on Los Tigres is Juan Gómez-Quiñones's (2000) well-grounded and more critical essay. Finally, the collection of largely ethnographic essays in *Latino Cultural Citizenship* offers grounded social analyses of several Latino communities, including San Jose and East Los Angeles in California. While by and large they do not focus on expressive culture, they do offer ethnographic entry points and a conceptual framework—cultural citizenship—for delving into the everyday poetics of these communities. Sadly, this important work is also almost wholly ignored in the Chabram-Dernersesian volumes (Flores and Benamayor 1997).

16. For the younger Chicano/a studies, the turning away from these methods may also have been reinforced by Rosaldo's own later critique of anthropology and his turn to literary criticism and the writing of poetry (1989: 25–45). Yet Rosaldo certainly was not advocating the total abandonment of fieldwork and ethnographic methods, only a much more self-conscious awareness of the ethnographer's subjectivity in the field and of the language employed in such work (1989: 46–67).

17. It may be of some relevance to note that Peña was born and partially raised in South Texas and that he came back to UT-Austin from rural central California. For her part, though a UC-Santa Cruz undergraduate, Nájera-Ramirez also has small-town, rural California origins. For the record, we should also note that three other California

Chicanas did come to study with Paredes; only one, Alicia González, completed the PhD, though not under his direction, and she embarked on a career largely in public sector folklore in Washington, DC.

18. Though most of his work is centered on Texas, Reyna's career continues at CSU-Bakersfield. He appears nowhere in Chicano cultural studies and is one illustrative case of a general exclusion of scholars at working-class institutions in California.

19. A now third generation of young, anthropologically oriented UT-Austin Chicano/a cultural studies scholars is also emerging, including Jennifer Nájera, Brenda Sendejo, Pablo González, Maria Cruz, Amanda Morrison, Virginia Raymond, Alex Chávez, Santiago Guerra, and Ana Nogar.

20. However, as a study of *corrido* narrativity, *"With His Pistol in His Hand"* did influence Chicano/a literary criticism (Saldívar 1990; Limón 1992; McKenna 1997; Alemán 1998).

CHAPTER 5

1. As I write in Long Beach, the Los Angeles City Council, with minimal community participation, is trying to severely restrict taco trucks in the city, depriving mostly Mexican immigrants and other working-class folk and students of inexpensive food and sites of such conversation. See http://www.npr.org/templates/story/story .php?storyId=90149577.

2. Here Reyna is using the term "Chicanos" to refer to all Mexican Americans, not to a particular and militant political tradition.

3. This city on the Gulf of Mexico had its beginnings in 1839 when an Anglo American named Henry Lawrence Kinney established a trading post doing business with the Mexican community to the south. As noted earlier the area also served as a launching point for the U.S.-Mexico War of 1846. Later, the growing city would take the Latin name "Corpus Christi" (Body of Christ), given to the nearby bay by Spanish explorers in 1519, the bay that would later make it a major port, especially for the surrounding oil industry. Thus its "Anglo" origins, its role in the war against Mexico, and its skilled-labor petrochemical industry produced a more lasting Anglo-dominant social structure than has been true for other parts of South Texas. As Zamora (2009) has shown, Mexican-American access to skilled employment in this industry was racially restricted throughout much of the twentieth century.

4. As José R. Reyna (1980: 32–34) reminds us, there is also a tradition of Mexican-American jokes about African Americans that are at best ambivalent.

5. The Dallas Cowboys seem to be particular favorites with Mexican Americans *across regions*. According to the *Los Angeles Times*, in terms of a television audience, the January 3, 2009, regular-season finale between the Dallas Cowboys and Philadelphia Eagles drew a Latino audience of 2.3 million, "the largest ever for a regular-season game" (http://www.latimes.com/sports/la-sp-nfl-mexico-facts29-2010jan29,0,2427221 .story). One suspects that they were not rooting for faraway Philadelphia. If and why

this Cowboys fandom among Latinos is the case might bear investigation, but one might begin by recalling that in the 1970s, the Cowboys may have had the first NFL Mexican-American player in the person of placekicker Efren Herrera after his great career at UCLA. And, of course, the first "cowboys," or *vaqueros*, were Mexicans in Texas!

6. http://www.latimes.com/sports/la-sp-nfl-mexico-facts29-2010jan29,0,2427221 .story.

7. http://www.latimes.com/news/opinion/web/la-oewcontreras8nov08,0,2142352 .story.

8. For the most detailed and analytical account of González's biography, see Cotera 2008: 103–144, 199–224.

9. Vigil 1985: 26, as quoted in Alonzo. Most of the poem is in Spanish. The English translations are Alonzo's.

10. However, in 2005, the well-known conjunto group Los Alegres de Teran also released a recording of the ballad. I do not include it in this discussion because it is a very short version of Variant A (see later discussion) and sung in the traditional *lento* tempo.

11. El Corrido de Gregorio Cortez

Voy a cantarles la historia
Donde Gregorio Cortez,
En mil novecientos uno
Mató un sheriff de ley.
En una investigación,
Por el robo de un caballo,
Mató al sheriff mayor,
Por defender a su hermano.
El sheriff tiró primero,
Valido de la ocasión.
Dejando a Romaldo herido,
Sin niguna compassión.
Gregorio al ver a su hermano
Que por el suelo caía
Desenfundo su pistola
Dejando al sheriff sin vida.
Romaldo, muy mal herido,
Lo llevaron a prisión,
En la carcel de Karnes City
De las heridas murió.
Lo seguían con perros jaunes,
Para poderlo aprender.
Y ofrecieron recompensa,
Aquel que diera con él.

Lo citiaron en Ottine,
El la casa de Martín,
Para poderse escapar,
Ahi mató a otro sheriff.
Por ese Río Guadalupe,
Siguió rumbo a la frontera.
Llegó cansado a Cotulla
Y no faltó quien lo viera.
Por ganar la recompensa,
Mil dolares que ofrecían,
Jesus Gonzalez, "El Teco,"
Lo entregó a la policía.
Lo llevan a San Antonio,
Por vida le dan prisión.
Revocaron la sentencia,
Y a los ocho años salió.
Aquí se acaba el corrido,
De este hombre que les conté.
Decidido y muy valiente,
Era Gregorio Cortez.

12. Los Hermanos Cortez

En mil novecientos uno
A caballo lo buscaban.
El sheriff muy seguro,
A Cortez le preguntaba,
Como no hablaba el inglés,
Otro hombre interpretaba.
Su contestacíon fue buena,
La que Rumaldo les dió.
La tragedia fue la yegua,
La que Rumaldo cambió,
Por su caballo de rienda,
Conocido en la región.
El sheriff al instante,
Comenzaba a disparar.
Gregorio, por mala suerte,
Vió a su hermano agonizer.
Y al sheriff le dió muerte,
En defense personal.
Para a prender a Cortez,

Mil dolares ofrecieron.
Los rinches con perros jaunes,
Desde Laredo vinieron,
Hasta el pueblo de González,
Y matarlo no pudieron.
En la presa del Rendado,
Lo querían matar de sed.
Los rinches se descuidaron,
Con aquel gato Montez,
Fue al agua con el gando,
Y hasta les tomó el café.
Cincuenta años sin clemencia,
Lo mandarin al penal.
Con valor y inteligencia,
Lo nombraron capataz.
Doce años tuvo sentencia,
Y le dieron libertad.

13. Sommer is quoting from page 605 of a manuscript on the life of the famous Texas-Mexican singer Lydia Mendoza, coedited by Nicolopulos and later published (Mendoza 1993).

CHAPTER 6

1. I am very grateful to John Moran González for reminding me of this scene.

2. In 1969 Paredes did travel to Spain to attend a meeting of the International Congress of Americanists (personal recollection).

3. Given my concerns in Chapter 2, it is of more than passing interest for me that Chávez, a New Mexican, took part in the American beachhead landings in the Philippines in 1944, the site of the Bataan Death March in 1941–1942.

4. In a 1975 letter to a colleague, Paredes wrote, "Thanks for the news about Jovita González. I have been meaning to get in touch with her for years but never seem to have the opportunity. Neither she nor I attend the meetings of the Texas Folklore Society anymore." Américo Paredes, Personal Correspondence, October 13, 1975. Paredes Papers, Box 16, Folder 7.

5. We should also note that Paredes's most famous poem, the critical "The Mexico-Texan," appeared anonymously in the LULAC newsletter after circulating in "the vernacular political discourse of south Texas" (Saldívar 2006: 457 n. 10). It is telling that the so-called "assimilationist" LULAC had no problems publishing this biting poem.

6. It is to be noted that Perales was indeed a lawyer and did return to South Texas

after a stint in the Civil Service in Washington, DC, so one can only hope that Paredes did not have Perales in mind as he imagined George's parallel career in *George Washington Gómez*, for it would be a terribly wrong comparison.

7. In his recent *State of Minds: Texas Culture and Its Discontents* (2011), Don Graham offers an assessment of Dobie's influence on the curriculum in the English department at UT-Austin at that time.

8. It is unclear whether Paredes visited with Dobie as a student from 1950 to 1956 or later as faculty member between 1957 and 1964, or both.

9. Paredes, Personal Correspondence, Letter to Ronnie Dugger, February 11, 1964. Paredes Papers, Box 74, Folder 2.

10. Paredes, Personal Correspondence, Letter from Ronnie Dugger, February 12, 1964. Paredes Papers, Box 74, Folder 2.

11. Paredes, Personal Correspondence, Letter to Ronnie Dugger, February 11, 1964. Paredes Papers, Box 74, Folder 2.

12. Paredes, Personal Correspondence, Letter to Austin Fife, September 21, 1964. Paredes Papers, Box 74, Folder 2.

13. See, for example, Madrid-Barela 1973 and the paintings of César A. Martínez (Quirarte and Rote 1999).

14. Paredes (1978b) would later write of his displeasure with Paz that particular evening.

15. See especially Saldívar 2006: 52–53.

Bibliography

Abrahams, Roger D. 1964a. *Deep Down in the Jungle: Negro Narrative Folklore from the Streets of Philadelphia*. Hatboro, PA: Folklore Associates.

———. 1964b. "Introductory Remarks." In "Folksong and Folksong Scholarship: Changing Approaches and Attitudes." *A Good Tale and a Bonnie Tune*, edited by Mody C. Boatright, Wilson M. Hudson, and Allen Maxwell, 199–201. Dallas: Southern Methodist University Press.

———. 1981. "Shouting Match at the Border: The Folklore of Display Events." In *"And Other Neighborly Names": Social Process and Cultural Image in Texas Folklore*, edited by Richard Bauman and Roger D. Abrahams, 303–321. Austin: University of Texas Press.

———. 2005. *Everyday Life: A Poetics of Vernacular Practices*. Philadelphia: University of Pennsylvania Press.

Los Alegres de Teran. 2005. "El Corrido de Gregorio Cortez." *Corridos Famosos*. Mexico City: EMI Music.

Aleman, Jesse. 1998. "Chicano Novelistic Discourse: Dialogizing the Corrido Critical Paradigm." *MELUS* 23: 49–65.

Alonzo, Armando. 1998. *Rancheros and Settlers in South Texas, 1734–1900*. Albuquerque: University of New Mexico Press.

Alonzo, Juan J. 2002. "Américo Paredes' *The Shadow*: Social and Subjective Transformation in Greater Mexico." *Aztlán* 27: 27–57.

———. 2009. *Badmen, Bandits and Folk Heroes: The Ambivalence of Mexican American Identity in Literature and Film*. Tucson: University of Arizona Press.

Antoni, Klaus. 1991. "Momotaro (The Peach Boy) and the Spirit of Japan: Concerning the Function of a Fairy Tale in Japanese Nationalism of the Early Showa Age." *Asian Folklore Studies* 50: 155–188.

Asad, Talal, ed. 1973. *Anthropology and the Colonial Encounter*. London: Ithaca Press.

Bauman, Richard, and Américo Paredes, eds. 1972. *Toward New Perspectives in Folklore*. Austin: University of Texas Press.

Bauman, Richard, and Roger D. Abrahams, eds. 1981. *"And Other Neighborly Names"*:

Social Process and Cultural Image in Texas Folklore. Austin: University of Texas Press.

Beevor, Antony. 2001. *The Battle for Spain: The Spanish Civil War, 1936–1939.* New York: Penguin Books.

Bell, Julian. 2008. "Back to Basics." *New York Review of Books* 55: 16.

Bell, Michael J. 1983. *The World from Brown's Lounge: An Ethnography of Black Middle-Class Play.* Urbana: University of Illinois Press.

Bendix, Regina. 1997. *In Search of Authenticity: The Formation of Folklore Studies.* Madison: University of Wisconsin Press.

Bermudez, Esmeralda. 2010. "Quite a Gig for Day Laborers." *Los Angeles Times,* January 10, 2010, A31–A35.

Blake, Debra J. 2008. *Chicana Sexuality and Gender: Cultural Refiguring in Literature, History, and Art.* Durham, NC: Duke University Press.

Blanton, Carlos. 2006. "George I. Sánchez, Ideology, and Whiteness in the Making of the Mexican American Civil Rights Movement, 1930–1960." *Journal of Southern History* 72: 569–604.

Bleys, Rudi C. 1996. *The Geography of Perversion: Male-to-Male Sexual Behaviour Outside the West and the Ethnographic Imagination, 1750–1918.* London: Cassell.

Bronner, Simon J. 1986. *American Folklore Studies: An Intellectual History.* Lawrence: University Press of Kansas.

Bruce-Novoa, Juan. 1994. "Dialogical Struggles, Monological Goals: Chicano Literature." In *An Other Tongue: Nation and Ethnicity in the Linguistic Borderlands,* edited by Alfred Arteaga, 225–245. Durham, NC: Duke University Press.

Calderón, Hector, and José Rosbel López-Morín. 2000. "Interview with Américo Paredes." *Nepantla* 1: 197–228.

Cantú, Norma, and Olga Nájera-Ramirez, eds. 2002. *Chicana Traditions: Continuity and Change.* Urbana: University of Illinois Press.

Caryl, Christian. 2008. "An Asian Star Is Born." *New York Review of Books* (LV: 20), December 18, 2008, 56–58.

Chabram-Dernersesian, Angie, ed. 2006. *The Chicana/o Cultural Studies Reader.* New York: Routledge.

———. 2007. *The Chicana/o Cultural Studies Forum: Critical and Ethnographic Perspectives.* New York: New York University Press.

Chang, Iris. 1997. *The Rape of Nanking: The Forgotten Holocaust of World War II.* New York: Basic Books.

Chappell, Ben. 2002. "Mexican American Lowriders: Postmodernism as Popular Practice." In *Postmodern Practices: Beiträge zu einer Vergehenden Epoche,* edited by Thomas Doerfler and Claudia Globisch, 229–245. Hamburg, Germany: LIT.

———. 2006. "Lowrider Cruising Spaces." In *Mobile Crossings: Representations of Chicana/o Cultures,* edited by Anja Bandau and Marc Priewe, 51–62. Trier, Germany: Wissenschaftlicher Verlag Trier.

———. 2008. "Lowrider Style: Cultural Poetics and the Politics of Scale." In *Cultural Studies: An Anthology,* edited by Michael Ryan, 634–645. Malden, MA: Blackwell.

Chávez, Alex. 2010. *Compañeros del Destino: Transborder Social Lives and Huapango Arribeño at the Interstices of Postmodernity.* PhD dissertation, University of Texas at Austin.

Cheng, Anne Anlin. 2001. *The Melancholy of Race: Psychoanalysis, Assimilation, and Hidden Grief.* New York: Oxford University Press.

Christophersen, Paul. 1952. *The Ballad of Sir Aldingar.* Oxford: Clarendon Press.

Coffin, Tristram. 1959. "Review of 'With His Pistol in His Hand': A Border Ballad and Its Hero, by Américo Paredes." *Midwest Folklore* 1: 244–245.

———. 1964. "Folksong and Folksong Scholarship: Changing Approaches and Attitudes." In *A Good Tale and a Bonnie Tune,* edited by Mody C. Boatright, Wilson M. Hudson, and Allen Maxwell, 201–209. Dallas: Southern Methodist University Press.

Cotera, María Eugenia. 2008. *Native Speakers: Ella Deloria, Zora Neale Hurston, Jovita González, and the Poetics of Culture.* Austin: University of Texas Press.

Davis, Steven L. 2009. *J. Frank Dobie: A Liberated Mind.* Austin: University of Texas Press.

de Certeau, Michel. 1984. *The Practice of Everyday Life.* Berkeley and Los Angeles: University of California Press.

Delpar, Helen. 1992. *The Enormous Vogue of Things Mexican: Cultural Relations Between the United States and Mexico, 1920–1935.* Tuscaloosa: University of Alabama Press.

De Leon, Arnoldo. 1983. *They Called Them Greasers: Anglo Attitudes Toward Mexicans in Texas, 1821–1900.* Austin: University of Texas Press, 1983.

———. 1997. *The Tejano Community, 1836–1900.* Dallas: Southern Methodist University Press.

Dobie, J. Frank. 1961. *The Voice of the Coyote.* Lincoln: University of Nebraska Press.

———. 1964. *Cow People.* Boston: Little, Brown.

Dorson, Richard M. 1967. "The Shaping of Folklore Traditions in the United States." *Folklore* 78: 161–183.

———. 1971. *American Folklore and the Historian.* Chicago: University of Chicago Press.

Douglas, Mary. 1968. "The Social Control of Cognition: Some Factors in Joke Perception." *Man* 3: 361–376.

Dower, John W. 1986. *War without Mercy: Race and Power in the Pacific War.* New York: Random House.

———. 1999. *Embracing Defeat: Japan in the Wake of World War II.* New York: W. W. Norton.

Dundes, Alan. 1969. "The Devolutionary Premise in Folklore Theory." *Journal of the Folklore Institute* 6: 5–19.

During, Simon, ed. 1993. "Introduction." In *The Cultural Studies Reader,* edited by Simon During, 1–25. New York: Routledge.

Easthope, Anthony. 1991. *Literary into Cultural Studies.* New York: Routledge.

Eliot, T. S. 1920. "Tradition and the Individual Talent." In *The Sacred Wood: Essays on Poetry and Criticism*, 16–35. London: Methuen.

Faubion, James D., and George E. Marcus, eds. 2009. *Fieldwork Is Not What It Used to Be: Learning Anthropology's Method in A Time of Transition*. Ithaca, NY: Cornell University Press.

Ferris, William R., Jr. 1970. "Review of *"With His Pistol in His Hand"*: A Border Ballad and Its Hero, by Américo Paredes." *Mississippi Folklore Register* 4: 37–38.

Fife, Austin E. 1960. "Review of *"With His Pistol in His Hand"*: A Border Ballad and Its Hero, by Américo Paredes." *Journal of American Folklore* 73: 78–79.

Fine, Elizabeth C. 1984. *The Folklore Text: From Performance to Print*. Bloomington: Indiana University Press.

Fiske, John. 1992. "Cultural Studies and the Culture of Everyday Life." In *Cultural Studies*, edited by Lawrence Grossberg, Cary Nelson, and Paula Treichler, 154–173. New York: Routledge.

Flores, Richard R. 1994. "The *Corrido* and the Emergence of Texas-Mexican Social Identity." *Journal of American Folklore* 105: 166–182.

———. 1995. *Los Pastores: History and Performance in the Mexican Shepherd's Play of South Texas*. Washington, DC: Smithsonian Institution Press.

———. 2002. *Remembering the Alamo: Memory, Modernity, and the Master Symbol*. Austin: University of Texas Press.

Flores, William V., and Rina Benamayor, eds. 1997. *Latino Cultural Citizenship: Claiming Identity, Space and Rights*. Boston: Beacon Press.

Foss, George. 1964. "The Transcription and Analysis of Folk Music." In *A Good Tale and a Bonnie Tune*, edited by Mody C. Boatright, Wilson M. Hudson, and Allen Maxwell, 237–269. Dallas: Southern Methodist University Press.

Fregoso, Rosa Linda. 2003. *meXicana Encounters: The Making of Social Identities on the Borderlands*. Berkeley and Los Angeles: University of California Press.

Freud, Sigmund. [1905] 1960. *Jokes and Their Relation to the Unconscious*. Edited and translated by James Strachey. New York: W. W. Norton.

García, Ignacio M. 1997. *Chicanismo: The Forging of a Militant Ethos Among Mexican-Americans*. Tucson: University of Arizona Press.

———. 2000. *Viva Kennedy: Mexican-Americans in Search of Camelot*. College Station: Texas A&M University Press.

———. 2002. *Hector P. Garcia: In Relentless Pursuit of Justice*. Houston: Arte Público.

García, Richard. 1991. *The Rise of the Mexican-American Middle Class, San Antonio, 1929–1941*. College Station: Texas A&M University Press, 1991.

Garza-Falcón, Leticia. 1998. *Gente Decente: A Borderlands Response to the Rhetoric of Dominance*. Austin: University of Texas Press.

Geertz, Clifford. 1977. *The Interpretation of Cultures*. New York: Basic Books.

Gencarella, Stephen Olbrys. 2009. "Constituting Folklore: A Case for Critical Folklore Studies." *Journal of American Folklore* 122: 172–196.

Gómez-Quiñones, Juan. 1977. "On Culture." *Revista Chicano- Riqueña* 5: 290–308.

———. 1978. *Mexican Students por La Raza: The Chicano Student Movement in Southern California, 1967–1977*. Santa Barbara: Editorial La Causa.

———. 2000. "Outside Inside—The Immigrant Workers: Creating Popular Myths, Cultural Expressions, and Personal Politics in Borderlands Southern California." In *Chicano Renaissance: Contemporary Cultural Trends*, edited by David R. Maciel, Isidro D. Ortiz, and María Herrera-Sobek. Tucson: University of Arizona Press.

González, John Moran. 2009. *Renaissance in the Borderlands: The Texas Centennial and the Emergence of Mexican-American Literature*. Austin: University of Texas Press.

González, Jovita, and Eve Raleigh. 1997. *Caballero: A Historical Romance*. Edited by José E. Limón and María E. Cotera. College Station: Texas A&M University Press.

Goodwin, Andrew. 1992. "Introduction to the Transaction Edition: The Uses and Abuses of In-Discipline." In *The Uses of Literacy*, by Richard Hoggart. New Brunswick, NJ: Transaction.

Graham, Don. 2011. *State of Minds: Texas Culture and Its Discontents*. Austin: University of Texas Press.

Gramsci, Antonio. 1985. *Selections from the Cultural Writings*. Trans. William Boelhower. Cambridge, MA: Harvard University Press.

Greenway, John. "Folksong as an Anthropological Province: The Anthropological Approach." In *A Good Tale and a Bonnie Tune*, edited by Mody C. Boatright, Wilson M. Hudson, and Allen Maxwell, 209–217. Dallas: Southern Methodist University Press.

Gutiérrez, David. 1995. *Walls and Mirrors: Mexican-Americans, Mexican Immigrants and the Politics of Ethnicity*. Berkeley and Los Angles: University of California Press.

Hall, Stuart, Dorothy Hobson, Andrew Lowe, and Paul Willis, eds. 1980. *Culture, Media and Language*. Birmingham: Centre for Contemporary Cultural Studies.

Hall, Stuart, and Tony Jefferson, eds. 1976. *Resistance Through Rituals: Youth Sub-Cultures in Post-War Britain*. Birmingham: Centre for Contemporary Cultural Studies.

Harlow, Barbara. 1987. *Resistance Literature*. New York: Routledge.

Harries, Meirion, and Susie Harries. 1987. *Sheathing the Sword: The Demilitarization of Japan*. London: Hamilton.

———. 1991. *Soldiers of the Sun: The Rise and Fall of the Imperial Japanese Army*. New York: Random House.

Hayes-Bautista, David E. 2004. *La Nueva California: Latinos in the Golden State*. Berkeley and Los Angeles: University of California Press.

Hebdige, Dick. 1979. *Subculture: The Meaning of Style*. London: Methuen.

Henkes, Barbara, and Richard Johnson. 2002. "Silences across Disciplines: Folklore, Cultural Studies, and History." *Journal of Folklore Research* 39: 125–146.

Hernandez, Guillermo E. 1999. "What Is a Corrido? Thematic Representation and Narrative Discourse." *Studies in Latin American Popular Culture*. 18: 69–95.

Herrera-Sobek, María. 1979. *The Bracero Experience: Elitelore versus Folklore*. Los Angeles: UCLA Latin American Center.

———. 1990. *The Mexican Corrido: A Feminist Analysis*. Bloomington: Indiana University Press.

———. 1993. *Northward Bound: The Mexican Immigrant Experience in Ballad and Song*. Bloomington: Indiana University Press.

———. 2000. "Américo Paredes: A Tribute." *Mexican Studies: Estudios Mexicanos* 16: 239–266.

Hoare, Quentin, and Geoffrey Nowell Smith, eds. 1971. *Selections from the Prison Notebooks of Antonio Gramsci*. New York: International.

Hoggart, Richard. [1957] 1992. *The Uses of Literacy*. New Brunswick, NJ: Transaction.

Horkheimer, Max, and Theodor Adorno. 2002. *Dialectic of the Enlightenment*. Palo Alto, CA: Stanford University Press.

Hornfischer, James D. 2006. *Ship of Ghosts: The Story of the USS Houston, FDR's Legendary Lost Cruiser, and the Epic Saga of Her Survivors*. New York: Bantam.

Huerta, Joel. 2005. *Red, Brown, and Blue: A History and Cultural Poetics of High School Football in Mexican America*. PhD dissertation, University of Texas at Austin.

Jameson, Fredric. 2007. *Signatures of the Visible*. New York: Routledge.

JanMohamed, Abdul R. 1995. "Negating the Negation as a Form of Affirmation in Minority Discourse: The Construction of Richard Wright as Subject." In *Richard Wright: A Collection of Critical Essays*, edited by Arnold Rampersad, 132–145. Englewood Cliffs, NJ: Prentice Hall.

Johannessen, Lene M. 2008. *Threshold Time: Passage of Crisis in Chicano Literature*. New York: Rodopi.

Johnson, Benjamin. 2005. *Revolution in Texas: How a Forgotten Rebellion and Its Bloody Suppression Turned Mexicans into Americans*. New Haven: Yale University Press.

Johnston, Robert D. 2003. *The Radical Middle Class: Populist Democracy and the Question of Capitalism in Progressive Era Portland, Oregon*. Princeton, NJ: Princeton University Press.

Laba, Martin. 1986. "Popular Culture and Folklore: The Social Dimension." In *Media Sense: The Folklore–Popular Culture Continuum*, 9–18. Bowling Green, OH: Bowling Green State University Popular Press.

Labov, William. 1966. "Hypercorrection by the Lower Middle Class as a Factor in Linguistic Change." In *Sociolinguistics: Proceedings of the UCLA Sociolinguistics Conference, 1964*, edited by William Bright, 84–113. The Hague: Mouton.

Lamadrid, Enrique R., Miguel Gandert, Ramón Gutiérrez, Lucy R. Lippard, Chris Wilson, and Helen R. Lucero, eds. 2000. *Nuevo México Profundo: Rituals of an Indo-Hispano Homeland*. Albuquerque: Museum of New Mexico Press.

Lear, Jonathan. 2008. *Radical Hope: Ethics in the Face of Cultural Devastation*. Cambridge, MA: Harvard University Press.

LeClerc, Gustavo, Raúl H. Villa, and Michael J. Dear, eds. 1999. *Urban Latino Cultures: La Vida Latina en L.A.* Thousand Oaks, CA: Sage.

Limón, José E. 1973. "Stereotyping and Chicano Resistance: An Historical Dimension." *Aztlán* 4: 257–270.

———. 1977. "El folklore y los mexicanos en los Estados Unidos: Una perspectiva cultural marxista." In *La otra cara de México: El pueblo chicano*, edited by David Maciel, 224–242. Mexico City: Editorial El Caballito.

———. 1980. "Américo Paredes: A Man from the Border." *Revista Chicano-Riqueña* 8: 1–5.

———. 1981. "The Folk Performance of 'Chicano' and the Cultural Limits of Political Ideology." In *"And Other Neighborly Names": Social Process and Cultural Image in Texas Folklore*, edited by Richard Bauman and Roger D. Abrahams, 197–225. Austin: University of Texas Press.

———. 1983a. "The Rise, Fall, and 'Revival' of the Mexican-American Corrido: A Review Essay." *Studies in Latin American Popular Culture* 2: 202–207.

———. 1983b. "Western Marxism and Folklore: A Critical Introduction." *Journal of American Folklore* 96: 34–52.

———. 1989. "Carne, Carnales, and the Carnivalesque: Bakhtinian Batos, Disorder and Narrative Discourses." *American Ethnologist* 16: 471–486.

———. 1992. *Mexican Ballads, Chicano Poems: History and Influence in Mexican-American Social Poetry.* Berkeley: University of California Press.

———. 1994. *Dancing with the Devil: Society and Cultural Poetics in Mexican-American South Texas.* Madison: University of Wisconsin Press.

———. 2006. "Américo Paredes: Ballad Scholar." *Journal of American Folklore* 120: 3–18.

———. 2008. "Border Literary Histories, Globalization, and Critical Regionalism." *American Literary History* 20: 160–182.

———. 2009. "Imagining the Imaginary: A Reply to Ramón Saldívar." *American Literary History* 21: 595–603.

———. 2011. "'This is our música, guy!': Tejanos and Ethno/Regional Musical Nationalism." In *Transnational Encounters: Music and Performance at the U.S.-Mexico Border*, edited by Alejandro L. Madrid, 111–126. New York: Oxford University Press.

Limón, Renata. 2010. *The Science of Folklore: Aurelio M. Espinosa on Spain and the American Southwest.* Master's thesis, University of California at Berkeley.

Lipsitz, George. 2006a. "Con Safos: Can Cultural Studies Read the Writing on the Wall?" In *The Chicana/o Cultural Studies Reader*, edited by Angie Chabram-Dernersesian, 47–60. New York: Routledge.

———. 2006b. "'Home Is Where the Hatred Is': Work, Music, and the Transnational Economy." In *The Chicana/o Cultural Studies Reader*, edited by Angie Chabram-Dernersesian, 299–312. New York: Routledge.

———. 2007. Transcript of conversation. In *The Chicana/o Cultural Studies Forum: Critical and Ethnographic Perspectives*, edited by Angie Chabram-Dernersesian. New York: New York University Press.

Lombardi-Satriani, Luigi. 1974. "Folklore as the Culture of Contestation." *Journal of the Folklore Institute* 11: 99– 121.

López-Morín, José R. 2006. *The Legacy of Américo Paredes*. College Station: Texas A&M University Press.

Loza, Steven. 1993. *Barrio Rhythm: Mexican American Music in Los Angeles*. Urbana: University of Illinois Press.

Macías, Anthony. 2008. *Mexican American Mojo: Popular Music, Dance, and Urban Culture in Los Angeles, 1935–1968*. Durham, NC: Duke University Press.

Madrid-Barela, Arturo. 1973. "In Search of the Authentic Pachuco: An Interpretive Essay." *Aztlán* 4: 31–57.

Marez, Curtis. 1996. "Brown: The Politics of Working-Class Chicano Style." *Social Text* 48: 109–132.

Maya, Jesus, and Timoteo Cantú. [1949] 1991. "Gregorio Cortez." *Tejano Roots*. El Cerrito, CA: Arhoolie Productions.

McCracken, Ellen. 2009. *The Life and Writing of Fray Angélico Chávez: A New Mexico Renaissance Man*. Albuquerque: University of New Mexico Press.

McDowell, John H. 1981. "The *Corrido* of Greater Mexico as Discourse, Music, and Event." In *"And Other Neighborly Names": Social Process and Cultural Image in Texas Folklore*, edited by Richard Bauman and Roger D. Abrahams, 44–75. Austin: University of Texas Press.

McKenna, Teresa. 1997. *Migrant Song: Politics and Process in Contemporary Chicano Literature*. Austin: University of Texas Press.

———, ed. 1982. *Mexican Folklore and Folk Art in the United States*. Special thematic issue of *Aztlán* 13 (1–2).

Medrano, Manuel F. 2010. *Américo Paredes: In His Own Words, an Authorized Biography*. Denton: University of North Texas Press.

Meléndez, Gabriel. 2010. "Américo Paredes and Fray Angélico Chávez: Sangre, sotanas, guitarras y pistolas on the Camino Real to Aztlán." In *Nuevas reflexiones en torno a la literatura y cultura chicana*, edited by Julio Cañero, 131–141. Madrid: Instituto Franklin de Estudios Norteamericanos, Universidad de Alcalá.

Mendoza, Louis. 2001. *Historia: The Literary Making of Chicana and Chicano History*. College Station: Texas A&M University Press.

Mendoza, Lydia. 1993. *Lydia Mendoza: A Family Autobiography*. Compiled and introduced by Chris Strachwitz with James Nicolopulos. Houston: Arte Público.

Miller, Elaine K. 1973. *Mexican Folk Narrative from the Los Angeles Area*. Austin: University of Texas Press.

Montejano, David. 1987. *Anglos and Mexicans in the Making of Texas, 1836–1986*. Austin: University of Texas Press.

Morley, David, and Kuan-Hsing Chen, eds. 1996. *Stuart Hall: Critical Dialogues in Cultural Studies*. New York: Routledge.

Mullen, Bill V. 2004. *Afro-Orientalism*. Minneapolis: University of Minnesota Press.

Mullen, Bill V., and Cathryn Watson, eds. 2005. *W. E. B. DuBois on Asia: Crossing the World Color Line*. Jackson: University Press of Mississippi.

Muñoz, Carlos. 1989. *Youth, Identity and Power: The Chicano Generation*. New York: Verso.

Murphy, Gretchen. 2007. "How the Irish Became Japanese: Winfred Eaton's Racial Reconstructions in a Transnational Context." *American Literature* 79: 29–56.

Naranjo, Ruben, and Los Gamblers. 2001. "Los Hermanos Cortez." *Dulce Adorada*. Corpus Christi, TX: Hacienda Records.

Narváez, Peter, and Martin Laba, eds. 1986. *Media Sense: The Folklore-Popular Culture Continuum*. Bowling Green, OH: Bowling Green State University Popular Press.

Nelson, Cary, Paula Treichler, and Lawrence Grossberg. 1992. *Cultural Studies*. New York: Routledge.

O'Connor, Alan. 1989. *Raymond Williams: Writing, Culture, Politics*. New York: Basil Blackwell.

Olguín, B. V. 2010. *La Pinta: Chicana/o Prisoner Literature, Culture and Politics*. Austin: University of Texas Press.

Oring, Elliot. 1975. "The Devolutionary Premise: A Definitional Delusion?" *Western Folklore* 34: 36–44.

———. 1992. *Jokes and Their Relations*. Lexington: University Press of Kentucky.

Ortner, Sherry B. 2006. *Anthropology and Social Theory: Culture, Power, and the Acting Subject*. Durham, NC: Duke University Press.

O'Sullivan, John. 1845. "Annexation." *United States Magazine and Democratic Review* 17: 5- 10.

Paredes, Américo. 1886–1999. Américo Paredes Papers, 1886–1999. Benson Latin American Collection, General Libraries, University of Texas at Austin.

———. 1942. "The Mexico-Texan *Corrido*." *Southwest Review* 27: 470–481.

———. 1956. "El Corrido de Gregorio Cortez: A Ballad of Border Conflict." PhD dissertation, University of Texas at Austin.

———. [1958] 1971. *"With His Pistol in His Hand": A Border Ballad and its Hero*. Austin: University of Texas Press.

———. 1961. "On *Gringo, Greaser*, and Other Neighborly Names." In *Singers and Storytellers*, edited by Mody C. Boatright, Wilson M. Hudson, and Allen Maxwell, 285–290. Dallas: Southern Methodist University Press.

———. 1963. "El cowboy norteamericano en el folklore y la literatura." *Cuadernos del Instituto Nacional de Antropología* 4: 227–240.

———. 1965. "Review of *Legends of Texas* and *Happy Hunting Ground*, edited by J. Frank Dobie." *Journal of American Folklore* 78: 163–164.

———. 1966. "The Anglo-American in Mexican Folklore." In *New Voices in American Studies*, edited by Ray B. Browne, Donald A. Winkelman, and Allen Hayman, 113–127. Lafayette, IN: Purdue University Press.

———. 1968. "Folk Medicine and the Intercultural Jest." In *Spanish-Speaking in the United States*, edited by June Helm, 104–119. Proceedings of the 1968 Annual Meeting of the American Ethnological Society. Seattle: University of Washington Press.

————. 1969. "Concepts about Folklore in Latin America and the United States." *Journal of the Folklore Institute* 6: 2—38.

————. 1970. *The Folktales of Mexico*. Chicago: University of Chicago Press.

————. 1971. "Mexican Legendry and the Rise of the Mestizo." In *American Folk Legend: A Symposium*, 97–107. Berkeley and Los Angeles: University of California Press.

————. 1976. *A Texas-Mexican Cancionero: Folksongs of the Lower Border*. Champaign-Urbana: University of Illinois Press.

————. 1977. "Yamashita, Zapata, and the Arthurian Legend." *Western Folklore* 36: 160–163.

————. 1978a. "On Ethnographic Work Among Minority Groups: A Folklorist's Perspective." In *New Directions in Chicano Scholarship*, edited by Ricardo Romo and Raymund Paredes, 1–32. La Jolla, CA: University of California at San Diego Chicano Studies.

————. 1978b. "The Problem of Identity in a Changing Culture: Popular Expressions of Cultural Conflict Along the Lower Rio Grande Border." In *Views Across the Border: The United States and Mexico*, edited by Stanley Ross, 68–94. Albuquerque: University of New Mexico Press.

————. 1979. "The Folk Base of Chicano Literature." In *Modern Chicano Writers: A Collection of Critical Essays*, edited by Joseph Sommers and Tomás Ybarra-Frausto, 4–17. Englewood Cliffs, NJ: Prentice Hall.

————. 1982. "Folklore, *Lo Mexicano*, and Proverbs." *Aztlán* 13: 1–11.

————. 1985. *Con su pistola en la mano: Un corrido fronterizo y su heroe*. Mexico City: Instituto Nacional de Antropología e Historia.

————. 1990. *George Washington Gómez: A Mexico-Texan Novel*. Houston: Arte Público.

————. 1991. *Between Two Worlds*. Houston: Arte Público.

————. 1993a. *Folklore and Culture on the Texas-Mexican Border*, edited by Richard Bauman. Austin: University of Texas at Austin Center for Mexican American Studies.

————. 1993b. *Uncle Remus con Chile*. Houston: Arte Público.

————. 1994. *"The Hammon and the Beans" and Other Stories*. Houston: Arte Público.

————. 2007. *Cantos de adolescencia / Songs of Youth (1932–1937)*. Translated and edited by B. V. Olguín and Omar Vásquez Barbosa. Houston: Arte Público.

Paredez, Deborah. 2009. *Selenidad: Selena, Latinos, and the Performance of Memory*. Durham, NC: Duke University Press.

Paz, Octavio. 1985. *The Labyrinth of Solitude and Other Writings*. New York: Grove Press.

Peacock, James L. 2007. *Grounded Globalism: How the U.S. South Embraces the World*. Athens: University of Georgia Press.

Peña, Manuel H. 1981. "Folksong and Social Change: Two Corridos as Interpretive Sources." *Aztlán* 13: 13–42.

———. 1985. *The Texas-Mexican Conjunto: History of a Working Class Music*. Austin: University of Texas Press.

———. 1999. *Música Tejana: The Cultural Economy of Artistic Transformation*. College Station: Texas A&M University Press.

Perez, Domino. 2008. *There Was a Woman: La Llorona from Folklore to Popular Culture*. Austin: University of Texas Press.

Perez, Hector. 1998. "Voicing Resistance on the Border: A Reading of Américo Paredes' *George Washington Gómez*." *MELUS* 23: 27–48.

Portales, Marco. 2000. *Crowding Out Latinos: Mexican Americans in the Public Consciousness*. Philadelphia: Temple University Press.

Porter, James. 1993. "Convergence, Divergence, and Dialectic in Folksong Paradigms: Critical Directions for Transatlantic Scholarship." *Journal of American Folklore* 106: 61–98.

Quirarte, Jacinto, and Carey Clements Rote. 1999. *César A. Martínez: A Retrospective*. San Antonio, TX: Marion Koogler McNay Museum.

Rabinow, Paul, and George E. Marcus, with James D. Faubion and Tobias Rees. 2008. *Designs for an Anthropology of the Contemporary*. Durham, NC: Duke University Press.

Radway, Janice. 1984. *Reading the Romance: Women, Patriarchy and Popular Literature*. Chapel Hill: University of North Carolina Press.

Ramírez, Catherine S. 2009. *The Woman in the Zoot Suit: Gender, Nationalism, and the Cultural Politics of Memory*. Durham, NC: Duke University Press.

Ramos, Rubén, and the Texas Revolution. 1992. "El Corrido de Gregorio Cortez." *The Cat's Out of the Bag*. Miami: Sony Discos.

Renwick, Roger deV. 1992. "Folksong Scholarship Today: A Rich Palimpsest." *Journal of Folklore Research* 29: 73–81.

———. 2001. *Recentering Anglo/American Folksong: Sea Crabs and Wicked Youth*. Jackson: University Press of Mississippi.

Reyna, José. 1973. "Mexican American Prose Narratives in Texas: The Jest and Anecdote." Ph.D. dissertation, University of California at Los Angeles.

———. 1980. *Raza Humor: Chicano Joke Tradition in Texas*. San Antonio, TX: Penca Books.

Richmond, W. Edson. 1964. "The Comparative Approach: Its Aims, Techniques, and Limitations." In *A Good Tale and a Bonnie Tune*, edited by Mody C. Boatright, Wilson M. Hudson, and Allen Maxwell, 217–227. Dallas: Southern Methodist University Press.

Rickels, Laurence A. 1991. *The Case of California*. Minneapolis: University of Minnesota Press.

Rivas-Rodríguez, Maggie, and Emilio Zamora, eds. 2009. *Beyond the Latino World War II Hero: The Social and Political Legacy of a Generation*. Austin: University of Texas Press.

Rivera, John-Michael. 2006. *The Emergence of Mexican America: Recovering Stories of Mexican Peoplehood in U.S. Culture*. New York: New York University Press.

Rivera, Tomás. [1971] 1992. . . . *y no se lo tragó la tierra* (. . . *and the Earth Did Not Devour Him*). Trans. Evangelina Vigil-Piñon. Houston: Arte Público.

Robe, Stanley. 1971. *Antología del Saber Popular: A Selection of Various Genres of Mexican Folklore Across Borders*. Los Angeles: UCLA Chicano Studies Research Center.

Rodríguez, Ralph E. 2009. "Chicano Studies and the Need to Not Know." *American Literary History* 22: 180–190.

Romano-V., Octavio Ignacio. 1968. "The Anthropology and Sociology of the Mexican-American: The Distortion of Mexican-American History." *El Grito* 2: 43–56.

———. 1970. "Social Science, Objectivity and the Chicanos." *El Grito* 4: 4–16.

Rosaldo, Renato. 1989. *Culture and Truth: The Remaking of Social Analysis*. Boston: Beacon Press.

Gilberto Rosas. 2006a. "The Managed Violences of the Borderlands: Treacherous Geographies, Policeability, and the Politics of Race." *Latino Studies* 4: 401–418.

———. 2006b. "The Thickening Borderlands: Diffused Exceptionality and 'Immigrant' Social Struggles during the 'War on Terror.'" *Cultural Dynamics* 18: 335–349.

———. 2007. "The Fragile Ends of War: Forging the US-Mexico Border and Borderlands Consciousness." *Social Text* 25: 81–102.

Said, Edward W. 1994. *Representations of the Intellectual*. New York: Pantheon Books.

Sakade, Florence, ed. [1953] 1958. "Peach Boy." In *Japanese Children's Favorite Stories*, 9–16. Rutland, VT, and Tokyo: Charles E. Tuttle.

Saldívar, José David. 1997. *Border Matters: Remapping American Cultural Studies*. Berkeley: University of California Press.

Saldívar, Ramón. 1990. *Chicano Narrative: The Dialectics of Difference*. Madison: University of Wisconsin Press.

———. 1994. "Introduction." In *The Hammon and the Beans and Other Stories*, by Américo Paredes. Houston: Arte Público.

———. 1999. "Transnational Migrations and Border Identities: Immigration and Postmodern Culture." *South Atlantic Quarterly* 98: 217–230.

———. 2006. *The Borderlands of Culture: Américo Paredes and the Transnational Imaginary*. Durham, NC: Duke University Press.

———. 2009. "Asian Américo: Paredes in Asia and the Borderlands: A Response to José E. Limón." *American Literary History* 21: 584–594.

Sandell, David P. 2009a. "Poetics, Politics and the Life of Latino Catholics in California." *Aztlán* 34: 125–154.

———. 2009b. "Rituals, Stories, and the Poetics of a Journey Home Among Latino Catholics." *Anthropology of Consciousness* 20: 53–80.

———. 2010. "Where Mourning Takes Them: Migrants, Borders, and an Alternative Reality." *Ethos* 38: 179–204.

———. Forthcoming. "Mexican Pilgrimages, Migration, and Discovery of the Sacred." *Journal of American Folklore*.

San Miguel, Guadalupe. 2001. *"Let Them All Take Heed": Mexican-Americans and the Campaign for Educational Equality in Texas, 1910–1981*. College Station: Texas A&M University Press.

Schedler, Christopher. 2000. "Inscribing Mexican-American Modernism in Américo Paredes' Novel, *George Washington Gómez*." *Texas Studies in Literature and Language* 42: 154–172.

Sennett, Richard. 2008. *The Craftsman*. New Haven: Yale University Press.

Simeone, W. E. 1960. "Review of *"With His Pistol in His Hand"*: *A Border Ballad and Its Hero*, by Américo Paredes." *Southern Folklore Quarterly* 24: 176–177.

Soldatenko, Michael. 2009. *Chicano Studies: The Genesis of a Discipline*. Tucson: University of Arizona Press.

Sommer, Doris. 1999. *Proceed with Caution, When Engaged by Minority Writing in the Americas*. Cambridge: Harvard University Press.

Sommers, Joseph, and Tomás Ybarra-Frausto, eds. 1979. *Modern Chicano Writers: A Collection of Critical Essays*. Twentieth Century Views. Englewood Cliffs, NJ: Prentice Hall.

Soto, Sandra K. 2010. *Reading Like a Queer: Chicana/o Culture, Racialized Sexuality, and the De-Mastery of Desire*. Austin: University of Texas Press.

Sparks, Colin. 1996. "The Evolution of Cultural Studies . . ." In *What Is Cultural Studies? A Reader*, edited by John Storey, 14–30. New York: Arnold.

Stocking, George. 1987. *Victorian Anthropology*. New York: Free Press.

Storey, John. 1996. "Cultural Studies: An Introduction." In *What Is Cultural Studies? A Reader*, 1–13. New York: Arnold.

SUN Ge. 2000. "How Does Asia Mean? (Part I)." *Inter-Asia Cultural Studies* 1 (2).

Tatum, Charles, M. 2001. *Chicano Popular Culture: Que Hable el Pueblo*. Tucson: University of Arizona Press.

Taylor, Archer. 1931. *"Edward" and "Sven I Rosengaard."* Chicago: University of Chicago Press.

Tenayuca, Emma, and Homer Brooks. 1939. "The Mexican Question in the Southwest." *The Communist* 18: 257–268.

Tijerina, Andres. 1994. *Tejanos and Texas under the Mexican Flag, 1821–1836*. College Station: Texas A&M University Press.

Toelken, Barre. 1986. "Context and Meaning in the Anglo-American Ballad." In *The Ballad and the Scholars: Approaches to Ballad Study*, 29–52. Los Angeles: William Andrews Clark Memorial Library, UCLA.

Trujillo, Michael. 2009. *Land of Disenchantment: Latina/o Identities and Transformations in Northern New Mexico*. Albuquerque: University of New Mexico Press.

Vaca, Nicolás C. 1970a. "The Mexican-American in the Social Sciences, 1912–1970, Part I: 1912–1935." *El Grito* 3: 3–24.

———. 1970b. "The Mexican-American in the Social Sciences, 1912–1970, Part II: 1936–1970." *El Grito* 4: 17–51.

Valdez, Diana Washington. 2007. "Ex-Judge, ex-ACLU Board Member Honored." *El Paso Times*, June 28.

Velasco, Juan. 2006. "The X in Race and Gender: Rethinking Chicano/a Cultural Pro-
duction Through the Paradigms of Xicanisma and Me(x)icaness." In *The Chicana/o
Cultural Studies Reader*, edited by Angie Chabram-Dernersesian, 203–210. New
York: Routledge.

Vigil, Evangelina. 1985. *Thirty an' Seen a Lot*. Houston: Arte Público.

Villa, Raul Homero. 2000. *Barrio-Logos: Space and Place in Urban Chicano Literature and Culture*. Austin: University of Texas Press.

Westbrook, David A. 2008. *Navigators of the Contemporary: Why Ethnography Matters*. Chicago: University of Chicago Press.

Wilgus, D. K. 1964. "The Rationalistic Approach." In *A Good Tale and a Bonnie Tune*,
edited by Mody C. Boatright, Wilson M. Hudson, and Allen Maxwell, 227–237.
Dallas: Southern Methodist University Press.

———. 1986. "The Comparative Approach." In *The Ballad and the Scholars: Approaches to Ballad Study*, 1–28. Los Angeles: William Andrews Clark Memorial
Library, UCLA.

Williams, Raymond. 1958. *Culture and Society: 1780–1950*. London: Chatto and
Windus.

———. 1970. "Introduction." In *Dombey and Son*, by Charles Dickens, edited by
Peter Fairclough, 11–34. Harmondsworth, UK: Penguin.

———. 1975. *The Country and the City*. Oxford: Oxford University Press.

———. 1977. *Marxism and Literature*. New York: Oxford University Press.

———. 1979. *Politics and Letters: Interviews with New Left Review*. London: Verso.

———. 1989. *The Politics of Modernism: Against the New Conformists*. London:
Verso.

———. [1981] 1995. *The Sociology of Culture*. Chicago: University of Chicago Press.

Willis, Paul. 1977. *Learning to Labour: How Working Class Kids Get Working Class
Jobs*. Farmborough: Saxon House.

Young, Robert C. 1995. *Colonial Desire: Hybridity in Theory, Culture, and Race*. New
York: Routledge.

Zamora, Emilio. 1995. *The World of the Mexican Worker in Texas*. College Station:
Texas A&M University Press, 1995.

———. 2009. *Claiming Rights and Righting Wrongs in Texas: Mexican Workers and
Job Politics During World War II*. College Station: Texas A&M University Press.

Zumwalt, Rosemary Levy. 1988. *American Folklore Scholarship: A Dialogue of Dissent*. Bloomington: Indiana University Press.

Index

Ingram Content Group UK Ltd.
Milton Keynes UK
UKHW042248260323
418963UK00011B/152